Pocket
NEW YORK CITY

TOP SIGHTS • LOCAL LIFE • MADE EASY

Regis St Louis, Cristian Bonetto

In This Book

QuickStart Guide

Your keys to understanding the city – we help you decide what to do and how to do it

Need to Know
Tips for a smooth trip

Neighborhoods
What's where

Explore New York City

The best things to see and do, neighborhood by neighborhood

Top Sights
Make the most of your visit

Local Life
The insider's city

The Best of New York City

The city's highlights in handy lists to help you plan

Best Walks
See the city on foot

New York City's Best...
The best experiences

Survival Guide

Tips and tricks for a seamless, hassle-free city experience

Getting Around
Travel like a local

Essential Information
Including where to stay

Our selection of the city's best places to eat, drink and experience:

◎ **Sights**

✖ **Eating**

🍷 **Drinking**

★ **Entertainment**

🛍 **Shopping**

These symbols give you the vital information for each listing:

☏	Telephone Numbers	👪	Family-Friendly
⊙	Opening Hours	🐾	Pet-Friendly
🅿	Parking	🚌	Bus
⊖	Nonsmoking	🚢	Ferry
@	Internet Access	Ⓜ	Metro
🛜	Wi-Fi Access	Ⓢ	Subway
🥗	Vegetarian Selection	🚊	Tram
🔤	English-Language Menu	🚆	Train

Find each listing quickly on maps for each neighborhood:

Bar Hemingway

16 🍷 Map p233, B2

Legend has it that Hemi self, wielding a machine rate this timber-pan ered bar during showpiece is a en by Papa a town. Dress s.com; Hôtel Rit ⊙6.30pm-2a

6 ◎ Plac

Lonely Planet's New York City

Lonely Planet Pocket Guides are designed to get you straight to the heart of the city.

Inside you'll find all the must-see sights, plus tips to make your visit to each one really memorable. We've split the city into easy-to-navigate neighborhoods and provided clear maps so you'll find your way around with ease. Our expert authors have searched out the best of the city: walks, food, nightlife and shopping, to name a few. Because you want to explore, our 'Local Life' pages will take you to some of the most exciting areas to experience the real New York City.

And of course you'll find all the practical tips you need for a smooth trip: itineraries for short visits, how to get around, and how much to tip the guy who serves you a drink at the end of a long day's exploration.

It's your guarantee of a really great experience.

Our Promise

You can trust our travel information because Lonely Planet authors visit the places we write about, each and every edition. We never accept freebies for positive coverage, so you can rely on us to tell it like it is.

QuickStart Guide 7

Explore New York City 21

Worth a Trip:

The Best of New York City 205

New York City's Best Walks

New York City's Best...

Survival Guide 235

QuickStart Guide

Welcome to New York City

One of the world's most captivating cities, New York offers an intoxicating blend of hallowed concert halls, wildly inventive restaurants and roaring nightlife. Yet this is just the beginning of a whole world of possibilities, encompassing cutting-edge couture, back-lit Broadway stages and late-night jazz clubs. If you can dream it up, you can make it happen in the Big Apple.

The High Line (p86)
CRISTINAMURACA/SHUTTERSTOCK ©

New York City Top Sights

Empire State Building (p130)

The striking art-deco skyscraper has appeared in dozens of films and still provides one of the best views in town – particularly around sunset when the twinkling lights of the city switch on.

Central Park (p178)

One of the world's most renowned green spaces, Central Park checks in with 843 acres of rolling meadows, boulder-studded outcrops, elm-lined walkways and lakes. The challenge? Where to begin.

New York Harbor (p24)

Soaring Lady Liberty has welcomed millions of immigrants, sailing into New York Harbor in the hope of a better life. Neighboring Ellis Island pays tribute to the indelible courage of these teeming masses.

Times Square (p128)

Sizzling lights, electrifying energy: this is the America of the world's imagination. Just beyond the glittering billboards of Times Square lies NYC's dream factory: Broadway, the theatrical epicenter of America.

GRANT FAINT/GETTY IMAGES ©

National September 11 Memorial & Museum (p26)

A soaring tower, an evocative museum, and North America's largest human-made waterfalls are as much a symbol of hope and renewal as they are a tribute to the victims of terrorism.

Museum of Modern Art (p132)

Quite possibly the greatest hoarder of modern masterpieces on earth, MoMA is a cultural promised land. Van Gogh, Picasso and Warhol are just the beginning.

ERIKA CROSS/SHUTTERSTOCK ©

The High Line (p86)

Once-unsightly rail tracks have been transformed into grassy catwalks in the sky. It's the paradigm of urban renewal gone right and one of the city's best-loved public spaces.

Metropolitan Museum of Art (p158)

With more than two million objects in its collections, the Met is simply dazzling. Its great works span the world, from ancient Greek sculptures to Guinean tribal carvings.

Brooklyn Bridge (p28)

Completed in 1883, this Gothic Revival masterpiece has inspired poetry, music and plenty of art. Against the towering backdrop of Lower Manhattan, views at sunrise or sunset are pure magic.

Guggenheim Museum (p162)

A sculpture in its own right, architect Frank Lloyd Wright's swirling white building is a worthy match for the bounty of 20th-century art housed inside. Interior, Solomon R Guggenheim Museum, New York ©SRGF, NY

MoMA PS1 (p202)

Hop across the East River for some of the city's most cutting-edge exhibitions. Set in a former schoolhouse, MoMA PS1 is full of surprises and hosts a celebrated summer series of art and music.

New York City Local Life

Insider tips to help you find the real city

New York's great treasures aren't just its iconic sights, but its wild assortment of heady art galleries, candlelit speakeasies, vintage markets and quirky boutiques. There's much to discover for those wanting to delve beneath the surface.

Shop Local SoHo
(p48)

▶ Original boutiques
▶ Gourmet snacks

Join downtown's fashion crowd in Nolita and SoHo, where you'll find a treasure chest of eye-catching shops, cafes and eateries. Hit the backstreets for literary-minded booksellers, weird curiosity shops, perfume purveyors of uncommon scents, perfectly pulled espressos and hidden street art.

Chelsea Galleries
(p88)

▶ Today's art stars
▶ Spanish tapas

Once a derelict corner of Manhattan, western Chelsea is now the epicenter of the NYC art world, with more than 200 galleries scattered along its streets. Spend a day exploring the best of the best, stopping for tapas and rioja along the way.

Harlem (p196)

▶ African American history
▶ Inspiring architecture

Northern Manhattan is home to a soaring (but unfinished) cathedral, an African-infused market, reinvented soul food, one riotously fun concert hall and photogenic streets where history was made in the great Harlem renaissance.

South Brooklyn
(p198)

▶ Lovely parks
▶ Vintage wares

Some Brooklynites rarely venture into Manhattan, and after a stroll through this quartet of neighborhoods, you'll see why. Leafy parks, buzzing cafes, bizarre shops, sunny backyard bars and one massive flea market are just a few reasons why Brooklyn is booming.

Williamsburg
(p200)

▶ Cocktail dens
▶ Brooklyn crafts

Just across the bridge from the Lower East Side, Williamsburg is the heart of Brooklyn creativity. This walk takes you to Brooklyn's first brewery, a secret art library, a much-loved vintage store and various drinking spots, including a tasting room that specializes in locally made spirits.

Vintage cocktail glasses

Apollo Theater (p197)

Other great places to experience the city like a local:

New York City Day Planner

Day One

Spend the morning exploring the wonders of **Central Park** (p178). Start on the southeast corner, check out the **Central Park Zoo** (p179), stroll up the elegant Mall, stop for a rowboat paddle at the **Loeb Boathouse** (p186), check out model boaters on the Conservatory Water and remember John Lennon at **Strawberry Fields** (p179). Leave the park for a glimpse of great mysteries of earth and sky at the **American Museum of Natural History** (p184).

It's now time to uncover some of the city's architectural wonders: **Grand Central Terminal** (p136), the **Chrysler Building** (p137), the **New York Public Library** (p137) and **Rockefeller Center** (p136). Round off the afternoon with a visit to Midtown's greatest art repository at **MoMA** (p132).

Spend the evening under the starry lights of Broadway, checking out a blockbuster show or something distinctly ahead of the curve at **Playwrights Horizons** (p150). Soak up the Las Vegas–like atmosphere of **Times Square** (p128) from above the TKTS Booth; swig cocktails at **Rum House** (p146); then climb to the top of the **Empire State Building** (p130) to bid the city goodnight.

Day Two

Start at the staggering **Metropolitan Museum of Art** (p158). Wander through the Egyptian and Roman collections; take in European masters; then head up to the rooftop (in summer) for a view over Central Park. Afterwards, visit the nearby **Neue Galerie** (p166) for a feast of German and Austrian art in a 1914 mansion.

Head down to SoHo for an afternoon of shopping along **Prince** and **Spring Streets** amid crowds seeking the best brands in the world. Wander over to Chinatown's **Mulberry Sreet**, which feels worlds away from mainstream consumerism, but is – in reality – only a few blocks over. Stroll by the neighborhood's Buddhist temples, stopping for custard tarts and durian ice cream.

If you have concert tickets, then skip dinner downtown and have a drink at well-placed gastropub **The Smith** (p188). Then it's off to **Lincoln Center** (p184) across the street for opera at the Metropolitan Opera House or a symphony in Avery Fisher Hall. Later, dine on modern American cuisine at high-class **Dovetail** (p188), and follow it up with drinks at the elegant **Manhattan Cricket Club** (p189).

Short on time?
We've arranged New York City's must-sees into these day-by-day itineraries to make sure you see the very best of the city in the time you have available.

Day Three

As the party people are crawling back to their shoebox apartments after a raucous night out, make your way to the **Lower East Side Tenement Museum** (p68) to learn about life in the area long before gentrification. Fast-forward into the future at the avant-garde-loving **New Museum of Contemporary Art** (p68).

Stop for lunch at one of the creative eateries that the LES is famous for: **Dimes** (p72) or **El Rey** (p70) are delicious options. Afterwards, zoom down to City Park, the starting point for a sunset walk over the awe-inspiring **Brooklyn Bridge** (p28). Descend into Dumbo for more great views from Brooklyn's waterfront.

In the evening, head to the East Village. Take a stroll along gritty **St Marks Place** (p70); enjoy a pick-me-up beer at a buzzing cafe such as **MUD** (p71); then catch a show at **La MaMa ETC** (p80), an icon of the downtown arts scene. Afterwards, feast on gourmet Indian street food at **Babu Ji** (p72), then hit a few neighborhood cocktail dens such as **Rue B** (p75) and **Pouring Ribbons** (p76).

Day Four

Catch the Staten Island Ferry in the early morning and watch the sun come up over Lower Manhattan. Then go skyward for a marvelous view from the **One World Observatory** (p32). Afterwards, visit the moving **National September 11 Memorial & Museum** (p26).

Head up to the Meatpacking District and visit the gorgeous new **Whitney Museum of American Art** (p92). Afterwards, take the nearby steps up to the **High Line** (p86) for a wander along a once-abandoned rail line. Along the way stop for coffee and snack breaks, and to take in the intriguing views over the streetscape. Descend in the West 20s for gallery-hopping in Chelsea, and refuel on gourmet goodies inside the **Chelsea Market** (p92).

Stroll the lovely, meandering streets of Greenwich Village, working up an appetite for a meal at atmospheric **Minetta Tavern** (p99), followed by live jazz at **Mezzrow** (p106), **Smalls** (p104) or the **Village Vanguard** (p105). End the night with a craft cocktail at stylish **Employees Only** (p100), before dancing at **Cielo** (p104), one of the city's best little clubs.

Need to Know

For more information, see Survival Guide (p236)

Currency
US dollar (US$)

Language
English

Visas
The US Visa Waiver Program allows nationals of 38 countries to enter the US without a visa.

Money
ATMs widely available; credit cards accepted at most hotels, stores and restaurants. Farmers markets and some restaurants and bars are cash-only.

Cell Phones
Most US cell (mobile) phones besides the iPhone operate on CDMA, not the European standard GSM. Check compatibility with your phone service provider.

Time
Eastern Standard Time (GMT/UTC minus five hours)

Plugs & Adaptors
The US electric current is 110V to 115V, 60Hz AC. Outlets are made for flat two-prong plugs (which often have a third, rounded prong for grounding).

Tipping
Restaurant servers 15% to 20%, barkeeps $1 per beer or $2 per specialty cocktail, taxi drivers 10% to 15%, and hotel housekeepers $3 to $5 per day.

❶ Before You Go

Your Daily Budget

Budget less than $100
▶ Dorm bed: $40–70
▶ Food-truck taco: from $3
▶ Bus or subway ride: $2.75

Midrange $100–$300
▶ Double room in a midrange hotel: from $200
▶ Dinner for two at a midrange eatery: $130
▶ Craft cocktail at a lounge: $14–18
▶ Discount TKTS ticket to a Broadway show: $80

Top End more than $300
▶ Luxury stay at a high-end hotel: $325–850
▶ Tasting menu at a top-end restaurant: $85–325
▶ Metropolitan Opera orchestra seats: $100–390

Useful Websites

Lonely Planet (www.lonelyplanet.com/usa/new-york-city) Destination information, hotel bookings, traveller forum and more.

NYC: The Official Guide (www.nycgo.com) New York City's official tourism portal.

New York Magazine (www.nymag.com) Comprehensive listings for bars, restaurants, entertainment and shopping.

Advance Planning

Two months before Book your hotel and snag Broadway tickets.

Three weeks before Score a table at your top-choice high-end restaurant.

One week before Scan the web and Twitter for the latest openings and events.

② Arriving in New York City

Three bustling airports, two main train stations and a monolithic bus terminal welcome millions of visitors each year.

✈ From John F Kennedy International Airport (JFK)

Destination	Best Transport
Brooklyn	Subway LIRR to Atlantic Terminal
Lower East Side	Subway J/Z line
Lower Manhattan	Subway A line
Midtown	LIRR to Penn Station
Greenwich Village	Village Subway A line
Upper West Side	Subway A line
Upper East Side	Subway E, then 4/5/6 lines
Harlem	Subway E, then B or C lines

✈ From LaGuardia Airport (LGA)

Destination	Best Transport
Harlem	Bus M60
Upper East Side	Bus M60 & Subway 4/5/6 line
Midtown	Bus Q70 & Subway F, 7 or E lines
Union Square	Bus Q70 then Subway R line
Greenwich Village	Bus Q70 then Subway F line
Brooklyn	Taxi

✈ From Newark International Airport (EWR)

Take the AirTrain to Newark Airport rail station, then board any train bound for NYC's Penn Station. Shared shuttles and buses are also available. From Midtown, hop on a subway to reach your final destination.

③ Getting Around

Once you've arrived in NYC, getting around is fairly easy. The extensive subway system is cheap and (usually) efficient, and you can also get around by bike, ferry, bus or on foot.

S Subway

The subway system is iconic, inexpensive and open around the clock. Check out www.mta .info for public transportation information; download the useful NextStop app, with map, arrival countdowns and service alerts.

🚌 Bus

Buses are a good choice when traveling 'crosstown' (going east or west across the city) or for travel along First and Tenth Aves.

🚕 Taxi

Outside of rush hour, taxi travel can be the fastest and most convenient way to get around; it's a good option when you'd rather stay above ground. It can be quite difficult to grab a taxi in inclement weather.

🚲 Bike

New York's excellent bike-sharing network **Citi Bike** (www.citibikenyc.com; 24hr/7 days $11/27) has hundreds of kiosks in Manhattan and parts of Brooklyn. Just select access (24-hour or seven-day), swipe your credit card, grab a bike and go. Find nearby docks with the Citi Bike app.

🛥 Ferry

There are free rides to Staten Island, and decent service aboard the **East River Ferry** (www.eastriverferry.com; one-way $4-6) at stops between Lower Manhattan, E 34th St and the Queens and Brooklyn waterfront. There's also the pricey hop-on, hop-off **New York Water Taxi** (📞212-742-1969; www. nywatertaxi.com; hop-on, hop-off 1-day pass $31).

New York City Neighborhoods

Upper West Side & Central Park (p176)

Home to Lincoln Center and Central Park – the city's antidote to the endless stretches of concrete.

⊙ Top Sights

Central Park

West Village, Chelsea & the Meatpacking District (p84)

Quaint streets and well-preserved brick townhouses lead to neighborhood cafes mixed with trendy nightlife options.

⊙ Top Sights

The High Line

SoHo & Chinatown (p46)

Hidden temples and steaming dumpling houses dot Chinatown. Next door are SoHo's streamlined streets and retail storefronts.

Lower Manhattan & the Financial District (p22)

Home to the National September 11 Memorial & Museum, the Brooklyn Bridge and the Statue of Liberty.

⊙ Top Sights

New York Harbor

National September 11 Memorial & Museum

Brooklyn Bridge

Museum of Modern A

Times Square ⊙

Empire State Building ⊙

⊙ The High Line

National September 11 Memorial & Museum ⊙

⊙ Brooklyn Bridge

⊙ New York Harbor

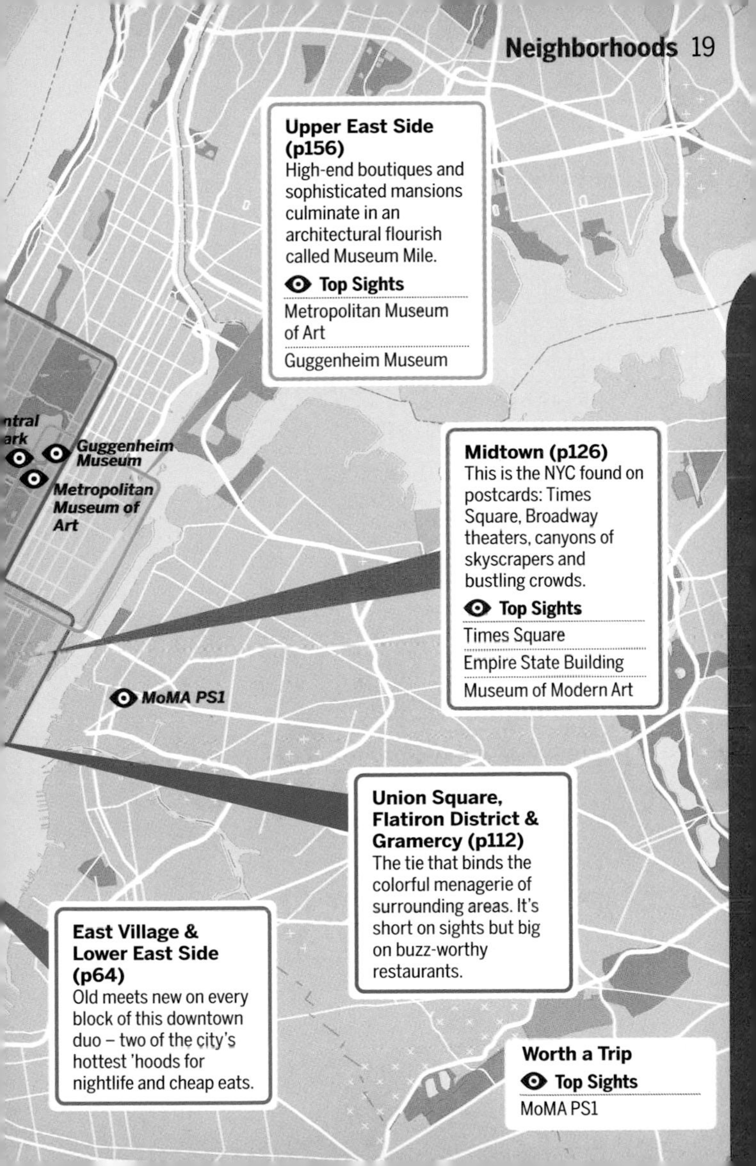

Upper East Side (p156)
High-end boutiques and sophisticated mansions culminate in an architectural flourish called Museum Mile.

⊙ Top Sights

Metropolitan Museum of Art

Guggenheim Museum

Midtown (p126)
This is the NYC found on postcards: Times Square, Broadway theaters, canyons of skyscrapers and bustling crowds.

⊙ Top Sights

Times Square

Empire State Building

Museum of Modern Art

Central Park

⊙ ⊙ Guggenheim Museum
⊙ ⊙
⊙ Metropolitan Museum of Art

⊙ MoMA PS1

Union Square, Flatiron District & Gramercy (p112)
The tie that binds the colorful menagerie of surrounding areas. It's short on sights but big on buzz-worthy restaurants.

East Village & Lower East Side (p64)
Old meets new on every block of this downtown duo – two of the city's hottest 'hoods for nightlife and cheap eats.

Worth a Trip
⊙ Top Sights
MoMA PS1

Explore
New York

View over Central Park from Top of the Rock (p136)
ONIONASTUDIO/GETTY IMAGES ©

Explore

Lower Manhattan & the Financial District

Gleaming with bold, new architectural icons, Manhattan's southern tip is back in business. It's in the Financial District that you'll find the National September 11 Memorial and Museum, One World Observatory and Wall St, and Ellis Island and the Statue of Liberty are just offshore. To the north lie the warehouse conversions of Tribeca, full of vibrant restaurants, low-lit bars, and tiny shops and galleries.

The Sights in a Day

☼ Start the day early with a sunrise stroll out across the majestic **Brooklyn Bridge** (p28). Afterwards, stop for French pastries, perfectly pulled espressos and other gourmet goodies at **Le District** (p38). Grab a few snacks for later then head out on the ferry to visit the **Statue of Liberty** (p24), followed by a stroll through history on Ellis Island.

☀ Head back to Manhattan and wander over to the **Fraunces Tavern** (p38), a historic pub where you can have a first-rate meal amid 18th-century decor. Walk it off on a leisurely stroll past Wall St and the spindly bell tower of **Trinity Church** (p34) before reaching the moving **National September 11 Memorial** (p26). Learn about the tragic events that transpired here inside the adjoining museum. Afterwards, head skyward to the **One World Observatory** (p32) for a view across New York's forever-altered skyline.

☾ In the evening, take in dinner and a show in Tribeca. Go early to Michelin-starred **Bâtard** (p40), before catching an innovative production at the **Soho Rep** (p43), a venerable Off-Broadway venue. End the night over bespoke cocktails at **Weather Up** (p42).

◉ Top Sights

New York Harbor (p24)

National September 11 Memorial & Museum (p26)

Brooklyn Bridge (p28)

♥ Best of New York City

Eating
Locanda Verde (p39)

Bâtard (p40)

Brookfield Place (p39)

Drinking
Dead Rabbit (p40)

Ward III (p40)

Smith & Mills (p40)

Shopping
Century 21 (p43)

Shinola (p44)

Getting There

S Subway Fulton St is the main interchange station, servicing the A/C, J/Z, 2/3 and 4/5 lines. The 1 train terminates at South Ferry, from where the Staten Island Ferry departs.

⚓ Boat The Staten Island Ferry Terminal is at the southern end of Whitehall St. Services to Liberty and Ellis Islands depart from nearby Battery Park.

Top Sights
New York Harbor

Since its unveiling in 1886, Lady Liberty has welcomed millions of immigrants sailing into New York Harbor in the hope of a better life. She now welcomes millions of tourists, many of whom head up to her crown for one of New York City's finest skyline and water views. Close by lies Ellis Island, the American gateway for more than 12 million new arrivals between 1892 and 1954. These days it's home to one of the city's most moving museums, paying tribute to these immigrants and their indelible courage.

👁 Map p30, B8

📞 212-363-3200, ferry tickets 📞 877-523-9849

www.nps.gov/stli

ferry adult/child incl Statue of Liberty & Ellis Island $18/9, incl Liberty crown $21/12

🕗 8:30am-5:30pm

Ⓢ 1 to South Ferry; 4/5 to Bowling Green

Statue of Liberty

Don't Miss

Statue of Liberty

Folks who reserve their tickets to the statue in advance are able to climb the 354 steps to Lady Liberty's crown, from where the city and harbor are breathtaking. That said, crown access is extremely limited, and the only way in is to reserve your spot in advance – and the further in advance you can do it, the better, as a six-month lead time is allowed. Each customer may only reserve a maximum of four crown tickets, and children must be at least 4ft tall to access the crown. If you miss out on crown tickets, you may have better luck booking tickets to the pedestal, which also offers commanding views.

Ellis Island's Immigration Museum

Ellis Island's three-level Immigration Museum is a poignant tribute to the immigrant experience. It is estimated that 40% of Americans today have at least one ancestor who was processed at Ellis Island, confirming the major role this tiny harbor island has played in the making of modern America. The museum's self-guided audio tour features narratives from a number of sources, including historians, architects and the immigrants themselves, bringing to life the center's hefty collection of personal objects, official documents, photographs and film footage. It's an evocative experience to relive personal memories – both good and bad – in the very halls and corridors in which they occurred. If you're very short on time, focus on the outstanding Through America's Gate and Peak Immigration Years exhibitions on the 2nd floor.

☑ Top Tips

▶ The ferry ride from Battery Park in Lower Manhattan lasts only 15 minutes, but a trip to both the Statue of Liberty and Ellis Island is an all-day affair, and only those setting out on the ferry by 1pm will be able to visit both sites.

▶ Reservations to visit the Statue of Liberty are strongly recommended, as you get a specific visit time and a guarantee that you'll get in.

▶ If you don't have crown or pedestal tickets, don't fret. All ferry tickets to Liberty Island offer basic access to the grounds, including self-guided audio tours, which give loads of historical info on the statue (there's even an audioguide for kids).

✕ Take a Break

Skip the cafeteria fare at Lady Liberty and pack a picnic lunch. Or visit early and return to Lower Manhattan for foodie market Seaport Smorgasburg (p38) or the gourmet emporium Inside Brookfield Place (p39).

Top Sights
National September 11 Memorial & Museum

The National September 11 Memorial is a dignified tribute to the victims of the worst terrorist attack on American soil. Titled *Reflecting Absence,* the memorial's two massive reflecting pools are symbols of hope and renewal as well as tributes to the thousands who lost their lives. Beside them stands the Memorial Museum, a striking, solemn space documenting that horrific day in 2001.

◉ Map p30, B5

www.911memorial.org

180 Greenwich St

memorial free, museum adult/child $24/15

◷ 9am-8pm Sun-Thu, to 9pm Fri & Sat

Ⓢ E to World Trade Center; R to Cortlandt St; 2/3 to Park Pl

National September 11 Memorial and Museum, designed by architect Michael Arad and landscape architect Peter Walker

Don't Miss

Reflecting Pools

Surrounded by a plaza planted with 400 swamp white oak trees, the September 11 Memorial's reflecting pools occupy the very footprints of the ill-fated twin towers. From their rim, a steady cascade of water pours 30ft down toward a central void. The flow of the water is richly symbolic, beginning as hundreds of smaller streams, merging into a massive torrent of collective confusion, and ending with a slow journey toward an abyss. Bronze panels frame the pools, inscribed with the names of those who died in the terrorist attacks of September 11, 2001, and in the World Trade Center car bombing on February 26, 1993.

Memorial Museum

Between the reflective pools stands the entrance to the National September 11 Memorial Museum, its subterranean multimedia galleries documenting the terrorist attacks. Among the relics is the 'survivors' staircase', used by hundreds of workers to flee the WTC site. At the bottom of these stairs, the interactive In Memoriam gallery sheds light on the victims' lives. You'll also find the last steel column removed from the clean-up, adorned with the messages and mementos of recovery workers, responders and loved ones of the victims.

One World Trade Center

At the northwest corner of the WTC site is architect David M Childs' One World Trade Center (1 WTC). Not only the loftiest building in America, this tapered, 1776ft-tall giant is currently the tallest building in the Western Hemisphere and the fourth tallest in the world by pinnacle height. Head up to One World Observatory for sublime views from over 100 stories above the earth.

☑ Top Tips

▶ In the museum, look out for the so-called 'Angel of 9/11', the eerie outline of a woman's anguished face on a twisted girder believed to originate from the point where American Airlines Flight 11 slammed into the North Tower.

▶ Take time to appreciate the design of the new WTC Transportation Hub, rising beside the museum. Conceived by Spanish starchitect Santiago Calatrava, it was inspired by the image of a child releasing a dove.

▶ Last entry is two hours before close.

▶ Entry to the museum is free from 5pm to 8pm on Tuesdays.

✖ Take a Break

Escape the swarm of restaurants serving the lunching Wall St crowd and head to Tribeca for a variety of in-demand eats, such as Locanda Verde (p39).

Top Sights
Brooklyn Bridge

A New York icon, the Brooklyn Bridge was the world's first steel suspension bridge. When it opened in 1883, the 1596ft span between its two support towers was the longest in history. Although its construction was fraught with disaster, the bridge became a magnificent example of urban design, inspiring poets, writers and painters. Today, the Brooklyn Bridge continues to dazzle – many regard it as the most beautiful bridge in the world.

◉ Map p30, E4

S 4/5/6 to Brooklyn Bridge-City Hall; J/Z to Chambers St; R to City Hall

Don't Miss

Crossing the Bridge

For many visitors to NYC, crossing the Brooklyn Bridge is a rite of passage. The neo-Gothic wonder was designed by Prussian-born engineer John Roebling, who died of tetanus poisoning before construction even began. His son, Washington Roebling, supervised construction of the bridge, which lasted 14 years and managed to survive budget overruns and the deaths of 20 workers. The younger Roebling himself suffered from the bends while helping to excavate the riverbed for the bridge's western tower and remained bedridden for much of the project. When the bridge opened in June 1883, a shout from the crowd that the bridge was collapsing caused mayhem and the trampling death of 12 pedestrians.

Brooklyn Bridge Park

Across the bridge in Brooklyn is one of the borough's most celebrated new assets, the 85-acre Brooklyn Bridge Park (www.brooklynbridgepark. org). Stretching 1.3 miles from Jay St in Dumbo to the west end of Atlantic Ave in Cobble Hill, the park's highlights include the Empire Fulton Ferry, a state park featuring a grassy lawn with skyline views and the lovingly restored 1922-vintage Jane's Carousel, set inside a glass pavilion designed by Pritzker Prize–winning architect Jean Nouvel. Just south of Empire Fulton Ferry is Pier 1, a 9 acre space complete with playground, lushly landscaped walkways, and a hillside offering mesmerizing views over Lower Manhattan. From July through August, free outdoor films are screened on Pier 1, against the stunning Manhattan skyline. Other free open-air events take place throughout summer.

☑ Top Tips

▶ Walking across the bridge, stay on the side of the walkway marked for pedestrians. One half is designated for cyclists, and used by commuters and tourists alike.

▶ To beat the crowds, come early morning, when you'll have those views largely to yourself.

✕ Take a Break

From May to October, Brooklyn Bridge Park features a few seasonal concessions, such as wood-fired pizza, beer and Italian treats at **Fornino** (☏718-422-1107; www.fornino.com; Pier 6, Brooklyn Bridge Park; pizzas $12-25; ⊗10am-10pm Apr-Oct; ☒B45 to Brooklyn Bridge Park/Pier 6, Ⓢ2/3, 4/5 to Borough Hall). Year-round you can try classic and creative pizzas at **Juliana's** (☏718-596-6700; www.julianaspizza. com; 19 Old Fulton St, btwn Water & Front Sts, Dumbo; pizza $17-32; ⊗11:30am-11pm; ⒮A/C to High St), near Pier 1.

Pier 16

South Street
Seaport 9

Pier 15

East River

Ferry to
Hoboken (NJ)

Pier 11

Franklin D Roosevelt Dr

Heekman St

South St

S South St

Fulton St

16 35

John St

Front St

Fletcher St

Water St

Pearl St

Cliff St

Platt St

Maiden La

Museum of
American Finance

Pier 6

Gouverneur La

Old Slip

Ferry to
Governors Island

Louise
Neyelson
Plaza

Cedar St

Pine St

Water St

Hanover
Sq

Vietnam
Veterans
Plaza

John St

Dutch

S William St

21

Stone St

Fraunces
Tavern Museum

LOWER
MANHATTAN

William St

10

Federal
Hall

12

Broad St

5

Beaver St

Whitehall St

S Liberty St

Nassau St

Wall St

Wall St

13

Stock
Exchange

New St

New York
Stock Exchange

24

Whitehall St

Peter Minuit
Plaza

South Ferry

15 Staten
Island Ferry

Zuccotti
Park

Trinity 7

Church

Rector St

Exchange Pl

Pearl St

State St

S

State St

Hugh L. Carey
Tunnel

Broadway

Cedar St

Thames St

Trinity Pl

Greenwich St

Morris
St

Bowling
Green

FINANCIAL
DISTRICT

National
Museum of the
American Indian

Battery Pl

Battery
Park

Castle
Clinton

New York
Harbor

Ferry to:
Statue of Liberty

Memorial 31
National September 11
Memorial & Museum 17

North
Cove

Liberty St

Carlisle St

Rector St

Washington St

Edgar St

Greenwich St

West Side Hwy

Skyscraper
Museum 6

2nd Pl

Battery Pl

Pier A 26

Ferry to:
Ellis Island

Upper
New York Bay

BATTERY PARK
CITY

Liberty St

South End Ave

W Thames St

Albany St

Museum of
Jewish Heritage 1

Robert F Wagner
Jr Park

Battery Park City Esplanade

Hudson River

E

D

C

B

A

5

6

7

8

Sights

Museum of Jewish Heritage
MUSEUM

1 ◉ Map p30, B7

An evocative waterfront museum, exploring all aspects of modern Jewish identity and culture, from religious traditions to artistic accomplishments. The museum's core exhibition includes a detailed exploration of the Holocaust, with personal artifacts, photographs and documentary films providing a personal, moving experience. Outdoors is the Garden of Stones installation. Created by artist Andy Goldsworthy and dedicated to those who lost loved ones in the Holocaust, its 18 boulders form a narrow pathway for contemplating the fragility of life. (☑646-437-4202; www.mjhnyc.org; 36 Battery Pl; adult/child $12/free, 4-8pm Wed free; ☺10am-5:45pm Sun-Tue & Thu, to 8pm Wed, to 5pm Fri mid-Mar–mid-Nov, to 3pm Fri rest of year; ♿; ⑤4/5 to Bowling Green; R to Whitehall St)

One World Observatory
VIEWPOINT

2 ◉ Map p30, B4

Spanning levels 100 to 102 of the highest building in the western hemisphere, One World Observatory offers dazzling views from its sky-high perch. Choose a clear day and expect to see all five boroughs and surrounding states. Not surprisingly, it's a hugely popular site. Purchase tickets online: you'll need to choose the date and time of your visit. (☑844-696-1776; www.oneworldobservatory.com; cnr West & Vesey Sts; adult/child $32/26; ☺9am-8pm, last ticket sold 7:15pm; ⑤E to World Trade Center; 2/3 to Park Pl; A/C, J/Z, 4/5 to Fulton St; R to Cortlandt St)

National Museum of the American Indian
MUSEUM

3 ◉ Map p30, C7

An affiliate of the Smithsonian Institution, this elegant tribute to Native American culture is set in Cass Gilbert's spectacular 1907 Custom House, one of NYC's finest beaux-arts buildings. Beyond a vast elliptical rotunda, sleek galleries play host to changing exhibitions documenting Native American art, culture, life and beliefs. The museum's permanent collection includes stunning decorative arts, textiles and ceremonial objects that document the diverse native cultures across the Americas. (☑212-514-3700; www.nmai.si.edu; 1 Bowling Green; admission free; ☺10am-5pm Fri-Wed, to 8pm Thu; ⑤4/5 to Bowling Green; R to Whitehall St)

Woolworth Building
HISTORIC BUILDING

4 ◉ Map p30, C4

The world's tallest building upon completion in 1913, Cass Gilbert's 60-story, 792ft-tall Woolworth Building is a neo-Gothic marvel, elegantly clad in masonry and terra-cotta. Surpassed in height by the Chrysler Building in 1930, its landmarked lobby is a breathtaking spectacle of dazzling,

Museum of Jewish Heritage

Byzantine-like mosaics. The lobby is only accessible on prebooked guided tours, which also offer insight into the building's more curious original features, among them a dedicated subway entrance and a secret swimming pool. (☎203-966-9663; http://woolworthtours. com; 233 Broadway, at Park Pl; 30/60/90min tours $20/30/45; ⑤R to City Hall; 2/3 to Park Pl; 4/5/6 to Brooklyn Bridge-City Hall)

Fraunces Tavern Museum   MUSEUM

5 ⊙ Map p30, C7

Combining five early-18th-century structures, this unique museum/ restaurant/bar pays homage to the nation-shaping events of 1783, when the British relinquished control of New York at the end of the Revolutionary War, and General George Washington gave a farewell speech to the officers of the Continental Army in the 2nd-floor dining room on December 4. (☎212-425-1778; www. frauncestavernmuseum.org; 54 Pearl St, btwn Broad St & Coenties Slip; adult/under 6yr/6-18yr $7/free/4; ⊙noon-5pm Mon-Fri, 11:30am-5pm Sat & Sun; ⑤J/Z to Broad St; 4/5 to Bowling Green; R to Whitehall St-South Ferry; 1 to South Ferry)

Skyscraper Museum   MUSEUM

6 ⊙ Map p30, B7

Fans of phallic architecture will appreciate this compact, high-gloss gallery, examining skyscrapers as objects of design, engineering and urban renewal. Temporary exhibitions dominate the space, with past exhibitions exploring everything from New York's new generation of super-slim residential towers, to the world's new breed of supertalls. Permanent fixtures include information on the design and construction of the Empire State Building and World Trade Center. (📞212-968-1961; www.skyscraper.org; 39 Battery Pl; admission $5; ⊙noon-6pm Wed-Sun; Ⓢ4/5 to Bowling Green; R to Whitehall St)

Trinity Church CHURCH

7 ◉ Map p30, B6

New York City's tallest building upon completion in 1846, Trinity Church features a 280ft-high bell tower and a richly colored stained-glass window over the altar. Famous residents of its serene cemetery include founding father Alexander Hamilton, while its excellent music series includes Concerts at One (1pm Thursdays) and magnificent choir concerts, including an annual December rendition of Handel's *Messiah*. (www.trinitywallstreet.org; Broadway, at Wall St; ⊙church 7am-6pm Mon-Fri, 8am-4pm Sat, 7am-4pm Sun, churchyard 7am-4pm Mon-Fri, 8am-3pm Sat, 7am-3pm Sun; Ⓢ R to Rector St; 2/3, 4/5 to Wall St)

St Paul's Chapel CHURCH

8 ◉ Map p30, C4

After his inauguration in 1789, George Washington worshipped at this classic revival brownstone chapel, which found new fame in the aftermath of September 11. With the World Trade

---

Understand
Building Lady Liberty

One of America's most powerful symbols of kinship and freedom, 'Liberty Enlightening the World' was a joint effort between America and France to commemorate the centennial of the Declaration of Independence. It was created by commissioned sculptor Frédéric-Auguste Bartholdi. The artist spent most of 20 years turning his dream – to create the hollow monument and mount it in New York Harbor – into reality. Bartholdi's work on the statue was delayed by structural challenges – a problem resolved by the metal framework mastery of railway engineer Gustave Eiffel (of, yes, the famous tower). The work of art was finally completed in France in 1884. It was shipped to NYC as 350 pieces packed into 214 crates; reassembled over a span of four months; and placed on a US-made granite pedestal. Its spectacular October 1886 dedication included New York's first ticker-tape parade and a flotilla of almost 300 vessels. The monument made it onto the UN's list of World Heritage Sites in 1984.

Center destruction occurring just a block away, the mighty structure became a spiritual support and volunteer center, movingly documented in its exhibition 'Unwavering Spirit: Hope & Healing at Ground Zero.' (☏212-602-0800; www.trinitywallstreet.org; Broadway, at Fulton St; ⏰10am-6pm Mon-Sat, 7am-6pm Sun; ⓢA/C, J/Z, 2/3, 4/5 to Fulton St; R to Cortlandt St; E to World Trade Center)

South Street Seaport

AREA

9 ◉ Map p30, E5

This enclave of cobbled streets, maritime warehouses and shops combines the best and worst in historic preservation. It's not on the radar for most New Yorkers, but tourists are drawn to the nautical air, the frequent street performers and the mobbed restaurants. (www.southstreetseaport.com; ⓢA/C, J/Z, 2/3, 4/5 to Fulton St)

Museum of American Finance

MUSEUM

10 ◉ Map p30, C6

Money makes this interactive museum go round. It focuses on historic moments in American financial history, and its permanent collections include rare historic currency (including Confederate currency used by America's southern states during the Civil War), stock and bond certificates from the Gilded Age, the oldest known photograph of Wall St and a stock ticker from c 1875. (☏212-908-4110; www.moaf.

◉ Local Life
Governors Island

The former military outpost **Governors Island** (off Map p30; ☏212-825-3045; http://govisland.com; admission free; ⏰10am-6pm Mon-Fri, 10am-7pm Sat & Sun; ⓢ4, 5 to Bowling Green; 1 to South Ferry) is one of New York's most popular seasonal playgrounds. Each summer, daily ferries make the seven-minute trip from Lower Manhattan to the 172-acre oasis, where you'll find grassy lawns, waterfront paths, a historic fort and a hammock grove. Throughout the summer, the island hosts concerts, outdoor art exhibitions and other events (plus food trucks). Bike rental is available on the island. Ferries depart from 10 South St, from the building next to the Staten Island Ferry Terminal.

org; 48 Wall St, btwn Pearl & William Sts; adult/child $8/free; ⏰10am-4pm Tue-Sat; ⓢ2/3, 4/5 to Wall St)

African Burial Ground

MEMORIAL

11 ◉ Map p30, C3

In 1991, construction workers here uncovered more than 400 stacked wooden caskets, just 16ft to 28ft below street level. The boxes contained the remains of enslaved Africans (nearby Trinity Church graveyard had banned the burial of Africans at the time). Today, a memorial and visitor center honors an estimated 15,000 Africans buried here during the 17th and 18th

centuries. (📞212-637-2019; www.nps.
gov/afbg; 290 Broadway, btwn Duane & Elk
Sts; admission free; 🕐memorial 9am-5pm
Mon-Sat, visitor center 10am-4pm Tue-Sat;
Ⓢ1/2/3, A/C, J/Z to Chambers St; R to City
Hall; 4/5/6 to Brooklyn Bridge-City Hall)

Federal Hall   MUSEUM

12 ⊙ Map p30, C6

A Greek Revival masterpiece, Federal
Hall houses a museum dedicated to
postcolonial New York. Themes include
George Washington's inauguration,
Alexander Hamilton's relationship with
the city, and the struggles of John Peter
Zenger – jailed, tried and acquitted of
libel on this site for exposing government corruption in his newspaper.
There's also a visitor information hall
with city maps and brochures. (www.
nps.gov/feha; 26 Wall St, entrance on Pine St;
🕐9am-5pm Mon-Fri; Ⓢ J/Z to Broad St; 2/3,
4/5 to Wall St)

New York
Stock Exchange   HISTORIC BUILDING

13 ⊙ Map p30, C6

Home to the world's best-known
stock exchange (the NYSE), Wall St
is an iconic symbol of US capitalism.
Behind the portentous Romanesque
facade about one billion shares
change hands daily, a sight no longer
accessible to the public due to security
concerns. Feel free to gawp outside
the building, protected by barricades
and the hawk-eyed NYPD (New York
Police Department). (www.nyse.com;

11 Wall St; 🕐closed to the public; Ⓢ J/Z to
Broad St; 2/3, 4/5 to Wall St)

Irish Hunger
Memorial   MEMORIAL

14 ⊙ Map p30, A4

Artist Brian Tolle's compact laby-
rinth of low limestone walls and
patches of grass pays tribute to the
Great Irish Famine and Migration
(1845–52), which prompted hundreds
of thousands of immigrants to leave
Ireland for better opportunities in the
New World. Representing abandoned
cottages, stone walls and potato fields,
the work was created with stones
from each of Ireland's 32 counties.
(290 Vesey St, at North End Ave; admission
free; Ⓢ2/3 to Park Pl; E to World Trade
Center; A/C to Chambers St)

Staten Island
Ferry   FERRY

15 ⊙ Map p30, D8

Staten Islanders know these hulking,
dirty-orange ferryboats as commuter
vehicles, while Manhattanites like
to think of them as their secret,
romantic vessels for a spring-day
escape. Yet many a tourist is clued
into the charms of the Staten Island
Ferry, whose 5.2-mile journey between
Lower Manhattan and the Staten
Island neighborhood of St George is
one of NYC's finest free adventures.
(www.siferry.com; Whitehall Terminal, 4 South
St, at Whitehall; admission free; 🕐24hr; Ⓢ1
to South Ferry)

Understand
Clues to the Past

Manhattan's Financial District is more than just gleaming towers, stock markets and a lust for profit. It's New York City's cradle and the setting for many important historical tales. Wall St once marked the northern boundary of the fledgling Dutch settlement of New Amsterdam. On it, Federal Hall is the very site on which George Washington became America's first president. Yet beneath these famous facts lie some lesser-known historical anecdotes.

What's in a Name?

Wall St is one of many streets harboring clues to the past. Originally known as Mother-of-Pearl St for the bounty of iridescent shells found in the vicinity, crooked Pearl St traces the foot of a long-gone hill. The leveling of hills became a common practice in the 18th century as Manhattan's population grew and demand for land increased. Dug up and dumped into the East River, the soil created space for the aptly named Water St. By the end of the 18th century, the shore had been pushed back even further to create Front St. Home to the New York Stock Exchange, Broad St was once a canal, crossed by a bridge at...Bridge St.

Blast from the Past

Buildings, too, can tell a tale. Take the former headquarters of JP Morgan Bank on the southeast corner of Wall and Broad Sts. The pockmarks on the building's Wall St facade are the remnants of the so-called Morgan Bank bombing – America's deadliest terrorist attack until the Oklahoma City bombing of 1995. At exactly 12.01pm on September 16, 1920, 500 pounds of lead sash weights and 100 pounds of dynamite exploded from a horse-drawn carriage. Thirty-eight people were killed and around 400 injured. Among the latter was John F Kennedy's father, Joseph P Kennedy. The bomb's detonation outside America's most influential financial institution at the time led many to blame anti-capitalist groups, from Italian anarchists to stock-standard Bolsheviks. The crime has never been solved; the decision to reopen both the bank and New York Stock Exchange the following day led to a swift clean-up of both debris and any crucial clues.

Eating

Seaport Smorgasburg
MARKET $

16 🍴 Map p30, E5

Brooklyn's hipster food market has jumped the East River, injecting touristy South Street Seaport with some much-needed local cred. Cooking up a storm from May to late September, its offerings include anything from lobster rolls, ramen and pizza, to slow-smoked Texan-style brisket sandwiches. Add a splash of historic architecture and you have one of downtown's coolest cheap feeds. (www.smorgasburg.com; Fulton St, btwn Front & South Sts; dishes $6-19; ⊗11am-8pm May-Sep; Ⓢ A/C, J/Z, 2/3, 4/5 to Fulton St)

Brookfield Place
FAST FOOD, MARKET $$

17 🍴 Map p30, A5

The World Financial Center is now Brookfield Place, a polished, high-end office and retail complex that's home to two fabulous food halls. For Gallic flavors, hit **Le District** (☎212-981-8588; http://ledistrict.com; Brookfield Place, 200 Vesey St; sandwiches $6-15, market mains $16-24, Beauborg dinner mains $18-45; ⊗6:30am-11pm Mon-Fri, 8:30am-11pm Sat, 8:30am-10pm Sun; 🛜; Ⓢ E to World Trade Center; 2/3 to Park Pl; R to Cortlandt St; A/C, 4/5, J/Z to Fulton St), a sprawling wonderland of high-gloss pastries, stinky cheese, pretty tartines and lusty *steak frites*. One floor above is **Hudson Eats** (☎212-417-2445; http://brookfieldplaceny.com/directory/food; dishes from $7; ⊗10am-9pm Mon-Sat, noon-7pm Sun; 🛜;

Understand
Long Before New York

Long before the days of European conquest, the swath that would eventually become NYC belonged to Native Americans known as the Lenape – 'original people' – who resided in a series of seasonal campsites. They lived up and down the eastern seaboard; along the signature shoreline; and on hills and in valleys once sculpted by Ice Age glaciers – the area now called Hamilton Heights and Bay Ridge. The glaciers scoured off soft rock, leaving behind Manhattan's stark foundations of gneiss and schist.

Around 11,000 years before the first Europeans sailed through the Narrows, the Lenape people foraged, hunted and fished the regional bounty here. Spear points, arrowheads, bone heaps and shell mounds testify to their presence. Some of their pathways still lie beneath streets such as Broadway. In the Lenape language of Munsee, the term Manhattan may have translated as 'hilly island.' Others trace the meaning to a more colorful phrase: 'place of general inebriation.'

S E to World Trade Center; 2/3 to Park Pl; R to Cortlandt St; A/C, 4/5, J/Z to Fulton St), a fashionable enclave of quality fast bites, from sushi and tacos to salads and burgers. (📞212-417-7000; brookfield placeny.com; 200 Vesey St; 📶; S E to World Trade Center; 2/3 to Park Pl; R to Cortlandt St; A/C, 4/5, J/Z to Fulton St)

Fraunces Tavern AMERICAN $$

Can you really pass up a chance to eat at the tavern (see 5 ⊙ Map p30, C7) where George Washington (it's been documented) supped in 1762? Expect heaping portions of tavern stew, clam chowder, slow-roasted chicken pot pie, followed by a rather cheeky classic sundae for two (brownie bits, peanuts, bananas, cherries and hot fudge). The bar, filled with friendly locals, is great for a snack and a drink. (📞212-968-1776; www.frauncestavern.com; 54 Pearl St, at Broad St; mains lunch $14-38, dinner $20-38; ⊙11am-10pm; S R to Whitehall St)

Da Mikele PIZZA $$

18 ✕ Map p30, B2

An Italo-Tribeca hybrid where pressed tin and recycled wood meet retro Vespa, Da Mikele channels the *dolce vita* (sweet life) with its weeknight aperitivo (5pm to 7pm), where your drink includes a complimentary spread of lip-smacking bar bites. The real reason to head here, however, is for the pizzas. We're talking light, beautifully charred revelations, simultaneously crisp and chewy, and good enough to make a Neapolitan

A classic meal at Fraunces Tavern

SIVAN ASKAYO/LONELY PLANET ©

weep. (📞212-925-8800; http://luzzosgroup. com; 275 Church St, btwn White & Franklin Sts; pizzas $17-21; ⊙noon-10:30pm Sun-Wed, to 11:30pm Thu-Sat; 📶; S 1 to Franklin St; A/C/E, N/Q/R, J/Z, 6 to Canal St)

Locanda Verde ITALIAN $$$

19 ✕ Map p30, A2

Step through the velvet curtains into a scene of loosened button-downs, black dresses and slick barmen behind a long, crowded bar. This celebrated brasserie showcases modern, Italo-inspired fare such as housemade pappardelle with lamb bolognese, mint and sheep's milk ricotta, and Sicilian-style halibut with heirloom squash and almonds. Weekend brunch features no less creative fare: try scampi and grits or lemon ricotta pancakes with blueberries. (📞212-925-3797; www.locandaverdenyc.com; 377 Greenwich St, at Moore St; mains lunch $19-29, dinner $29-36; ⏰7am-11pm Mon-Thu, to 11:30pm Fri, 8am-11:30pm Sat, 8am-11pm Sun; 🚇A/C/E to Canal St; 1 to Franklin St)

Bâtard
MODERN AMERICAN $$$

20 ✖ Map p30, B1

Austrian chef Markus Glocker heads this warm, Michelin-starred hot spot, where a pared-back interior puts the focus squarely on the food. It's attention well deserved. Glocker's dishes are beautifully balanced and textured, whether it's sweet Maine lobster paired with salsify and gritty potato crisps, or tender venison wrapped in a skin of Swiss chard and golden phyllo pastry for added comfort. (📞212-219-2777; www.batardtribeca.com; 239 W Broadway , btwn Walker & White Sts; 2-/3-/4-courses $55/69/79; ⏰5:30-10:30pm Mon-Sat; 🚇1 to Franklin St; A/C/E to Canal St)

Drinking

Dead Rabbit
COCKTAIL BAR

21 🍸 Map p30, C7

Named in honor of a dreaded Irish-American gang, this most-wanted rabbit is regularly voted one of the world's best bars. During the day, hit the sawdust-sprinkled taproom for specialty beers, historic punches and pop-inns (lightly hopped ale spiked with different flavors). Come evening, scurry upstairs to the cozy Parlor for more than 70 meticulously researched cocktails. Tip: head in before 5:30pm to avoid a long wait for a Parlor seat. (📞646-422-7906; www.deadrabbitnyc.com; 30 Water St; ⏰taproom 11am-4am, parlor 5pm-2am Mon-Wed, to 3am Thu-Sat; 🚇R to Whitehall St; 1 to South Ferry)

Ward III
COCKTAIL BAR

22 🍸 Map p30, B3

Dark and bustling, Ward III channels old-school jauntiness with its elegant libations, vintage vibe (including old Singer sewing tables behind the bar), and gentlemanly house rules (No 2: 'Don't be creepy'). Reminisce over a Moroccan martini, or sample the bar's coveted collection of whiskeys. If you need to line the stomach, top-notch bar grub is served till close. (📞212-240-9194; www.ward3tribeca.com; 111 Reade St, btwn Church St & W Broadway; ⏰4pm-4am Mon-Fri, 5pm-4am Sat, to 2am Sun; 🚇A/C, 1/2/3 to Chambers St)

Smith & Mills
COCKTAIL BAR

23 🍸 Map p30, A2

Petite Smith & Mills ticks all the cool boxes: unmarked exterior, kooky industrial interior and expertly crafted cocktails with a penchant for the classics. Space is limited so head in early if you fancy kicking back on a plush banquette. A seasonal menu spans light snacks to a particularly notable burger pimped with caramelized on-

One World Observatory (p32)

ions. (☎212-226-2515; www.smithandmills.com; 71 N Moore St, btwn Hudson & Greenwich Sts; ⏲11am-2am Sun-Wed, to 3am Thu-Sat; Ⓢ1 to Franklin St)

Bluestone Lane CAFE

24 ⓠ Map p30, C6

While the NYSE busies itself with stocks, its tiny Aussie neighbor does a roaring trade in killer coffee. Littered with retro Melbourne memorabilia and squeezed into the corner of an art-deco office block, it's never short of smooth suits and homesick antipodeans craving a cup of decent, velvety joe. (☎646-684-3771; http://bluestone laneny.com; 30 Broad St, entrance on New St; ⏲7am-5pm Mon-Fri, 9am-3pm Sat & Sun; Ⓢ J/Z to Broad St; 2/3, 4/5 to Wall St)

Terroir Tribeca WINE BAR

25 ⓠ Map p30, A2

Award-winning Terroir keeps oenophiles upbeat with its well-versed, well-priced wine list. Drops span the Old World and New, among them natural wines and inspired offerings from smaller producers. Best of all, there's a generous selection of wines by the glass, making a global wine tour a whole lot easier. (☎212-625-9463; www.wineisterroir.com; 24 Harrison St, at Greenwich St; ⏲4pm-1am Mon-Sat, to 11pm Sun; Ⓢ1 to Franklin St)

Pier A Harbor House
BAR

26 🍷 Map p30, B8

Looking dashing after a major restoration, Pier A is now a super-spacious, casual eating and drinking house located right on New York Harbor. If the weather's on your side, try for a seat on the waterside deck. Here, picnic benches, sun umbrellas and an eyeful of New York skyline combine to make a brilliant spot to sip craft beers or one of the house cocktails that are available on tap. (📞212-785-0153; www.piera.com; 22 Battery Pl; ⏰11am-4am; 🛜; 🚇4/5 to Bowling Green; R to Whitehall St; 1 to South Ferry)

Weather Up
COCKTAIL BAR

27 🍷 Map p30, B3

Softly lit subway tiles, amiable bar-keeps and seductive cocktails make for a bewitching trio at Weather Up. Sweet talk the staff while enjoying a Whizz Bang (scotch whiskey, dry ver-mouth, housemade grenadine, orange bitters and absinthe). Failing that, comfort yourself with some satisfying snacks. (📞212-766-3202; www.weatherupnyc.com; 159 Duane St, btwn Hudson St & W Broadway; ⏰5pm-late Mon-Sat; 🚇1/2/3 to Chambers St)

Keg No 229
BEER HALL

28 🍷 Map p30, E5

If you know that a Flying Dog Raging Bitch is a craft beer – not a nickname for your ex – this curated beer bar is for you. From Elysian Space Dust to Abita Purple Haze, its battalion of drafts, bottles and cans are a who's who of boutique American brews. Across the street, Bin No 220 is its wine-loving sibling. (📞212-566-2337; www.kegno229.com; 229 Front St, btwn Beekman St & Peck Slip; ⏰11:30am-midnight Sun-Wed, to 2am Thu-Sat; 🚇A/C, J/Z, 2/3, 4/5 to Fulton St; R to Cortlandt St)

Macao
COCKTAIL BAR

29 🍷 Map p30, B1

Though we love the 1940s-style 'gambling parlor' bar-restaurant, it's the downstairs 'opium den' (open Thursday to Saturday) that gets our hearts racing. A Chinese-Portuguese fusion of grub and liquor, both floors are a solid spot for late-night sipping and snacking, especially if you've got a soft spot for sizzle-on-the-tongue libations. (📞212-431-8642; www.macaonyc.com; 311 Church St, btwn Lispenard & Walker Sts; ⏰bar 5pm-2am Sun-Wed, to 4am Thu-Sat; 🚇A/C/E to Canal St)

Top Tip

Downtown TKTS

After cheap tickets to Broadway shows? Ditch the TKTS Booth in Times Square for the TKTS Booth at South Street Seaport. Queues usually move a little faster and you can purchase tickets for next-day matinees (something you can't do at the Times Square outlet). The TKTS Smartphone app offers real-time listings of what's on sale.

South Street Seaport (p35)

Entertainment

Soho Rep
THEATER

30 ⭐ Map p30, C1

This is one of New York's finest Off-Broadway companies. Soho Rep wows theater fans and critics with its annual trio of sharp, innovative new work. Kevin Spacey, Ed O'Neill and Kathleen Turner all made their professional debuts here, and the company's productions have garnered no shortage of Obie (Off-Broadway Theater) Awards. Check the website for info on current or upcoming shows. (Soho Repertory Theatre; ☏212-941-8632; http://sohorep. org; 46 Walker St, btwn Church St & Broadway; ⓢA/C/E, N/Q/R, 6, J/Z to Canal St)

Shopping

Century 21
FASHION

31 🔒 Map p30, B5

For penny-pinching fashionistas, this giant, cut-price department store is dangerously addictive. Raid the racks for designer duds at up to 65% off. Not everything is a knockout or a bargain, but persistence pays off. You'll also find accessories, shoes, cosmetics, homewares and toys. (☏212-227-9092; www.c21stores.com; 22 Cortlandt St, btwn Church St & Broadway; ⓩ7:45am-9pm Mon-Fri, 10am-9pm Sat, 11am-8pm Sun; ⓢA/C, J/Z, 2/3, 4/5 to Fulton St; R to Cortlandt St)

Shinola
ACCESSORIES

32 🔒 Map p30, A2

Well known for its coveted wrist-watches, Detroit-based Shinola branches out with a super-cool selection of Made-in-USA life props. You can bag anything from leather iPad cases, journal covers and toiletry bags, to grooming products, jewelry and limited-edition bicycles with customized bags. Added bonuses include complimentary monogramming of leather goods and stationery, and an in-house espresso bar, **Smile** (☎917-728-3023; www.thesmilenyc.com; 177 Franklin St, btwn Greenwich & Hudson Sts; ☺7am-7pm Mon-Fri, 8am-7pm Sat, 8am-6pm Sun; Ⓢ1 to Franklin St), to boot. (☎917-728-3000; www.shinola.com; 177 Franklin St,

btwn Greenwich & Hudson Sts; ☺11am-7pm Mon-Sat, noon-6pm Sun; Ⓢ1 to Franklin St)

Steven Alan
FASHION, ACCESSORIES

33 🔒 Map p30, B2

New York designer Steven Alan mixes his hip, heritage-inspired threads for men and women with a beautiful edit of clothes from indie-chic labels like France's Arpenteur and Scandinavia's Acne and Norse Projects. Accessories include hard-to-find fragrances, bags, jewelry and a selection of shoes by cognoscenti brands such as Common Projects and Isabel Marant Étoile. (☎212-343-0692; www.stevenalan.com; 103 Franklin St, btwn Church St & W Broadway; ☺11:30am-7pm Mon-Wed, Fri & Sat, 11:30am-8pm Thu, noon-6pm Sun; ⓈA/C/E to Canal St; 1 to Franklin St)

Philip Williams Posters
VINTAGE

34 🔒 Map p30, B3

You'll find over half a million posters in this cavernous treasure trove, from oversized French advertisements for perfume and cognac to Soviet film posters and retro-fab promos for TWA. Prices range from $15 for small reproductions to a few thousand bucks for rare, showpiece originals. There is a second entrance at 52 Warren St. (☎212-513-0313; www.postermuseum.com; 122 Chambers St, btwn Church St & W Broadway; ☺10am-7pm Mon-Sat; ⓈA/C, 1/2/3 to Chambers St)

Ⓠ Local Life
Flea Theater

One of NYC's top Off-Broadway companies, the **Flea Theater** (Map p30, C1; ☎tickets 212-352-3101; www.theflea.org; 41 White St, btwn Church St & Broadway; Ⓢ1 to Franklin St; A/C/E, N/Q/R, J/Z, 6 to Canal St) is famous for performing innovative, timely new works in its two performance spaces. Luminaries including Sigourney Weaver and John Lithgow have trodden the boards here, and the year-round program also includes music and dance performances.

View of Manhattan from Governors Island (p35)

Bowne Stationers & Co   GIFTS

35 🔒 Map p30, D5

Suitably set in cobbled South Street Seaport, this 18th-century veteran stocks vintage reproduction New York posters, city-themed notepads, pencil cases, cards, stamps and more. You can even bag New York–themed wrapping paper to wrap them in. Next door is the printing workshop, where you can order customized business cards or hone your printing skills at one of the monthly workshops. (📞646-315-4478; 211 Water St, btwn Beekman & Fulton Sts; ⏰11am-7pm; **S**2/3, 4/5, A/C, J/Z to Fulton St)

CityStore   SOUVENIRS

36 🔒 Map p30, C3

Score all manner of New York memorabilia, from authentic taxi medallions, manhole coasters and subway-themed socks to NYPD baseball caps and wine totes featuring Manhattan and Brooklyn themes. Topping it off is a great collection of city-themed books. (📞212-386-0007; http://a856-citystore.nyc.gov; Municipal Bldg, North Plaza, 1 Centre St; ⏰10am-5pm Mon-Fri; **S**J/Z to Chambers St; 4/5/6 to Brooklyn Bridge-City Hall)

Explore

SoHo & Chinatown

Like a colorful quilt of subneighborhoods sewn together in mis-matched patches, the areas orbiting SoHo (South of Houston) feel like a string of mini republics. Style-mavens boutique-hop in boom-ing Nolita (North of Little Italy), Italo-Americans channel Napoli in ever-shrinking Little Italy, and Chinese extended families gossip over *xiao long bao* (soup dumplings) in hyperactive Chinatown.

The Sights in a Day

Take a morning stroll through the bustling streets of Chinatown. Peek in at the giant gilded Buddha at the **Mahayana Temple** (p54), then grab a snack from **Xi'an Famous Foods** (p55) and take it to Columbus Park, where you can watch street musicians and mah-jongg players in action. Afterwards, learn about the past in the **Museum of Chinese in America** (p52).

Before lunch take a stroll up Mulberry St through tiny Little Italy and have a look inside the historic **St Patrick's Old Cathedral** (p54). In Nolita, lunch at the charming cafe **Ruby's** (p55), then check out the tiny boutiques along Mott and Mulberry Sts. Even more serious window-shopping awaits in SoHo. Skip the mainstream fare on Broadway and peruse the side-street wonders **3x1** (p49) and **Rag & Bone** (p61).

In the early evening, go time traveling at the **Merchant's House Museum** (p52), the best-preserved Federalist mansion in all of New York. Afterwards, linger over wine and sharing plates at **Estela** (p58). Cap off the night with a show at **Joe's Pub** (p60), or perhaps some indie cinema at **Film Forum** (p60), a downtown legend for its auteur offerings.

For a local's day in SoHo, see p48.

Local Life

Shop Local SoHo (p48)

Best of New York City

Museums

International Center of Photography (p52)

Merchant's House Museum (p52)

Leslie-Lohman Museum of Gay & Lesbian Art (p54)

Eating

Estela (p58)

Butcher's Daughter (p55)

Balthazar (p58)

Uncle Boons (p57)

Drinking

Apothéke (p59)

Mulberry Project (p59)

Getting There

S Subway For Chinatown, the subway lines drop you off at various points along Canal St (J/Z, N/Q/R and 6). The handiest SoHo stations are Prince St (N/R), Spring St (C/E) and Broadway-Lafayette (B/D/F/M).

Taxi Avoid taking cabs in Chinatown, as the traffic is intense.

Local Life
Shop Local SoHo

Shopaholics across the world lust for SoHo and its sharp, trendy whirlwind of flagship stores, coveted labels and strutting fashionistas. Look beyond the giant global brands, however, and you'll discover a whole other retail scene, one where talented artisans and independent, one-off enterprises keep things local, unique and utterly inspiring. Welcome to SoHo at its homegrown best.

....

1 Single Origin Brew
Charge up with single-origin coffee from **Café Integral** (☎646-801-5747; www.cafeintegral.com; 135 Grand St, btwn Crosby & Lafayette Sts; ☺8.30am-6pm Mon-Fri, 11am-5pm Sat; ⑤N/Q/R, J/Z, 6 to Canal St), a tiny espresso bar inside kooky shop-cum-gallery American Two Shot. You'll probably find owner César Martin Vega, who's obsessed with Nicaraguan coffee beans, at the machine.

❷ Perfect Jeans

3x1 (☎212-391-6969; www.3x1.us; 15 Mercer St, btwn Howard & Grand Sts; ⏰11am-7pm Mon-Sat, noon-6pm Sun; ⑤N/Q/R, J/Z, 6 to Canal St) lets you design your perfect pair of jeans. Choose hems for ready-to-wear pairs (women's from $195, men's from $245); customize fabric and detailing on existing cuts ($525 to $750); or create your most flattering pair from scratch ($1200).

❸ Curiosity Cabinet

Evolution (☎212-343-1114; www.theevolutionstore.com; 120 Spring St, btwn Mercer & Greene Sts; ⏰11am-8pm; ⑤N/R to Prince St; 6 to Spring St) keeps things quirky with natural-history collectibles usually seen in museum cabinets. This is the place to buy – or simply gawp at – framed beetles and butterflies, bugs frozen in amber-resin cubes, stuffed parrots, zebra hides and shark teeth, as well as stony wonders ranging from meteorites and fragments from Mars to 100-million-year-old fossils.

❹ Curbside Culture

The sidewalk engraving on the north-west corner of Prince St and Broadway is the work of Japanese-born sculptor Ken Hiratsuka, who has carved almost 40 sidewalks since moving to NYC in 1982. While this engraving took five or so actual hours of work, its completion took two years (1983–84), as Hiratsuka's illegal nighttime chiseling was often disrupted by police.

❺ Gourmet Snacks

Luxe grocer **Dean & DeLuca** (☎212-226-6800; www.deananddeluca.com; 560 Broadway, at Prince St; pastries from $2.75, sandwiches $11; ⏰7am-8pm Mon-Fri, 8am-8pm Sat & Sun; ⑤N/R to Prince St; 6 to Spring St) is one of the biggest names around town. If you're feeling peckish, ready-to-eat delectables include freshly baked cheese sticks, gourmet quesadillas and sugar-dusted almond croissants.

❻ Fragrance Flights

Drop into library-like apothecary **MiN New York** (☎212-206-6366; www.min.com; 117 Crosby St, btwn Jersey & Prince Sts; ⏰11am-7pm Tue-Sat, noon-6pm Mon & Sun; ⑤B/D/F/M to Broadway-Lafayette St; N/R to Prince St) and request a free 'fragrance flight,' a guided exploration of the store's extraordinary collection of rare, exclusive perfumes and grooming products. Look out for homegrown fragrances from the likes of Strangelove NYC and The Vagabond Prince.

❼ Books & Conversation

If MiN ignites a passion for fragrance, scan the shelves at **McNally Jackson** (☎212-274-1160; www.mcnallyjackson.com; 52 Prince St, btwn Lafayette & Mulberry Sts; ⏰10am-10pm Mon-Sat, to 9pm Sun; ⑤N/R to Prince St; 6 to Spring St) for a title on the subject. This is one of the city's best-loved independent bookstores, stocked with cognoscenti magazines and books, and its in-house cafe is ripe for quality downtime and conversation. In short, a pleasing downtown epilogue.

For reviews see
⊙ Sights	p52
✕ Eating	p55
⊙ Drinking	p59
⊙ Entertainment	p60
⊙ Shopping	p60

EAST VILLAGE

NOHO

NOLITA

SOHO

GREENWICH VILLAGE

1 International Center of Photography

Merchant's House Museum

St Patrick's 6 Old Cathedral

New York 9 Earth Room

New York City 5 Fire Museum

Grand St Ⓢ

Bowery

Bowery

Grand St

Elizabeth St

LITTLE ITALY

16 ✕

Broome St

Kenmare St

Hester St

Mahayana 8 Temple ◉

Manhattan Bridge Entrance

Columbus Plaza

Division

Chatham Square

E

Canal St

Mott St

12 ✕

Bayard St

Pell St

15 ✕✕ Doyers St

20 ✕

Mosco St

Mulberry St

21 ◉

CHINATOWN

35 ◉

Columbus Park 7 ◉

Baxter St

Hogan Pl

Center Market Pl

Centre St

Canal St

Canal St

Ⓢ

Centre St

eveland Pl

32 ◉

23 ◉

Old Police Headquarters ◉

Museum of 4 ◉ Chinese in America

Lafayette St

Ⓢ

33 ◉

Howard St

25 ◉

Canal St

Cortlandt Al

C

Broadway

Ⓢ

Broome St

Mercer St

Lispenard St

Walker St

White St

Franklin St

Leonard St

Greene S

Grand St

◉ 3

Leslie-Lohman Museum of Gay & Lesbian Art

Church St

Church St

B

Wooster

Sixth Ave (Ave of the Americas)

Canal St

Ⓢ

St Johns La

Beach St

Franklin St

W Broadway

Watts St

Hudson Square

Varick St

TRIBECA

A

Sights

International Center of Photography

GALLERY

1 🎯 Map p50, D3

ICP is New York's paramount platform for photography, with a strong emphasis on photojournalism and changing exhibitions on a wide range of themes. Past shows have included work by Sebastião Salgado, Henri Cartier-Bresson, Man Ray and Robert Capa. A new 11,000-sq-ft home on the Bowery places it close to the epicenter of the downtown art scene. (www.icp.org; 250 Bowery, btwn Houston & Prince Sts; adult/child $14/free, by donation Fri 5-8pm; ⏱10am-6pm Tue-Thu, Sat & Sun, to 8pm Fri; Ⓢ F to 2nd Ave; J/Z to Bowery)

Merchant's House Museum

MUSEUM

2 🎯 Map p50, D1

Built in 1832 and purchased by merchant Seabury Tredwell three years later, this red-brick mansion remains the most authentic Federal house in town. It's as much about the city's mercantile past as it is a showcase of 19th-century high-end domestic furnishings. Everything in the house is a testament to what money could buy, from the bronze gasoliers and marble mantelpieces, to the elegant parlor chairs, attributed to noted furniture designer Duncan Phyfe. Even the multilevel call bells for the servants work to this day. (✆212-777-1089; www.merchantshouse.org; 29 E 4th St, btwn Lafayette St & Bowery; adult/child $10/free; ⏱noon-5pm Fri-Mon, to 8pm Thu, guided tours 2pm Thu-Mon & 6.30pm Thu; Ⓢ 6 to Bleecker St; B/D/F/M to Broadway-Lafayette St)

Leslie-Lohman Museum of Gay & Lesbian Art

MUSEUM

3 🎯 Map p50, B6

Expected to double in size in 2016, the world's first museum dedicated to LGBT themes stages six to eight annual exhibitions of both homegrown and international art. Offerings have included solo-artist retrospectives as well as themed shows exploring the

🔍 Local Life
The Ghosts of Merchant's House

Perhaps just as well known as its antiques are the clan of ghosts and ghouls at the Merchant's House Museum. It is popularly believed that many of the former residents haunt the old mansion, making cameo appearances late in the evenings and sometimes at public events. In fact, at a Valentine's Day concert several years back many attendees spotted the shadow of a woman sitting in the parlor chairs – it was commonly believed to be the ghost of Gertrude Tredwell, the last inhabitant of the brownstone. Each year during the last couple of weeks of October, the museum offers special ghost tours after dark.

Mahayana Temple (p54)

likes of art and sex along the New York waterfront. Much of the work on display is from the museum's own collection, which consists of more than 24,000 works. The space also hosts queer-centric lectures, readings, film screenings and performances; check the website for updates. (📞 212-431-2609; www.leslielohman.org; 26 Wooster St, btwn Grand & Canal Sts; admission free; ⊙ noon-6pm Tue, Wed & Fri-Sun, to 8pm Thu; Ⓢ A/C/E, N/Q/R, 1 to Canal St)

Museum of Chinese in America   MUSEUM

4 ◉ Map p50, C6

In this space designed by architect Maya Lin (designer of the famed Viet-nam Memorial in Washington DC) is a multifaceted museum whose engaging permanent and temporary exhibitions shed light on Chinese American life, both past and present. Browse through interactive multimedia exhibits, maps, timelines, photos, letters, films and artifacts. The museum's anchor exhibit, 'With a Single Step: Stories in the Making of America,' provides an often intimate glimpse into topics including immigration, cultural identity and racial stereotyping. (📞 212-619-4785; www.mocanyc.org; 215 Centre St, btwn Grand & Howard Sts; adult/child $10/free, first Thu of month free; ⊙ 11am-6pm Tue, Wed & Fri-Sun, to 9pm Thu; Ⓢ N/Q/R, J/Z, 6 to Canal St)

KRZYSZTOF DYDYNSKI/GETTY IMAGES ©

New York City Fire Museum

MUSEUM

5 ◎ Map p50, A4

In a grand old firehouse dating from 1904, this ode to firefighters includes a fantastic collection of historic equipment and artifacts. Eye up everything from horse-drawn firefighting carriages and early stovepipe firefighter hats, to Chief, a four-legged firefighting hero from Brooklyn. Exhibits trace the development of the NYC firefighting system, and the museum's friendly staff (and the heavy equipment) make this a great spot to bring kids. (☎212-691-1303; www.nycfiremuseum.org; 278 Spring St, btwn Varick & Hudson Sts; adult/child $8/5; ⏰10am-5pm; ♿; ⑤C/E to Spring St)

St Patrick's Old Cathedral

CHURCH

6 ◎ Map p50, D3

Though St Patrick's Cathedral is now famously located on Fifth Ave in Midtown, its first congregation was housed here, in this recently restored Gothic Revival church. Designed by Joseph-François Mangin and constructed between 1809 and 1815, the church was once the seat of religious life for the Archdiocese of New York, as well as an important community center for new immigrants, mainly from Ireland. (☎212-226-8075; www.oldsaintpatricks.com; 263 Mulberry St, entrance on Mott St; ⏰6am-9pm; ⑤N/R to Prince St; B/D/F/M to Broadway-Lafayette St; 6 to Bleecker St)

Columbus Park

PARK

7 ◎ Map p50, D8

Mah-jongg meisters, slow-motion tai-chi practitioners and old aunties gossiping over homemade dumplings: it might feel like Shanghai, but this leafy oasis is core to NYC history. In the 19th century, this was part of the infamous Five Points neighborhood, the city's first tenement slums and the inspiration for Martin Scorsese's *Gangs of New York*. (Mulberry & Bayard Sts; ⑤J/Z, N/Q/R, 6 to Canal St)

Mahayana Temple

TEMPLE

8 ◎ Map p50, E7

Mahayana is the biggest Buddhist temple in Chinatown and its magnificent 16ft-high Buddha – sitting on a lotus and edged with offerings of fresh oranges, apples and flowers – is believed to be the largest in town. The temple itself faces the frenzied vehicle entrance to the Manhattan Bridge, and its entrance is guarded by two giant golden lions – symbols of protection. (☎212-925-8787; http://en.mahayana.us; 133 Canal St, at Manhattan Bridge Plaza; ⏰8:30am-6pm; ⑤B/D to Grand St; J/Z, 6 to Canal St)

New York Earth Room

GALLERY

9 ◎ Map p50, B3

Since 1980 the oddity of the New York Earth Room, the work of artist Walter De Maria, has been wooing the curious with something not easily found in the city: dirt (250 cu yd, or 280,000lb, of it, to be exact). Walking into the small space is a heady experience, as the scent will make you feel like you've entered a wet forest; the sight of such beautiful, pure earth in the midst of this crazy city is surprisingly moving. (☎212-989-5566; www.earthroom.org; 141 Wooster St, btwn Prince & W Houston Sts; admission free; ☉noon-3pm & 3:30-6pm Wed-Sun, closed mid-Jun–mid-Sep; ⓢN/R to Prince St)

Eating

Ruby's CAFE $
10 🍴 Map p50, D4

Almost always packed, this minute, cash-only cafe has all the bases covered: 'breakie' friendly avo toast (mashed avocado on ciabatta or eight-grain toast), buttermilk pancakes, competent pastas and salads, and (above all else) lusty burgers named after Australian surf beaches. Flat-white coffees and Aussie beers complete your Down Under dining adventure. (☎212-925-5755; www.rubyscafe.com; 219 Mulberry St, btwn Spring & Prince Sts; mains $10-15; ☉9:30am-11pm; ⓢ6 to Spring St; N/R to Prince St)

Tacombi MEXICAN $
11 🍴 Map p50, D3

Festively strung lights, foldaway chairs and Mexican men flipping tacos in an old VW Kombi: if you can't make it to the Yucatan shore, here's your Plan B. Casual, convivial and ever-popular, Tacombi serves up fine, fresh tacos, in-

cluding a fine *barbacoa* (roasted black Angus beef). Wash down the goodness with a pitcher of sangria and start plotting that south-of-the-border getaway. (☎917-727-0179; www.tacombi.com; 267 Elizabeth St, btwn E Houston & Prince Sts; tacos $4-6; ☉11am-midnight Mon-Wed, 11am-1am Thu & Fri, 10am-1am Sat, 10am-midnight Sun; ⓢF to 2nd Ave; 6 to Bleecker St)

Xi'an Famous Foods CHINESE $
12 🍴 Map p50, E8

Food bloggers short-circuit their keyboards at the mere thought of this small, no-fuss Chinatown joint. Star turn here is the spicy cumin lamb burger – tender lamb sautéed with ground cumin, toasted chili seeds, long-horn peppers, red onions and scallions, and stuffed into a crispy, flatbread bun. The hand-pulled noodles also enjoy a cult following. (http://xianfoods.com; 67 Bayard St, btwn Mott & Elizabeth Sts; dishes $2.75-10.25; ☉11:30am-9pm Sun-Thu, to 9:30pm Fri & Sat; ⓢJ/Z, N/Q, 6 to Canal St)

Butcher's Daughter VEGETARIAN $$
13 🍴 Map p50, D5

The butcher's daughter certainly has rebelled, peddling nothing but fresh herbivorous fare in her whitewashed cafe. While healthy it is, boring it's not: everything from the soaked organic muesli, to the spicy kale Caesar salad with almond Parmesan, to the dinnertime Butcher's burger (vegetable and black-bean patty with cashew cheddar cheese) is devilishly delish.

Understand

Tales of Two Neighborhoods

While the re-branding of New York City neighborhoods might be a favorite pastime of realtors and developers, some corners of Gotham have roots that burrow deep into the city's psyche. Chinatown and Little Italy are two such areas, their myriad tales an indelible part of New York City lore.

Five Points

Beneath the verdant appeal of Chinatown's Columbus Park lurks a dark and dirty history. In the 19th century, the site formed part of America's most wretched slum: Five Points. A diseased, unregulated jumble of slaughterhouses, tanneries, taverns and brothels, its ill repute drew a steady stream of high-end New Yorkers on voyeuristic 'slumming tours.' Among the foreign visitors was English scribe Charles Dickens, who later mused: 'Debauchery has made the very houses prematurely old.'

From Bust to Boom

The history of Chinese immigrants in New York City is long and tumultuous. The first Chinese people to arrive in America worked on the Central Pacific Railroad, while others hit the west coast in search of gold. When prospects dried up, many moved to NYC to work in factory assembly lines and laundry houses. Escalating racism led to the Chinese Exclusion Act (1882–1943), which made naturalization an impossibility and largely squashed the opportunity for mainland Chinese to find work in the US. With the introduction of the fairer Immigration and Nationality Act of 1965, Chinese migration boomed, and today over 150,000 citizens fill the tenement-like structures orbiting Mott St.

Crooners & Mobsters

Unlike Chinatown, neighboring Little Italy has been steadily shrinking over the last 50 years. Despite the changes, history looms large: Mulberry Street Bar at 176½ Mulberry St was a favorite haunt of the late Frank Sinatra, and alcohol was openly traded on the corner of Mulberry and Kenmare Sts during Prohibition (leading to its nickname, the 'Curb Exchange'), while 247 Mulberry St was once a hangout for infamous mobsters Lucky Luciano and John Gotti.

Pedestrians crossing a busy street in SoHo

(✆212-219-3434; www.thebutchersdaughter. com; 19 Kenmare St, at Elizabeth St; salads & sandwiches $12-14, dinner mains $16-18; ⊗8am-10pm Sun-Thu, to 11pm Fri & Sat; 🛜🗲; ⑤J to Bowery; 6 to Spring St)

Uncle Boons   THAI $$

14 🍽 Map p50, D4

New York's new favorite uncle, Boons serves up Michelin-star Thai in a fun, tongue-in-cheek combo of retro wood panels, Thai film posters and old family snaps. Spanning the old and the new, zesty, tangy dishes include fantastically crunchy *mieng kum* (betel leaf wrap with ginger, lime, toasted coconut, dried shrimp, peanuts and chili), *kao pat puu* (crab fried rice)

and banana blossom salad. (✆646-370-6650; www.uncleboons.com; 7 Spring St, btwn Elizabeth St & Bowery; small plates $12-16, large plates $21-28; ⊗5:30-11pm Mon-Thu, to midnight Fri & Sat, to 10pm Sun; 🛜; ⑤J/Z to Bowery; 6 to Spring St)

Nom Wah Tea Parlor   CHINESE $$

15 🍽 Map p50, E8

Hidden down a narrow lane, Nom Wah Tea Parlor might look like an old-school American diner, but it's actually the oldest dim-sum place in town. (✆212-962-6047; http://nomwah.com; 13 Doyers St; dim sum from $3.50; ⊗10:30am-9pm Sun-Thu, to 10pm Fri & Sat; ⑤J/Z to Chambers St; 4/5/6 to Brooklyn Bridge-City Hall)

Nyonya   MALAYSIAN $$

16   Map p50, D6

Take your palate to steamy Melaka at this bustling temple to Chinese-Malay Nyonya cuisine. Savor the sweet, the sour and the spicy in classics such as tangy Assam fish-head casserole, rich beef *rendang* (spicy dry curry) and refreshing *rojak* (savory fruit salad tossed in a piquant tamarind dressing). Vegetarians should be warned: there's not much on the menu for you. Cash only. (212-334-3669; www.ilovenyonya. com; 199 Grand St, btwn Mott & Mulberry Sts; mains $7-24; 11am-11:30pm Mon-Thu & Sun, to midnight Fri & Sat; N/Q/R, J/Z, 6 to Canal St; B/D to Grand St)

Estela   MODERN AMERICAN $$$

17   Map p50, D3

Estela might be hopeless at hide-and-seek (its location up some nondescript stairs hardly tricks savvy gourmands), but this busy, skinny wine bar kicks butt on the food and vino front.

> **☑ Top Tip**
> **Family-Style Dining**
> Chinatown has the best dining deals around and locals love to head downtown to satisfy their hankering for hole-in-the-wall fare. Experience the area's bustling dining dens with a handful of friends by eating 'family style' (order a ton of dishes and sample spoonfuls of each). You'll be sure the waiter left a zero off the bill.

Graze from a competent string of market-driven sharing plates, from phenomenal beef tartare (spiked with beef heart for added complexity) to moreish mussels escabeche on toast, to an impossibly sexy endive salad with walnuts and anchovy. (212-219-7693; www.estelanyc.com; 47 E Houston St, btwn Mulberry & Mott Sts; 5:30-11pm Sun-Thu, to 11:30pm Fri & Sat; B/D/F/M to Broadway-Lafayette St; 6 to Bleecker St)

Balthazar   FRENCH $$$

18   Map p50, C4

Still the king of bistros, bustling (OK, *loud*) Balthazar is never short of a mob. That's all thanks to three winning details: its location in SoHo's shopping-spree heartland; the uplifting Paris-meets-NYC ambience; and, of course, the something-for-everyone menu. Highlights include the outstanding raw bar, *steak frites,* Niçoise salad, as well as the roasted beet salad. (212-965-1414; www.balthazarny. com; 80 Spring St, btwn Broadway & Crosby St; mains $19-45; 7:30am-midnight Sun-Thu, 7:30am-1am Fri, 8am-1am Sat; 6 to Spring St; N/R to Prince St)

Il Buco Alimentari & Vineria   ITALIAN $$$

19   Map p50, D1

Whether it's wham-bam espresso at the front bar, a panino to go from the deli, or long-and-lazy Italian feasting in the sunken dining room, Il Buco's trendier spin-off delivers the goods.

Brickwork, hessian and giant industrial lamps set a hip-n-rustic tone, echoed in the menu's bold, nostalgic flavors. (☎212-837-2622; www.ilbucovineria.com; 53 Great Jones St, btwn Bowery & Lafayette St; sandwiches $12-16, dinner mains $32-34; ☺cafe 7am-late Mon-Fri, from 9am Sat & Sun, restaurant noon-3pm & 5:30pm-late Mon-Fri, 11am-3pm & 5:30pm-late Sat & Sun; ☎; Ⓢ6 to Bleecker St; B/D/F/M to Broadway-Lafayette St)

Drinking

Apothéke COCKTAIL BAR

20 Ⓠ Map p50, E8

It takes a little effort to track down this former opium-den-turned-apothecary bar on Doyers St. Inside, skilled barkeeps work like careful chemists, using local, seasonal produce from greenmarkets to produce intense, flavorful 'prescriptions.' Toast to your health with the likes of MVO Negative, a smoky concoction of Lapsang tea–infused gin, Antica Formula, Campari and Peychaud's Bitters. (☎212-406-0400; www.apothekenyc.com; 9 Doyers St; ☺6:30pm-2am Mon-Sat, 8pm-2am Sun; Ⓢ J/Z to Chambers St; 4/5/6 to Brooklyn Bridge-City Hall)

Mulberry Project COCKTAIL BAR

21 Ⓠ Map p50, D6

Lurking behind an unmarked door is this intimate, cavernous cocktail den, with its festive, 'garden-party' backyard one of the best spots to chill in the hood. Bespoke, made-to-order cocktails are the specialty, so disclose your preferences and let the barkeep do the rest. If you're peckish, choose from a competent list of bites that might include peach salad with pecorino cheese. (☎646-448-4536; www.mulberryproject.com; 149 Mulberry St, btwn Hester & Grand Sts; ☺5pm-2am Sun-Thu, to 4am Fri & Sat; Ⓢ N/Q/R, J/Z, 6 to Canal St)

Spring Lounge BAR

22 Ⓠ Map p50, D4

This neon-red rebel has never let anything get in the way of a good time. In Prohibition days, it peddled buckets of beer. In the '60s its basement was a gambling den. These days, it's best known for its kooky stuffed sharks, early-start regulars and come-one, come-all late-night revelry. (☎212-965-1774; www.thespringlounge.com; 48 Spring St, at Mulberry St; ☺8am-4am Mon-Sat, from noon Sun; Ⓢ6 to Spring St; N/R to Prince St)

La Compagnie des Vins Surnaturels WINE BAR

23 Ⓠ Map p50, C5

A snug mélange of Gallic-themed wallpaper, svelte armchairs and tea lights, La Compagnie des Vins Surnaturels is an offshoot of a Paris bar of the same name. Head sommelier Caleb Ganzer steers an impressive, French-heavy wine list, with some 600 drops and no shortage of arresting tipples by the glass. A short, sophisticated menu of bites includes housemade charcuterie and (if you're lucky) buffalo chicken

rillettes. (☏212-343-3660; www.compag
nienyc.com; 249 Centre St, btwn Broome &
Grand Sts; ⏰5pm-1am Mon-Wed, to 2am Thu-
Sat; Ⓢ6 to Spring St; N/R to Prince St)

Entertainment

Joe's Pub   LIVE MUSIC

24 ⭐ Map p50, C1

Part bar, part cabaret and performance
venue, intimate Joe's serves up both
emerging acts and top-shelf enter-
tainers. Performers have included
caustic comic Sandra Bernhard and
British songstress Adele. In fact, it was
right here that Adele gave her very
first American performance back in
2008. (☏212-539-8500, tickets 212-967-
7555; www.joespub.com; Public Theater, 425
Lafayette St, btwn Astor Pl & 4th St; Ⓢ6 to
Astor Pl; R/W to 8th-St-NYU)

Local Life
Film Forum
For a break from the staggering
consumerism of SoHo, feed your
mind something more nourish-
ing at the **Film Forum** (off Map p50;
☏212-727-8110; www.filmforum.com; 209
W Houston St, btwn Varick St & Sixth Ave;
Ⓢ1 to Houston St). The small three-
screen cinema shows an astounding array of independent films,
revivals and career retrospectives
from greats such as Sidney Lumet.
Screenings are often combined
with director talks or other film-
themed discussions.

Shopping

Opening Ceremony   FASHION, SHOES

25 🔒 Map p50, C6

Unisex Opening Ceremony is famed
for its never-boring edit of A-list
indie labels. The place showcases
a changing roster of names from
across the globe, both established and
emerging. Complementing them is
Opening Ceremony's own avant-garde
creations. No matter who is hanging
on the racks, you can always expect
show-stopping, 'where-did-you-get-
that?!' threads that are street-smart,
bold and refreshingly unexpected.
(☏212-219-2688; www.openingceremony.
us; 35 Howard St, btwn Broadway & Lafayette
St; ⏰11am-8pm Mon-Sat, noon-7pm Sun;
ⓈN/Q/R, J/Z, 6 to Canal St)

Other Music   MUSIC

26 🔒 Map p50, C1

This indie-run CD store feeds its loyal
fan base with a clued-in selection of,
well, other types of music: offbeat
lounge, psychedelic, electronica, indie
rock etc, available new and used.
Friendly staffers like what they do,
and may be able to help translate your
inner musical whims and dreams to
actual CD reality. OM also stocks a
small but excellent selection of new
and used vinyl. (☏212-477-8150; www.
othermusic.com; 15 E 4th St, btwn Lafayette
St & Broadway; ⏰11am-8pm Mon-Wed, 11am-
9pm Thu & Fri, noon-8pm Sat, noon-7pm Sun;
Ⓢ6 to Bleecker St; B/D/F/M to Broadway-
Lafayette St)

Man at work on a SoHo sidewalk

Rag & Bone FASHION

27 🔒 Map p50, B4

Downtown label Rag & Bone is a hit with many of New York's coolest, sharpest dressers – both men and women. Detail-oriented pieces range from clean-cut shirts and blazers, to graphic tees, monochromatic sweaters, feather-light strappy dresses, leathergoods and Rag & Bone's highly prized jeans. The tailoring is generally impeccable, with accessories including shoes, hats, bags and wallets. (📞212-219-2204; www.rag-bone.com; 119 Mercer St, btwn Prince & Spring Sts; ⏱11am-8pm Mon-Sat, noon-7pm Sun; Ⓢ N/R to Prince St)

MoMA Design Store GIFTS

28 🔒 Map p50, C4

The Museum of Modern Art's downtown retail space carries a huge collection of sleek, smart and clever objects for the home, office and wardrobe. You'll find modernist alarm clocks, sculptural vases and jewelry, surreal lamps, svelte kitchenware, plus brainy games, hand puppets, fanciful scarves, coffee-table tomes and loads of other unique gift ideas. (📞646-613-1367; www.momastore.org; 81 Spring St, at Crosby St; ⏱10am-8pm Mon-Sat, 11am-7pm Sun; Ⓢ N/R to Prince St; 6 to Spring St)

Uniqlo
FASHION

29 🔒 Map p50, C4

This enormous three-story Japanese emporium owes its popularity to good-looking, good-quality apparel at discount prices. You'll find Japanese denim, Mongolian cashmere, graphic T-shirts, svelte skirts, high-tech thermals and endless racks of colorful ready-to-wear items – with most things falling below the $100 mark. (☏877-486-4756; www.uniqlo.com; 546 Broadway, btwn Prince & Spring Sts; ⏰10am-9pm Mon-Sat, 11am-8pm Sun; Ⓢ N/R to Prince St; 6 to Spring St)

Housing Works Book Store
BOOKS

30 🔒 Map p50, C3

Relaxed, earthy and featuring a great selection of secondhand books, vinyl, CDs and DVDs you can buy for a good cause (proceeds go to the city's

Top Tip
Fashion Insiders
Serious shopaholics should consult the city's in-the-know retail blogs before hitting SoHo and surrounds – there's always some sort of 'sample sale' or offer going on, not to mention the opening of yet another boutique stocking fresh, emerging design talent. Get the lowdown online at Racked (www.ny.racked.com) and Glamourai (www.theglamourai.com).

HIV-positive and AIDS homeless communities), this creaky hideaway is a very local place to while away a few quiet afternoon hours (there's an in-house cafe). (☏212-334-3324; www.housingworks.org/usedbookcafe; 126 Crosby St, btwn E Houston & Prince Sts; ⏰9am-9pm Mon-Fri, 10am-5pm Sat & Sun; Ⓢ B/D/F/M to Broadway-Lafayette St; N/R to Prince St)

Screaming Mimi's
VINTAGE

31 🔒 Map p50, C1

If you dig vintage threads, you may just scream too. This funtastic shop carries an excellent selection of yester-year pieces – organized, ingeniously, by decade, from the 1950s to the '90s (ask to see the small, stashed-away collection of clothing from the 1920s, '30s and '40s). (☏212-677-6464; www.screamingmimis.com; 382 Lafayette St, btwn E 4th & Great Jones Sts; ⏰noon-8pm Mon-Sat, 1-7pm Sun; Ⓢ 6 to Bleecker St; B/D/F/M to Broadway-Lafayette St)

Fillmore & 5th
VINTAGE

32 🔒 Map p50, D5

Fashion is a fickle affair, as the racks at this Californian consignment store reveal. Near-new designer pieces are delivered daily and sold at mere-mortal prices, whether it's a Maison Kitsuné men's sweat top for $90, a Burberry blazer for $150, or a killer pair of Manolo Blahnik stilettos for $200. Always check the dedicated sale rack for the biggest savings. (☏646-791-5458; http://fillmore5th.com; 398 Broome St, at Centre St; ⏰11am-7pm

Mon-Sat, noon-6pm Sun; Ⓢ6 to Spring St;
N/R to Prince St)

Saturdays
FASHION, ACCESSORIES

33 🔒 Map p50, C5

SoHo's version of a surf shop sees
boards and wax paired up with designer grooming products, graphic art
and surf tomes, and Saturdays' own
line of high-quality, fashion-literate
threads for dudes. Styled-up, grab
a coffee from the in-house espresso
bar, hang in the back garden and fish
for some crazy, shark-dodging tales.
There's a second branch in the **West
Village** (📞347-246-5830; 17 Perry St;
🕙10am-7pm; Ⓢ1/2/3 to 14th St). (www.
saturdaysnyc.com; 31 Crosby St, btwn Broome
& Grand Sts; 🕙store 10am-7pm, coffee bar
8am-7pm Mon-Fri, 10am-7pm Sat & Sun; 📶;
ⓈN/Q/R, J/Z, 6 to Canal St)

Resurrection
VINTAGE

34 🔒 Map p50, D4

Boudoir-red Resurrection gives new
life to cutting-edge designs from past
decades. Striking, mint-condition pieces cover the eras of mod, glam-rock
and new-wave design, and design dei-
ties such as Marc Jacobs have dropped
by for inspiration. Top picks include
Halston dresses and Courrèges coats
and jackets. (📞212-625-1374; www.resur
rectionvintage.com; 217 Mott St, btwn Prince

Window-shopping in SoHo

& Spring Sts; 🕙11am-7pm Mon-Fri; Ⓢ6 to
Spring St; N/R to Prince St)

New Kam Man
HOMEWARES

35 🔒 Map p50, D7

Head past hanging ducks to the
basement of this classic Canal St food
store for cheap Chinese and Japanese
tea sets, plus kitchen products such as
chopsticks, bowls, stir-frying utensils
and rice cookers. (📞212-571-0330; www.
newkamman.com; 200 Canal St, btwn Mulberry & Motts Sts; 🕙9am-8:30pm; ⓈN/Q/R,
J/Z, 6 to Canal St)

Explore

East Village & Lower East Side

If you've been dreaming of those quintessential New York City moments – graffiti on crimson brick, skyscrapers rising overhead, tattooed buskers and grannies walking side by side, and cute cafes with rickety tables spilling out onto the sidewalks – then the East Village and the Lower East Side are your Holy Grail.

The Sights in a Day

☀ Connect to the old Jewish roots of the neighborhood with bagels and lox at **Russ & Daughters Cafe** (p72). Afterwards, delve deeper into New York's immigrant past in the fascinating **Lower East Side Tenement Museum** (p68). Then fast-forward into the future at the wild **New Museum of Contemporary Art** (p68), a showcase for the latest cutting-edge creations in the contemporary art world.

☀ Grab a healthy but delicious lunch at either **Dimes** (p72) or **El Rey** (p70), then wander down **St Marks Place** (p70) for a glimpse of the former countercultural epicenter of the East Village. Go window-shopping at one-of-a-kind clothing boutiques, jewelry shops and record stores (10th and 9th Sts are good starting points). Stop for a pick-me-up at **MUD** (p71) and engage in the discreet art of people-watching in **Tompkins Square Park** (p69).

☾ Explore the East Village's staggering culinary offerings by enjoying oysters and happy-hour drinks at **Upstate** (p71), creative Indian street food at **Babu Ji** (p72) or a multicourse feast (reserved ahead) at under-the-radar **Degustation** (p74). Finish off the night with moonshine and banjos at **Wayland** (p75), Japanese cocktails at **Bar Goto** (p75) and live jazz at **Rue B** (p75).

♥ Best of New York City

Museums
Lower East Side Tenement Museum (p68)

Eating
Degustation (p74)

Fung Tu (p74)

Momofuku Noodle Bar (p71)

Upstate (p71)

Drinking
Bar Goto (p75)

Rue B (p75)

Wayland (p75)

Ten Bells (p75)

Shopping
Still House (p80)

By Robert James (p81)

Getting There

Ⓢ Subway Trains don't go far enough east to carry you to most East Village locations, but it's a quick walk from the 6 at Astor Pl or the L at First Ave. The F line will let you off in the thick of the Lower East Side.

Ⓑ Bus If you're traveling from the west side, it's convenient to take the M14 (across 14th St) or the M21 (down Houston).

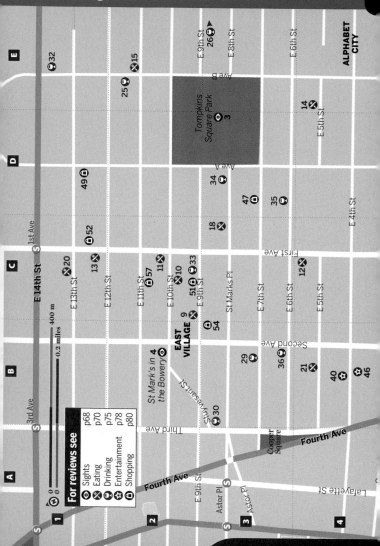

ALPHABET CITY

Tompkins Square Park

3

32

15

25

14

49

34

47

35

18

52

20

13

57

11

51

10

33

12

EAST VILLAGE

St Mark's in the Bowery **4**

9

54

29

36

21

40

46

30

Cooper Square

Fourth Ave

Fourth Ave

E 9th St

E 8th St

E 6th St

E 5th St

E 4th St

E 7th St

E 6th St

E 5th St

E 13th St

E 12th St

E 11th St

E 10th St

E 9th St

St Marks Pl

Ave B

Ave A

First Ave

Second Ave

Stuyvesant St

Third Ave

E 14th St

1st Ave

3rd Ave

Astor Pl

E 9th St

Astor Pl

Lafayette St

0   400 m
0   0.2 miles

For reviews see

⊙ Sights	p68
⊗ Eating	p70
ⓓ Drinking	p75
ⓔ Entertainment	p78
ⓘ Shopping	p80

Attorney St

Attorney St

E Houston St

Williamsburg Bridge

Clinton St

☒ 19

Suffolk St

Suffolk St

Stanton St

Rivington St

LOWER EAST SIDE

Norfolk St

E 2nd St

Essex St

28 ☉

Delancey-Essex Sts Ⓢ

Broome St

Grand St

☐ 50

☆ 42

37 ☉ 27

6 ☒

Ludlow St

☐ 53

Orchard St

☐ 56

☉ 48

E 2nd St

☆ 41

☒ 38

☒ 16

22 ☒ ▷

17 ☒

Allen St

Delancey St

Lower East Side
Tenement Museum 1 ☉

☒ 8

Eldridge St

☆ 43

New York City
Marble Cemetery

Museum at
Eldridge Street
Synagogue
☉ 5

E 1st St

23 ☒

24 ☉

7 ☒

31 ☐

Forsyth St

Forsyth St

☆ 39

Chrystie St

Sara D
Roosevelt
Park

Grand St Ⓢ

2nd Ave Ⓢ

Stanton St

Rivington St

45 ☆

Bowery Ⓢ

☐

Bowery

NOLITA

Bowery

New Museum of
Contemporary Art 2 ☉

Bowery

LITTLE
ITALY

Broome St

NOHO

E Houston St

Elizabeth St

Kenmare St

Bond St

Bleecker St

SOHO

Mott St

Spring St

Broadway-
Lafayette St Ⓢ

Jersey St

Prince St

Mulberry St

Spring St

Grand St

Spring St Ⓢ

Centre St

Lafayette St

Sights

Lower East Side Tenement Museum
MUSEUM

1 ⊙ Map p66, D7

This museum puts the neighborhood's heartbreaking but inspiring heritage on full display in three re-creations of turn-of-the-20th-century tenements. Re-creations include the late-19th-century home and garment shop of the Levine family from Poland, and two immigrant dwellings from the Great Depressions of 1873 and 1929. Visits to the tenements and other sites of interest are available only as part of scheduled tours (the price of which is included in the admission), with many daily departures. (☑877-975-3786; www.tenement.org; 103 Orchard St, btwn Broome & Delancey Sts; adult/student from $25/20;

🕙tours 10:15am-5pm Fri-Wed, to 6:30pm Thu; ⑤B/D to Grand St; J/M/Z to Essex St; F to Delancey St)

New Museum of Contemporary Art
MUSEUM

2 ⊙ Map p66, B6

Rising above the neighborhood, the New Museum is a sight to behold: a seven-story stack of off-kilter, white, ethereal boxes designed by Tokyo-based architects Kazuyo Sejima and Ryue Nishizawa of SANAA and the New York-based firm Gensler. It was a long-awaited breath of fresh air along what was a completely gritty Bowery strip when it arrived back in 2007 – though since its opening, many glossy new constructions have joined it, quickly transforming this once down-and-out avenue. (☑212-219-1222; www.

Ⓠ Local Life
LES Galleries

Rising star on the art scene, the Lower East Side has dozens of quality galleries. The **Sperone Westwater** (Map p66, B6; www.speronewestwater.com; 257 Bowery; 🕙10am-6pm Tue-Sat; ⑤F to 2nd Ave) gallery represents heavy-hitters such as William Wegman and Richard Long, and its new home was designed by British starchitect Norman Foster. Avant-garde **Salon 94** has two Lower East Side outposts: one secreted away on **Freeman Alley** (Map p66, B7; www.salon94.com; 1 Freeman Alley, off Rivington; 🕙11am-6pm Wed-Sat; ⑤F to 2nd Ave; J/Z to Bowery) and another on **Bowery** (Map p66, B6; www.salon94.com; 243 Bowery, cnr Stanton St; 🕙11am-6pm Tue-Sat, from 1pm Sun; ⑤F to 2nd Ave; J/Z to Bowery) near the New Museum. For a gallery with a conscience, visit **Anastasia Photo** (Map p66, D6; www.anastasia-photo.com; 143 Ludlow St, btwn Stanton & Rivington Sts; 🕙11am-7pm Tue-Sun; ⑤F to Delancey St; J/M/Z to Essex St), which has evocative exhibitions that cover subjects such as poverty in rural America, the ravages of war and disappearing cultures in Africa.

Acroyoga practice in Tompkins Square Park

newmuseum.org; 235 Bowery, btwn Stanton & Rivington Sts; adult/child $16/free, 7-9pm Thu by donation; ⏰11am-6pm Wed & Fri-Sun, to 9pm Thu; Ⓢ N/R to Prince St; F to 2nd Ave; J/Z to Bowery; 6 to Spring St)

Tompkins Square Park PARK

3 ◉ Map p66, D3

This 10.5-acre park is like a friendly town square for locals, who gather for chess at concrete tables, picnics on the lawn on warm days and spontaneous guitar or drum jams on various grassy knolls. It's also the site of basketball courts, a fun-to-watch dog run (a fenced-in area where humans can unleash their canines), a public swimming pool, frequent summer concerts and an always-lively kids' playground. (www.nycgovparks.org; E 7th & 10th Sts, btwn Aves A & B; ⏰6am-midnight; Ⓢ 6 to Astor Pl)

St Mark's in the Bowery CHURCH

4 ◉ Map p66, B2

Though it's most popular with East Village locals for its cultural offerings – such as poetry readings hosted by the Poetry Project or cutting-edge dance performances from Danspace and the Ontological Hysteric Theater – St Mark's is also a historic site. This Episcopal church stands on the site of the farm, or *bouwerij*, owned by Dutch Governor Peter Stuyvesant, whose crypt lies under the grounds. (☎212-674-6377; www.stmarksbowery.org; 131 E 10th

St, at Second Ave; ⏰10am-6pm Mon-Fri; Ⓢ L to 3rd Ave; 6 to Astor Pl)

Museum at Eldridge Street Synagogue

MUSEUM

5 ◉ Map p66, C8

This landmark house of worship, built in 1887, was once the center of Jewish life, before falling into squalor in the 1920s. Left to rot, the synagogue was restored following a 20-year-long, $20-million restoration that was completed in 2007, and it now shines with original splendor. Museum admission includes a tour of the synagogue, which departs hourly, with the last one starting at 4pm. (📞212-219-0302; www.eldridgestreet.org; 12 Eldridge St, btwn Canal & Division Sts; adult/child $12/8, Mon

Local Life
St Marks Place

St Marks Place (Map p66, C3; St Marks Pl, Ave A to Third Ave; Ⓢ N/R/W to 8th St-NYU; 6 to Astor Pl) is jam-packed with historical tidbits that would delight any trivia buff. A cast of colorful characters has left its mark at 4 St Marks Pl. Alexander Hamilton's son built the structure; James Fenimore Cooper lived here in the 1830s; and Yoko Ono's Fluxus artists descended upon the building in the 1960s. And don't miss the buildings at 96 and 98 St Marks Pl, which are immortalized on the cover of Led Zepellin's *Physical Graffiti* album.

free; ⏰10am-5pm Sun-Thu, 10am-3pm Fri; Ⓢ F to East Broadway)

Eating

El Rey

CAFE $

6 ✖ Map p66, D6

This white, minimalist space on Stanton feels more SoCal than LES, and has earned a huge following for its delectably inventive (and fairly priced) farm-to-table plates with plenty of vegan options. Stop by at lunchtime for a frittata with shaved fennel salad or roasted beets with granola and yogurt, or come at evening for octopus salad with black-bean puree. (📞212-260-3950; http://elreynyc.com; 100 Stanton St, btwn Orchard & Ludlow Sts; small plates $7-17; ⏰7am-10:30pm Mon-Fri, from 8am Sat & Sun; ✎; Ⓢ F to 2nd Ave)

Spaghetti Incident

ITALIAN $

7 ✖ Map p66, C6

Grab a seat at the marble-topped bar or one of the side tables and watch the cooks whip up tasty dishes of spaghetti beautifully topped with fresh ingredients such as kale pesto, chopped salmon and asparagus in a light cream sauce, or Italian sausage and broccoli rabe. The flavors (and prices!) are quite good. Salads, arancini (rice balls) and affordable wines round out the menu. (📞646-896-1446; www.spaghettiincidentnyc.com; 231 Eldridge St, btwn Stanton & E Houston Sts; mains $9-12; ⏰5:30-11:30pm Mon-Fri, from noon Sat & Sun; Ⓢ F to 2nd Ave)

Vanessa's Dumpling House
CHINESE $

8 🍴 Map p66, C8

Tasty dumplings – served steamed, fried or in soup – are whipped together in iron skillets at light speed and tossed into hungry mouths at unbeatable prices. (☎212-625-8008; www.vanessas. com; 118 Eldridge St, btwn Grand & Broome Sts; dumplings $1.25-5; ☺10:30am-10pm; ⓢB/D to Grand St; J to Bowery; F to Delancey St)

MUD
CAFE $

9 🍴 Map p66, C2

Offering trustworthy beans and an all-day breakfast that hits the spot after a late night out, this 9th St nook is a favorite among East Villagers looking for a quick caffeine fix or a friendly place to chat with old friends. The everyday brunch (coffee, craft beer or mimosa and any main course) is a deal at $18. (☎212-228-9074; www.onmud. com; 307 E 9th St, btwn Second & First Aves; mains $8-14; ☺8am-midnight; ⓢL to 3rd Ave; L to 1st Ave; 4/6 to Astor Pl)

Rai Rai Ken
RAMEN $

10 🍴 Map p66, C2

Rai Rai Ken's storefront may only be the size of its door, but it's pretty hard to miss since there's usually a small congregation of hungry locals lurking out the front. Inside, low-slung wooden stools are arranged around the noodle bar, where the cooks busily churn out piping-hot portions of tasty pork-infused broth. (☎212-477-7030; 218 E 10th St, btwn First & Second Aves; ramen $10-13; ☺noon-midnight Mon-Thu, to 2am Fri & Sat; ⓢL to 1st Ave; 6 to Astor Pl)

Momofuku Noodle Bar
NOODLES $$

11 🍴 Map p66, C2

With just 30 stools and a no-reservations policy, you will always have to wait to cram into this tiny phenomenon. Queue up for the namesake special: homemade ramen noodles in broth, served with poached egg, pork belly and pork shoulder or some interesting combos. The menu changes daily and includes buns (such as brisket and horseradish), snacks (smoked chicken wings) and desserts. (☎212-777-7773; www.momofuku.com/ noodle-bar/; 171 First Ave, btwn 10th & 11th Sts; mains $17-28; ☺noon-11pm Sun-Thu, to 1am Fri & Sat; ⓢL to 1st Ave; 6 to Astor Pl)

Upstate
SEAFOOD $$

12 🍴 Map p66, C4

Upstate serves outstanding seafood dishes and craft beers. The small, always-changing menu features the likes of beer-steamed mussels, seafood stew, scallops over mushroom risotto, softshell crab and wondrous oyster selections. There's no freezer – seafood comes from the market each day, so you know you'll be getting only the freshest ingredients. Lines can be long, so go early. (☎212-460-5293; www. upstatenyc.com; 95 First Ave, btwn 5th & 6th Sts; mains $15-30; ☺5-11pm; ⓢF to 2nd Ave)

Luzzo's

PIZZA $$

13 Map p66, C1

Fan-favorite Luzzo's occupies a thin sliver of real estate in the East Village, which gets stuffed to the gills each evening as discerning diners feast on thin-crust pies, kissed with ripe tomatoes and cooked in a coal-fired stove. (212-473-7447; www.luzzosgroup.com; 211 First Ave, btwn 12th & 13th Sts; pizzas $18-26; noon-11pm Sun-Thu, to midnight Fri & Sat; L to 1st Ave)

Lavagna

ITALIAN $$

14 Map p66, E4

Dark wood, flickering candles and a fiery glow from a somewhat open kitchen help make homey Lavagna a late-night hideaway for lovers. But it's laid-back enough to make it appropriate for children, at least in the early hours before the smallish space fills up. Delicious pastas, thin-crust pizzas and hearty mains, such as baby rack of lamb, are standard fare. (212-979-1005; www.lavagnanyc.com; 545 E 5th St, btwn Aves A & B; mains $19-35; 6-11pm Mon-Thu, to midnight Fri, noon-midnight Sat & Sun; ; S F to 2nd Ave)

Babu Ji

INDIAN $$

15 Map p66, E2

A playful spirit marks this excellent Australian-run Indian restaurant in Alphabet City. You can assemble a meal from street-food-style dishes such as *papadi chaat* (chickpeas, pomegranate and yogurt chutney) and potato croquettes stuffed with lobster, or feast on heartier dishes such as tandoori lamb chops or scallop coconut curry. (212-951-182; www.babujinyc.com; 175 Ave B, btwn 11th & 12 Sts; mains $16-25; 6pm-late Mon-Sat; S L to 1st Ave)

Russ & Daughters Cafe

EASTERN EUROPEAN $$

16 Map p66, D7

Sit down and feast on bagels and lox in the comfort of an old-school diner. Aside from rich slices of smoked fish, you can nibble on potato latkes, warm up over a bowl of borscht or feast on eggs Benny (poached eggs with smoked salmon, sautéed spinach and hollandaise sauce). (212-475-4881; 127 Orchard St, btwn Delancey & Rivington Sts; mains $13-20; 10am-10pm Mon-Fri, from 8am Sat & Sun; S F to Delancey St; J/M/Z to Essex St)

Dimes

CAFE $$

17 Map p66, D8

This tiny, sun-drenched eatery has a strong local following for its friendly service and healthy, good-value dishes. A design-minded group crowds in for spicy breakfast tacos (served till 4pm), bowls of granola with açaí (that strongly flavored, vitamin-rich Amazonian berry), creative salads (with sunchokes, anchovies, goat's cheese) and heartier dishes for dinner (striped bass with green curry, pulled pork with jasmine rice). (212-925-1300; www.dimesnyc.com; 49 Canal St, btwn Orchard & Ludlow Sts; mains breakfast $8-13,

Ginger scallion noodles at Momofuku Noodle Bar (p71)

dinner $14-23; ⊘8am-11pm Mon-Fri, from 9am Sat & Sun; 🖈)

Cafe Mogador
MOROCCAN $$

18 ✖ Map p66, C3

Family-run Mogador is a long-running NYC classic serving fluffy piles of couscous, char-grilled lamb and merguez sausage over basmati rice, as well as satisfying mixed platters of hummus and baba ghanoush. The standouts, however, are the tangines – traditionally spiced, long-simmered chicken or lamb dishes served up five different ways. (☎212-677-2226; www. cafemogador.com; 101 St Marks Pl; mains lunch $8-14, dinner $17-21; ⊘9am-midnight; Ⓢ6 to Astor Pl)

Clinton Street Baking Company
AMERICAN $$

19 ✖ Map p66, E5

Mom-and-pop shop extraordinaire, Clinton Street Baking Company gets the blue-ribbon in so many categories – best pancakes (blueberry! swoon!), best muffins, best po'boys (Southern-style sandwiches), best biscuits etc – that you're pretty much guaranteed a stellar meal no matter what time you stop by. In the evenings, you can opt for 'breakfast for dinner' (pancakes, eggs Benedict), fish tacos or the excellent buttermilk fried chicken. (☎646-602-6263; www.clintonstreetbaking.com; 4 Clinton St, btwn Stanton & Houston Sts; mains $12-20; ⊘8am-4pm & 6-11pm Mon-Sat, 9am-6pm

Sun; S J/M/Z to Essex St; F to Delancey St; F to 2nd Ave)

Redhead
SOUTHERN **$$**

20 Map p66, C1

Cozy corners of exposed brick and warm smiles from the staff mirror the home-style comfort food, which has a distinctly Southern bent. There are stacks of fried chicken and rounds of pucker-inducing cocktails on everyone else's table – you should follow suit. (☏212-533-6212; www.theredheadnyc.com; 349 E 13th St, btwn First & Second Aves; mains $15-25; ☺5:30pm-1am Mon-Sat, 5-10pm Sun; S L to 1st Ave; L to 3rd Ave; 6 to Astor Pl)

Local Life

Market Allure

Founded in 1940, the **Essex Street Market** (Map p66, D; ☏212-312-3603; www.essexstreetmarket.com; 120 Essex St, btwn Delancey & Rivington Sts; ☺8am-7pm Mon-Sat, 10am-6pm Sun; S F to Delancey St; J/M/Z to Essex St) is a slice of old-school LES, featuring local produce, smoked-fish purveyors and other non-edible surprises (such as an on-site barber). Although the interior lacks charm, there are some tempting gourmet goodies to be found here. Load up on artisanal cheeses at Saxelby Cheesemongers, fresh-baked breads from Pain d'Avignon, spinach pies and baklava from Boubouki and ice cream from Luca & Bosco.

Degustation
MODERN EUROPEAN **$$$**

21 Map p66, B4

Blending Iberian, French and New World recipes, Degustation does a beautiful array of tapas-style plates at this narrow 19-seat eatery. It's an intimate setting, with guests seated around a long wooden counter, and chef Nicholas Licata and team at center stage firing up crisp octopus, lamb belly with soft poached egg and paella with blue prawns and chorizo. (☏212-979-1012; http://degustation-nyc.com; 239 E 5th St, btwn 2nd & 3rd Aves; small plates $12-22, tasting menu $85; ☺6-11:30pm Mon-Sat, to 10pm Sun; S 6 to Astor Pl)

Fung Tu
FUSION **$$$**

22 Map p66, D8

Celebrated chef Jonathan Wu brilliantly blends Chinese cooking with global accents at this elegant little eatery on the edge of Chinatown. The complex sharing plates are superb (try scallion pancakes with cashew salad and smoked chicken or crepe roll stuffed with braised beef, pickled cucumbers and watercress) and pair nicely with creative cocktails such as the Fung Tu Gibson. (☏212-219-8785; www.fungtu.com; 22 Orchard St, btwn Hester & Canal Sts; small plates $13-18, mains $24-32; ☺6pm-midnight Tue-Sat, 4-10pm Sun; S F to East Broadway)

Prune
AMERICAN **$$$**

23 Map p66, C5

Expect lines around the block at the weekend, when the hungover show up to cure their ills with brunches and excellent Bloody Marys (in 11 varieties). The small room is always busy as diners pour in for grilled trout with mint and almond salsa, seared duck breast and rich sweetbreads. Reservations available for dinner only. (📞212-677-6221; www.prunerestaurant.com; 54 E 1st St, btwn First & Second Aves; mains brunch $14-22, dinner $25-32; ⏱10am-3:30pm Sat & Sun, 5:30-11pm daily; 🚇F/V to Lower East Side-2nd Ave)

Drinking

Bar Goto
BAR

24 🚇 Map p66, C6

Maverick mixologist Kenta Goto has cocktail connoisseurs spellbound at his eponymous hot spot. Expect meticulous, elegant drinks that revel in Goto's Japanese heritage (the sake-spiked Sakura Martini is utterly smashing), paired with authentic, Japanese comfort bites such as *okonomiyaki* (savory pancakes). (📞212-475-4411; http://bar goto.com; 245 Eldridge St, btwn E Houston & Stanton Sts; ⏱5pm-midnight Tue-Thu & Sun, to 2am Fri & Sat; 🚇F to 2nd Ave)

Rue B
BAR

25 🚇 Map p66, E2

There's live jazz (and the odd rockabilly group) every night from about 8:30pm at this tiny, amber-lit drinking den on a bar-dappled stretch of Avenue B. It draws a young, celebratory crowd, and the space is quite small, so mind the tight corners, lest the

trombonist ends up in your lap. (www.ruebnyc188.com; 188 Ave B, btwn 11th & 12 Sts; ⏱noon-4am; 🚇L to 1st Ave)

Wayland
BAR

26 🚇 Map p66, E3

Whitewashed walls, weathered floorboards and salvaged lamps give this urban outpost a Mississippi flair, which goes well with the live music (bluegrass, jazz, folk) played on Monday to Wednesday nights. The drinks, though, are the real draw – try the 'I hear banjos,' made of apple-pie moonshine, rye whiskey and applewood smoke, which tastes like a campfire (but slightly less burning). (📞212-777-7022; www.thewaylandnyc.com; 700 E 9th St, cnr Ave C; ⏱5pm-4am; 🚇L to 1st Ave)

Ten Bells
BAR

27 🚇 Map p66, D8

This charmingly tucked-away tapas bar has a grotto-like design, with flickering candles, dark tin ceilings, brick walls and a U-shaped bar that's an ideal setting for a conversation with a new friend. (📞212-228-4450; www.tenbellsnyc.com; 247 Broome St, btwn Ludlow & Orchard Sts; ⏱5pm-2am Mon-Fri, from 3pm Sat & Sun; 🚇F to Delancey St; J/M/Z to Essex St)

Berlin
CLUB

28 🚇 Map p66, D5

Like a secret bunker hidden beneath the ever-gentrifying streets of the East Village, Berlin is a throwback to the neighborhood's more riotous days of wildness and dancing. Once you find the unmarked entrance, head downstairs to the grotto-like space with vaulted brick ceilings, a long bar and tiny dance floor, with funk and rare grooves. (25 Ave A, btwn 1st & 2nd Aves; ⏱10pm-4am; **S**F to 2nd Ave)

Jimmy's No 43   BAR

29 🍺 Map p66, B3

Barrels and stag antlers line the walls up to the ceiling of this cozy basement beer hall as locals chug their drinks. Select from more than 50 imported favorites (a dozen on draft) to go with a round of delectable, locally sourced bar nibbles. (☎212-982-3006; www. jimmysno43.com; 43 E 7th St, btwn Third & Second Aves; ⏱5pm-1am Mon-Thu, 1pm-4am Fri & Sat, 1pm-1am Sun; **S**N/R to 8th St-NYU; F to 2nd Ave; 4/6 to Astor Pl)

Angel's Share   BAR

30 🍺 Map p66, B3

Show up early and snag a seat at this hidden gem, behind a Japanese restaurant on the same floor. It's quiet and elegant with creative cocktails, but you can't stay if you don't have a table or a seat at the bar, and they tend to go fast. (☎212-777-5415; 2nd fl, 8 Stuyvesant St, near Third Ave & E 9th St; ⏱6pm-1:30am Sun-Thu, to 2:30am Fri & Sat; **S**6 to Astor Pl)

Jadis   WINE BAR

31 🍺 Map p66, C6

French for 'in olden days,' Jadis channels a bit of European nostalgia with

its worn brick walls, antique fixtures and warmly lit interior. You'll find around two dozen or so wines by the glass, with French labels taking pride of place. Snacks include escargots, salads, pressed sandwiches, homemade quiches and rich cheeses. (☎212-254-1675; http://jadisnyc.com; 42 Rivington St, btwn Eldridge & Forsyth Sts; ⏱5pm-2am; **S**F to 2nd Ave; J/Z to Bowery)

Pouring Ribbons   COCKTAIL BAR

32 🍺 Map p66, E1

From the team behind Death & Co, Pouring Ribbons keeps the gimmicks and pretension low and the flavors exceptional. The encyclopedic cocktail menu could sate any appetite and includes a handy 'drink-decider' listing flavors such as 'refreshing' to 'comforting' on different axes. There is also possibly the largest collection of Chartreuse in NYC. (☎917-656-6788; www.pouringribbons.com; 2nd fl, 225 Avenue B; ⏱6pm-2am; **S**L to 1st Ave)

Immigrant   BAR

33 🍺 Map p66, C2

Wholly unpretentious, these twin boxcar-sized bars could easily become your neighborhood local if you decide to stick around town. The staff are knowledgeable and kind, mingling with faithful regulars while dishing out tangy olives and topping up glasses with imported snifters. (☎646-308-1724; 341 E 9th St, btwn First & Second Aves; ⏱5pm-1am Sun-Wed, to 2am Thu-Sat; **S**L to 1st Ave; 4/6 to Astor Pl)

Museum at Eldridge Street Synagogue (p70)

Ten Degrees Bar

WINE BAR

34 Map p66, D3

This small, candlelit St Marks charmer is a great spot to start out the night with leather couches, friendly bartenders and an excellent wine and cocktails list. Come from noon to 8pm for two-for-one drink specials (otherwise, it's $11 to $15 for cocktails), or get half-priced bottles of wine on Monday night. Go for the couches up front or grab a tiny table in the back nook. (☎212-358-8600; www.10degreesbar.com; 121 St Marks Pl, btwn First Ave & Ave A; ⏰noon-4am; **S** F to 2nd Ave; L to 1st Ave; L to 3rd Ave)

Death + Co

LOUNGE

35 Map p66, D3

Relax amid dim lighting and thick wooden slatting and let the bartenders – with their PhDs in mixology – work their magic as they shake, rattle and roll some of the most perfectly concocted cocktails (from $15) in town. (☎212-388-0882; www.deathandcompany.com; 433 E 6th St, btwn First Ave & Ave A; ⏰6pm-1am Sun-Thu, to 2am Fri & Sat; **S** F to 2nd Ave; L to 1st Ave; 6 to Astor Pl)

Mayahuel

COCKTAIL BAR

36 Map p66, B3

About as far from your typical spring break tequila bar as you can get,

Mayahuel is more like the cellar of a monastery. Devotees of the fermented agave can seriously indulge themselves experimenting with dozens of varieties (all cocktails $15); in between drinks, snack on quesadillas and tamales. (📞212-253-5888; www.mayahuelny.com; 304 E 6th St, at Second Ave; ⏲6pm-2am; 🚇L to 3rd Ave; L to 1st Ave; 6 to Astor Pl)

Barrio Chino   COCKTAIL BAR

37 🍸 Map p66, D8

An eatery that spills easily into a party scene, with an airy Havana-meets-Beijing vibe and a focus on fine-sipping tequilas. Or stick with fresh blood-orange or black-plum margaritas, guacamole and chicken tacos. (📞212-228-6710; www.barriochinonyc.com; 253 Broome St, btwn Ludlow & Orchard Sts; ⏲11:30am-4:30pm & 5:30pm-1am; 🚇F, J/M/Z to Delancey-Essex Sts)

Entertainment

Slipper Room   LIVE PERFORMANCE

38 ⭐ Map p66, C6

The Slipper Room is back, and looking better than ever thanks to a major renovation. The two-story club hosts a wide range of performances, including Seth Herzog's popular variety show Sweet at 9pm on Tuesday (admission $5 to $7) and several weekly burlesque shows, which feature a mash-up of acrobatics, sexiness, comedy and absurdity – shows are generally well worth the admission. Tickets available online. (📞212-253-7246; www.slipperroom.com; 167 Orchard St, entrance on Stanton St; admission $10-20; ⏲8pm-3am; 🚇F to 2nd Ave)

Anthology Film Archives   CINEMA

39 ⭐ Map p66, B5

Opened in 1970, this theater is dedicated to the idea of film as an art form. It screens indie works by new filmmakers and revives classics and obscure oldies, from Luis Buñuel to Ken Brown's psychedelia. (📞212-505-5181; www.anthologyfilmarchives.org; 32 Second Ave, at 2nd St; 🚇F to 2nd Ave)

🔍 Local Life
An Old-Fashioned Soak

Since 1892, the **Russian & Turkish Baths** (Map p66, C2; 📞212-674-9250; www.russianturkishbaths.com; 268 E 10th St, btwn First Ave & Ave A; per visit $40; ⏲noon-10pm Mon, Tue, Thu & Fri, from 10am Wed, from 9am Sat, from 8am Sun; 🚇L to 1st Ave; 6 to Astor Pl) has been the spa of choice for anyone who wants to romp in steam baths, refresh in an ice-cold plunge pool and then steam into pure bliss in a sauna. There's also a tiny sundeck. The baths are mostly open to both men and women (wearing shorts is required), with various times designated men or women only.

Bowery Ballroom (p80)

New York Theatre Workshop
THEATER

40 ⭐ Map p66, B4

Recently celebrating its 25th year, this innovative production house is a treasure to those seeking cutting-edge, contemporary plays with purpose. It was the originator of two big Broadway hits, *Rent* and *Urinetown,* and offers a constant supply of high-quality drama. (☎212-460-5475; www.nytw.org; 79 E 4th St, btwn Second & Third Aves; **S** F to 2nd Ave)

Rockwood Music Hall
LIVE MUSIC

41 ⭐ Map p66, C6

Opened by indie rocker Ken Rockwood, this breadbox-sized concert space has three stages that see a rapid-fire flow of bands and singer-songwriters. If cash and time are limited, head to stage 1, which has free shows, with a maximum of one hour per band (die-hards can see five or more performances a night). Music kicks off at 3pm on weekends and 6pm on weeknights. (☎212-477-4155; www.rockwoodmusichall.com; 196 Allen St, btwn Houston & Stanton Sts; ⊙6pm-2am Mon-Fri, from 3pm Sat & Sun; **S** F/V to Lower East Side-2nd Ave)

Pianos
LIVE MUSIC

42 ⭐ Map p66, D6

Nobody's bothered to change the sign at the door, a leftover from the location's previous incarnation as a piano shop. Now it's dedicated to a musical mix of genres and styles, leaning more toward pop, punk and new wave, but throwing in some hip-hop and indie for good measure. Sometimes you get a double feature – one act upstairs and another below. (☎212-505-3733; www.pianosnyc.com; 158 Ludlow St, at Stanton St; cover $8-12; ⏱2pm-4am; ⒮F to 2nd Ave)

Landmark Sunshine Cinema

CINEMA

43 Map p66, C5

A renovated Yiddish theater, the wonderful Landmark shows foreign and first-run mainstream art-house films on massive screens. It also has much-coveted stadium-style seating, so it doesn't matter what giant sits in front of you after the lights go out. (☎212-260-7289; www.landmarktheatres.com; 143 E Houston St, btwn Forsyth & Eldridge Sts; ⒮F/V to Lower East Side-2nd Ave)

Nuyorican Poets Café

LIVE PERFORMANCE

44 ⭐ Map p66, E5

Still going strong after 40-plus years, the legendary Nuyorican is home to poetry slams, hip-hop performances, plays, and film and video events. It's a piece of East Village history, but also a vibrant and still-relevant nonprofit arts organization. Buy tickets online for the more popular weekend shows. (☎212-780-9386; www.nuyorican.org; 236 E

3rd St; cover $8-25; ⏱shows 9pm or 10pm; ⒮F to Lower East Side-2nd Ave)

Bowery Ballroom

LIVE MUSIC

45 ⭐ Map p66, B7

This terrific, medium-sized venue has the perfect sound and feel for well-known indie-rock acts such as The Shins, Stephen Malkmus and Patti Smith. (☎212-533-2111; www.boweryballroom.com; 6 Delancey St, at Bowery St; ⒮J/Z to Bowery; B/D to Grand St)

La MaMa ETC

THEATER

46 ⭐ Map p66, B4

A long-standing home for onstage experimentation (ETC stands for Experimental Theater Club), La MaMa is now a three-theater complex with a cafe, an art gallery and a separate studio building that features cutting-edge dramas, sketch comedy and readings of all kinds. Ten $10 tickets are available for each show. Book early to score a deal! (☎646-430-5374; www.lamama.org; 74a E 4th St; admission $25; ⒮F to 2nd Ave)

Shopping

Still House

HOMEWARES

47 🔒 Map p66, D3

Step into this petite, peaceful boutique to browse sculptural glassware and pottery: handblown vases, geometric tabletop objects, ceramic bowls and cups, and other finery for the home. You'll also find minimalistic jewelry,

St Marks Place (p70)

delicately bound notebooks and small framed artworks for the wall. (📞212-539-0200; www.stillhousenyc.com; 117 E 7th St; 🕐noon-8pm; 🚇6 to Astor Pl)

By Robert James FASHION

48 Map p66, D8

Rugged, beautifully tailored menswear is the mantra of Robert James, who sources and manufactures right here in NYC (the design studio is just upstairs). The racks are lined with slim-fitting denim, handsome button-downs, and classic-looking sports coats. Lola, James' black lab, sometimes roams the store. He also has a store in Williamsburg. (📞212-253-2121; www.byrobertjames.com; 74 Orchard St;

🕐noon-8pm Mon-Sat, to 6pm Sun; 🚇F to Delancey St; J/M/Z to Essex St)

Obscura Antiques ANTIQUES

49 Map p66, D1

This small cabinet of curiosities pleases both lovers of the macabre and inveterate antique hunters. Here you'll find taxidermied animal heads, tiny rodent skulls and skeletons, butterfly displays in glass boxes, photos of dead people, disturbing little (dental?) instruments, German landmine flags (stackable so tanks could see them), old poison bottles and glass eyes. (📞212-505-9251; www.obscuraantiques.com; 207 Ave A, btwn 12th & 13th Sts; 🕐noon-8pm Mon-Sat, to 7pm Sun; 🚇L to 1st Ave)

Clothing stall, St Marks Place

Assembly
FASHION

50 🔒 Map p66, D6

Whitewashed floorboards and an air of stylish whimsy define this dapper men's and women's shop in the Lower East Side. There are lots of covetworthy wares on display, showcasing obscure designers from East and West. Look for canvas high tops by Shoes Like Pottery, satchels by Le Bas, chunky jewelry by Open House and outerwear by the shop's in-house label Assembly. (☏212-253-5393; www.assemblynewyork.com; 170 Ludlow St, btwn Stanton & Houston Sts; ☺noon-8pm; ⓢF to 2nd Ave)

Verameat
JEWELRY

51 🔒 Map p66, C2

Designer Vera Balyura creates exquisite little pieces with a dark sense of humor in this delightful little shop on 9th St. Tiny, artfully wrought pendants, rings, earrings and bracelets appear almost too precious, until a closer inspection reveals zombies, Godzilla robots, animal heads, dinosaurs and encircling claws – bringing a whole new level of miniaturized complexity to the realm of jewelry. (☏212-388-9045; www.verameat.com; 315 E 9th St, btwn First & Second Aves; ☺noon-8pm; ⓢ6 to Astor Pl; F to 2nd Ave)

No Relation Vintage
VINTAGE

52 🔒 Map p66, C1

Among the many vintage shops of the East Village, No Relation is a winner for its wide-ranging collections that run the gamut from denim and leather jackets to flannels, sneakers, plaid shirts, candy-colored T-shirts, varsity jackets, clutches and more. Sharpen your elbows: hipster crowds flock here on weekends. (☏212-228-5201; http://norelationvintage.com; 204 First Ave, btwn 12th & 13th Sts; ☺noon-8pm; ⓢL to 1st Ave)

Reformation
CLOTHING

53 🔒 Map p66, D6

This stylish boutique sells beautifully designed garments with minimal environmental impact. Aside from its green credentials, it sells unique tops, blouses, sweaters and dresses, with fair prices in comparison to other LES boutiques. (📞646-448-4925; www.thereformation.com; 156 Ludlow St, btwn Rivington & Stanton Sts; 🕐noon-8pm Mon-Sat, to 7pm Sun; Ⓢ F to Delancey St; F to 2nd Ave; J/M/Z to Essex St)

Dinosaur Hill   CHILDREN
54 🔒 Map p66, B3

A small, old-fashioned toy store that's inspired more by imagination than Disney movies, this shop has loads of great gift ideas: Czech marionettes, shadow puppets, micro building blocks, calligraphy sets, toy pianos, art and science kits, kids' music CDs from around the globe, and wooden blocks in half-a-dozen different languages, plus natural-fiber clothing for infants. (📞212-473-5850; www.dinosaurhill.com; 306 E 9th St; 🕐11am-7pm; Ⓢ6 to Astor Pl)

John Derian   HOMEWARES
55 🔒 Map p66, B5

John Derian is famed for its decoupage – pieces from original botanical and animal prints stamped under glass. The result is a beautiful collection of one-of-a-kind plates, paperweights, coasters, lamps, bowls and vases. (📞212-677-3917; www.johnderian.com; 6 E 2nd St, btwn Bowery & Second Ave;

🕐11am-7pm Tue-Sun; Ⓢ F/V to Lower East Side-2nd Ave)

Moo Shoes   SHOES
56 🔒 Map p66, D8

This earth- and animal-friendly boutique sells surprisingly stylish microfiber (faux leather) shoes, handbags and wallets. Look for elegant ballet flats from Love Is Mighty, rugged men's Oxfords by Novacos, and sleek Matt & Nat wallets. (📞212-254-6512; www.mooshoes.com; 78 Orchard St, btwn Broome & Grand Sts; 🕐11:30am-7:30pm Mon-Sat, noon-6pm Sun; Ⓢ F to Delancey St; J/M/Z to Essex St)

Odin (East Village)   FASHION
57 🔒 Map p66, C2

Named after the mighty Norse god, Odin offers a bit of magic for men seeking a new look. The large boutique carries stylish downtown labels such as Phillip Lim, Band of Outsiders and Edward, and is a great place to browse for up-and-coming designers. Other eye candy at the minimalist store includes Comme des Garçons wallets, sleek sunglasses, Sharps grooming products and Taschen coffee-table books. (📞212-475-0666; www.odinnewyork.com; 328 E 11th St; 🕐noon-9pm Mon-Sat, to 7pm Sun; Ⓢ L to 1st Ave; L, N/Q/R, 4/5/6 to 14th St-Union Sq)

Explore

West Village, Chelsea & the Meatpacking District

Quaint, twisting streets and well-preserved town houses offer endless options for intimate dining and drinking in the West Village. The Meatpacking District next door has trendy nightlife options galore. Further up is Chelsea, home to a vibrant gay scene and the epicenter of the NYC art scene, blossoming all along the West 20s.

The Sights in a Day

☀ Start the morning with French toast and the newspapers at West Village favorite **Café Cluny** (p98). Wander north along the cobblestone streets to the Renzo Piano–designed **Whitney Museum of American Art** (p92). Check out the stellar permanent collection before refueling at the **Chelsea Market** (p92) nearby.

☀ Afterwards, walk it off on the **High Line** (p86), a wildly landscaped greenway perched over the city streets. Walk up to about 26th St before exiting to street level, where former warehouses comprise Chelsea's vast art scene. Zigzag your way along the cross-streets between Tenth and Eleventh Aves, stopping in at galleries that catch your eye. Pause for tapas at **Tía Pol** (p89).

☾ In the evening, head down to **Washington Square Park** (p92) for a stroll through one of Manhattan's most picturesque little corners. There's a bounty of great little restaurants to choose from nearby, including **Jeffrey's Grocery** (p96) and **Blue Hill** (p98). With NYC's best jazz clubs also in the area, you should catch a set after dinner: try **Smalls** (p104) or the **Village Vanguard** (p105). End the night with a fun-loving crowd crooning campy show tunes at **Duplex** (p105).

For a local's day in Chelsea, see p88.

👁 Top Sights
The High Line (p86)

🔍 Local Life
Chelsea Galleries (p88)

💜 Best of New York City

Eating
Jeffrey's Grocery (p96)
Gansevoort Market (p95)
Blue Hill (p98)
RedFarm (p99)
Chelsea Market (p92)

Drinking
Employees Only (p100)
Buvette (p100)
Frying Pan (p100)

Getting There

🚇 **Subway** Take the A/C/E or 1/2/3 lines and disembark at 14th St (along either service) if you're looking for a good place to start exploring.

🚌 **Bus** Try M14 or M8 if you're traveling across town and want to access the westernmost areas of Chelsea and the West Village by public transportation.

Top Sights
The High Line

It's hard to believe that the High Line – a shining example of brilliant urban renewal – was once a dingy rail line that anchored a rather unsavory district of slaughterhouses. Today, this eye-catching attraction is one of New York's best loved green spaces, drawing visitors far and wide who come to stroll, sit and picnic 30ft above the city, while enjoying fabulous views of Manhattan's ever-changing urban landscape.

◉ Map p90, C3

☏212-206-9922

www.thehighline.org

Gansevoort St

⊙7am-11pm Jun-Sep, to 10pm Apr, May, Oct & Nov, to 7pm Dec-Mar

▣M11 to Washington St; M11, M14 to 9th Ave; M23, M34 to 10th Ave; ⑤L, A/C/E to 14th St-8th Ave; C/E to 23rd St-8th Ave

Don't Miss

The Industrial Past

The tracks that would one day become the High Line were commissioned in the 1930s when the municipal government decided to raise the street-level tracks after years of accidents that gave Tenth Ave the nickname 'Death Avenue.' The project drained over $150 million in funds (equivalent to around $2 billion by today's dime) and took roughly five years to complete. After two decades of effective use, the rail line was obsolete by the 1980s. In 1999 a plan was made to convert the scarring strands of metal into a public green space, though it would be another decade before the park finally became a reality.

Public Art

In addition to being a haven of hovering green, the High Line is also an informal art space featuring a variety of installations, both site-specific and stand-alone. For detailed information about the public art on display at the time of your visit, check out http://art.thehighline.org.

More Than Just a Public Space

The High Line's civic influence extends far beyond being the trendsetter in the island's re-green-ification. As you walk along the High Line you'll find staffers wearing shirts with the signature double-H logo who can point you in the right direction or offer you additional information about the converted rails. There are also myriad staffers behind the scenes organizing public art exhibitions and activity sessions. Special tours and events explore a variety of topics: history, horticulture, design, art and food. Check the event schedule on www.thehighline.org for the latest details.

☑ Top Tips

▶ Beat the crowds by starting early at 30th or 34th St, wandering south and exiting at 14th St for a bite at Chelsea Market (p92) before exploring the West Village. If you're peckish, head in the reverse direction, gelato in hand.

▶ If you're interested in helping support the High Line, you can become a member of the Friends of the High Line through the website. 'Spike' level members receive discounts at nearby stores such as Diane von Furstenberg, Amy's Bread and 192 Books (p110).

✕ Take a Break

The High Line invites gastronomic establishments from around the city to set up stalls for to-go items. Expect a showing of the finest coffee and ice cream establishments during the warmer months. A cache of eateries is stashed within the brick walls of Chelsea Market at the 14th St exit of the High Line.

Local Life
Chelsea Galleries

Chelsea is home to the highest concentration of art galleries in the entire city. Most lie in the 20s, on the blocks between Tenth and Eleventh Aves, and openings for new shows are typically held on Thursday evenings. Pick up Art Info's *Gallery Guide* (with map), available for free at most galleries. Take the C/E or 1 subway to 23rd St to start your walk.

❶ Pace

In a dramatically transformed garage, the **Pace Gallery** (☎212-929-7000; www .pacegallery.com; 534 W 25th St, btwn Tenth & Eleventh Aves; ◷10am-6pm Tue-Sat) has worked with some of the leading artists of recent years including Sol LeWitt, David Hockney, Chuck Close and Robert Rauschenberg. It has three locations on W 25th St, and one in Midtown. This branch often focuses on large-scale installations.

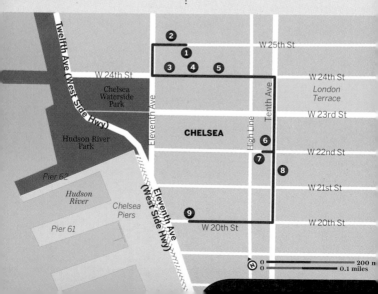

❷ Cheim & Read

Sculptures of every shape, size and material abound at **Cheim & Read** (☎212-242-7727; www.cheimread.com; 547 W 25th St, btwn Tenth & Eleventh Aves; ⏰10am-6pm Tue-Sat) and monthly rotations keep the exhibits fresh – expect blazing light installations and inspired photography displays.

❸ Gagosian

Gagosian (☎212-741-1111; www.gagosian.com; 555 W 24th St; ⏰10am-6pm Tue-Sat) offers a different vibe than most of the one-off galleries, as it's part of a constellation of showrooms that spreads well across the globe. Also check out the 21st St location, which easily rivals some of the city's museums with its large-scale installations.

❹ Mary Boone

Check out **Mary Boone Gallery** (☎212-752-2929; www.maryboonegallery.com; 541 W 24th St; ⏰10am-6pm Tue-Sat), whose owner found fame in the '80s with her eye for Jean-Michel Basquiat and Julian Schnabel. It's considered one of the main 'blue-chip' galleries in the area.

❺ Barbara Gladstone

The curator of the eponymous **Barbara Gladstone Gallery** (☎212-206-9300; www.gladstonegallery.com; 515 W 24th St, btwn Tenth & Eleventh Aves; ⏰10am-6pm Tue-Sat) has learned a thing or two in her 30 years in the Manhattan art world. Ms Gladstone consistently puts together the most talked-about and well-critiqued displays around.

❻ Tía Pol

Wielding Spanish tapas amid closet-sized surrounds, **Tía Pol** (☎212-675-8805; www.tiapol.com; 205 Tenth Ave, btwn 22nd & 23rd Sts; small plates $5-14; ⏰noon-11pm Tue-Sun, from 5:30pm Mon) has a great wine list and a tantalizing array of small plates.

❼ Matthew Marks

Famous for exhibiting big names such as Jasper Johns and Ellsworth Kelly, **Matthew Marks** (☎212-243-0200; www.matthewmarks.com; 522 W 22nd St; ⏰10am-6pm Tue-Sat) is a true Chelsea pioneer.

❽ 192 Books

This small but delightful **bookshop** (☎212-255-4022; www.192books.com; 192 Tenth Ave, btwn 21st & 22nd Sts; ⏰11am-7pm) makes a fine reprieve from art-gazing. You'll find an edifying selection of literary works covering many genres, plus artist monographs and kids' books.

❾ David Zwirner

One of the major players in the art world, **David Zwirner** (☎212-517-8677; www.davidzwirner.com; 537 W 20th St, btwn Tenth & Eleventh Aves; ⏰10am-6pm Tue-Sat) opened a five-story, LEED-certified gallery with 30,000 sq ft of exhibition space in 2013. He stages some of New York's best gallery shows. Infinity Mirrored Room was a major recent event that drew three-hour lines to see Yayoi Kusama's otherworldly light installations. He also has a location at 525 W 19th St.

Pier 66
28

Twelfth Ave (West Side Hwy)

Hudson River Park

Schooner Adirondack
8

Pier 62

Pier 61

Pier 60

Pier 59

Eleventh Ave (West Side Hwy)

Hudson River

Hudson River Park

West Side Hwy

W 27th St
39 15 44

Eleventh Ave

Chelsea Waterside Park

High Line

62 20

18

55

Chelsea Market 4

W 13th St
37 38
Little W 12th St

High Line 1

Whitney Museum of American Art

30

W 12th St

Bethune St

Washington St

Hudson St

Charles St

Chelsea Park

CHELSEA

Tenth Ave

10

W 26th St
W 25th St
W 24th St
W 23rd St
W 22nd St
W 21st St
W 20th St
W 19th St
W 18th St
W 17th St
W 16th St
W 15th St

Ninth Ave

Chelsea Market

W 14th St

MEATPACKING DISTRICT

Gansevoort St
9

Horatio St
Jane St

Abingdon Sq

Bank St

25
32

W 11th St
Perry St

23

W 10th St

Christopher St

Barrow St   Morton St

Hudson River Park 2

43

Eighth Ave

W 26th St
W 25th St

23rd

23r

W 22nd St
22

47
33 50

8th Av
14th

8th

Eighth Ave

19
WEST VILLAG
60

Bleecker

Greenwich

Hudson

For reviews see

👁	Top Sights	p86
◉	Sights	p92
✖	Eating	p95
🍷	Drinking	p100
★	Entertainment	p104
🔒	Shopping	p108

0 ———— 500 m
0 ———— 0.25 miles

E W 27th St
F E 27th St
G
H E 26th St

Seventh Ave
Broadway
Madison Ave
Lexington Ave
Third Ave
Second Ave

1
E 25th St
E 24th St

Madison Square Park

23rd St
23rd St
23rd St
23rd St
23rd St
E 23rd St

E 22nd St

FLATIRON DISTRICT
E 21st St
Park Ave S
E 21st St
Gramercy Park
E 20th St
E 20th St

Fifth Ave
Sixth Ave (Avenue of the Americas)

GRAMERCY PARK
E 19th St
E 19th St

2

18th St
E 18th St
E 18th St

Irving Pl

63 🔒
E 17th St
E 17th St

5 💿
UNION SQUARE
Stuyvesant Square
E 16th St
E 16th St

Rubin Museum of Art
Union Square
E 15th St
E 15th St
E 15th St

6th Ave-14th St
14th St-Union Sq

14th St
14th St
E 14th St
3rd Ave
E 14th St

3
W 13th St
E 13th St

58
W 12th St
53 🔒
E 12th St
EAST VILLAGE

Greenwich Ave
W 11th St
University Pl
E 11th St
Fourth Ave
Third Ave
E 11th St

4
42 ✕
16 ✕
29 ✕
W 10th St
E 10th St
6 💿
Grace Church
Stuyvesant St
E 10th St
E 10th St

3
17 ✕
31 ✕
11 ✕
W 9th St
E 9th St
E 9th St
St Marks Pl

46 ✕
56 🔒
54 🔒
W 8th St
64 🔒
E 8th St
8th St-NYU
Astor Pl
Cooper Square
E 7th St

4

40 ✕
57 ✕
36 ✕
14 ✕
Waverly Pl
E 6th St
Second Ave

41 ✕
Washington Sq N
21 ✕
3 Washington Square Park
Waverly Pl
Lafayette St
Bowery
E 5th St

Christopher St-Sheridan Sq
Washington Pl
W 4th St
Washington Sq S
Washington Pl
7 💿
E 4th St

GREENWICH VILLAGE
45 🌟
51 🌟
New York University
NOHO

27 🌟
48 🌟
Minetta La
W 3rd St
Great Jones St

12 🌟
Cornelia St
Bond St
E 2nd St

61 🔒
24 ✕
49 🌟
Sullivan St
Thompson St
LaGuardia Pl
Mercer St
Bleecker St
Bleecker St
E 1st St

5

Seventh Ave
Carmine St
Downing St
W Houston St
52 🌟
Broadway-Lafayette St
2nd Ave

Likes Pl
35 🌟
Bedford St
E Houston St

Sights

Whitney Museum of American Art
MUSEUM

1 ◉ Map p90, C3

After years of construction, the Whitney's new downtown location opened to much fanfare in 2015. Perched near the foot of the High Line, this architecturally stunning building – designed by Renzo Piano – makes a suitable introduction to the museum's superb collection. Inside the spacious, light-filled galleries, you'll find works by all the great American artists, including Edward Hopper, Jasper Johns, Georgia O'Keeffe and Mark Rothko. (☏212-570-3600; www.whitney.org; 99 Gansevoort St; adult/child $22/free;

⊙10:30am-6pm Mon, Wed & Sun, to 10pm Thu-Sat; ⑤L to 8th Ave)

Hudson River Park
PARK

2 ◉ Map p90, D5

The High Line may be all the rage these days, but one block away from that famous elevated green space, there stretches a five-mile-long ribbon of green that has dramatically transformed the city over the past decade. Covering 550 acres, and running from Battery Park at Manhattan's southern tip to 59th St in Midtown, the Hudson River Park is Manhattan's wondrous backyard. The long riverside path is a great spot for cycling, running and strolling. (www.hudsonriverpark.org)

Washington Square Park
PARK

3 ◉ Map p90, F4

What was once a potter's field and a square for public executions is now the unofficial town square of the Village, and plays host to lounging NYU students, tuba-playing street performers, curious canines and their owners, speed-chess pros, and bare-footed children who splash about in the fountain on warm days. (Fifth Ave at Washington Sq N; ⑤A/C/E, B/D/F/M to W 4th St-Washington Sq; N/R to 8th St-NYU)

Chelsea Market
MARKET

4 ◉ Map p90, C3

In a shining example of redevelopment and preservation, the Chelsea Market has transformed a former factory into

---

◯ Local Life

Robert Hammond on the High Line

Co-founder and executive director of Friends of the High Line Robert Hammond shares his High Line highlights: 'What I love most about the High Line are its hidden moments, like at the Tenth Ave cut-out near 17th St. Most people sit on the bleachers, but if you turn the other way, you can see the Statue of Liberty far away in the harbor. Architecture buffs will love looking down 18th St, and up on 30th is my favorite moment – a steel cut-out where you can see the cars underneath.'

Rubin Museum of Art

a shopping concourse that caters to foodies. More than two dozen food vendors ply their temptations, from ramen to ice cream and more (see p99). (www.chelseamarket.com; 75 Ninth Ave, at 15th St; ⊙7am-9pm Mon-Sat, 8am-8pm Sun; ⑤A/C/E to 14th St; L to 8th Ave)

Rubin Museum of Art   GALLERY

5 ◉ Map p90, E2

The Rubin is the first museum in the Western world to dedicate itself to the art of the Himalayas and surrounding regions. Its impressive collections include embroidered textiles from China, metal sculptures from Tibet, Pakistani stone sculptures and intricate Bhutanese paintings, as well as ritual objects and dance masks from various Tibetan regions, spanning from the 2nd to the 19th centuries. (☎212-620-5000; www.rmanyc.org; 150 W 17th St, btwn Sixth & Seventh Aves; adult/child $15/free, 6-10pm Fri free; ⊙11am-5pm Mon & Thu, to 9pm Wed, to 10pm Fri, to 6pm Sat & Sun; ⑤1 to 18th St)

Grace Church   CHURCH

6 ◉ Map p90, G3

This Gothic Revival Episcopal church, designed in 1843 by James Renwick Jr, was made of marble quarried by prisoners at 'Sing Sing,' the state penitentiary in the town of Ossining, 30 miles up the Hudson River (which, legend has it, is the origin of the expression 'being sent upriver'). After years of neglect, Grace Church has been beautifully restored. (☎212-254-2000; www.gracechurchnyc.org; 802 Broadway, at 10th St; ⊙10am-5pm, services daily; ⑤N/R to 8th St-NYU; 6 to Astor Pl)

New York University UNIVERSITY

7 ◉ Map p90, G4

In 1831 Albert Gallatin, formerly Secretary of the Treasury under President Thomas Jefferson, founded an intimate center of higher learning open to all students, regardless of race or class background. He'd scarcely recognize the place today, as it's swelled to a student population of around 50,000, with more than 16,000 employees, and schools and colleges at six Manhattan locations. (NYU; ☎212-998-4550; www.nyu.edu; information center 50 W 4th St; ⑤A/C/E, B/D/F/M to W 4th St-Washington Sq; N/R to 8th St-NYU)

Schooner Adirondack BOATING

8 ◉ Map p90, B2

The two-masted *'Dack* hits the New York Harbor with four two-hour sails daily from May to October. The 1920s-style, 80ft *Manhattan* yacht sails daily at 3:30pm and 6pm, with other tours throughout the week. Call or check the website for the latest times. (☎212-913-9991; www.sail-nyc.com; Chelsea Piers, Pier 62 at W 22nd St; tours $48-78; ⑤C, E to 23rd St)

Understand
The History of Washington Square Park

Although quite ravishing today, Washington Square Park has had a long and eclectic history. When the Dutch settled Manhattan to run the Dutch East India Company, they gave what is now the park to their freed black slaves. At the turn of the 19th century, it became a burial ground, quickly reaching capacity during an outbreak of yellow fever. More than 20,000 bodies remain buried under the park today. By 1830 the grounds were used for military parades, before quickly transforming into a park for the wealthy elite whose lavish town houses began springing up on the surrounding streets.

Colloquially known as the Washington Square Arch, the iconic Stanford White Arch now dominates the park with its 72ft of beaming white Dover marble. Originally designed in wood to celebrate the centennial of George Washington's inauguration in 1889, the arch proved so popular that it was replaced with stone six years later. In 1916 artist Marcel Duchamp famously climbed to the top of the arch by its internal stairway and declared the park the 'Free and Independent Republic of Washington Square.'

Eating

Gansevoort Market
MARKET $

9 Map p90, C3

Inside a brick building in the heart of the Meatpacking District, this sprawling market is the latest and greatest food emporium to land in NYC. Inside a raw, industrial space lit by skylights, several dozen gourmet vendors sling tapas, arepas, tacos, pizzas, meat pies, ice cream, pastries and more. (www.gansmarket.com; 52 Gansevoort St, btwn Greenwich & Washington Sts; mains $5-20; ⏰8am-8pm; 🚇A/C/E to 14th St; L to 8th Ave)

Jun-Men
RAMEN $

10 Map p90, C1

This tiny, ultramodern ramen joint whips up delectably flavored noodle bowls, in variants of pork shoulder, spicy miso or uni mushroom (with sea urchin). Don't skip the appetizers: the yellowtail ceviche and barbecue pork buns are outstanding. Service is speedy, and it's fun to watch the adroit prep team in action in the tiny kitchen at center stage. (☎646-852-6787; www.junmenramen.com; 249 Ninth Ave, btwn 25th & 26th Sts; ramen $14-18; ⏰11:30am-3pm & 5-10pm Mon-Thu, to 11pm Fri & Sat; 🚇C/E to 23rd St)

Umami
BURGERS $

11 Map p90, F4

That mysterious fifth taste sensation will be more than satisfied at this stylish burger bar. Combos such as the Truffle (truffled aioli and house-made truffle cheese) and the bacon-topped Manly are first-rate, as is the veg-friendly Black Bean. With creative cocktails, microbrews on draft and tasty sides (including beet salad and tempura onion rings), you're clearly not in the burger land of your childhood. (☎212-677-8626; www.umamiburger.com; 432 Sixth Ave, btwn 9th & 10th Sts; burgers $10-15; ⏰11:30am-11pm Sun-Thu, to midnight Fri & Sat; 🚇1 to Christopher St-Sheridan Sq; F/M to 14th St; L to 6th Ave)

Moustache
MIDDLE EASTERN $

12 Map p90, E5

Small and delightful Moustache serves up rich, flavorful sandwiches (leg of lamb, merguez sausage, falafel), thin-crust pizzas, tangy salads and hearty specialties such as *ouzi* (phyllo stuffed with chicken, rice and spices) and moussaka. The best start to a meal: a platter of hummus or baba ghanoush, served with fluffy, piping hot pitas. It's a warm, earthy space with copper-topped tables and brick walls. (☎212-229-2220; http://moustachepitza.com; 90 Bedford St, btwn Grove & Barrow Sts; mains $10-17; ⏰noon-midnight; 🚇1 to Christopher St-Sheridan Sq)

Taïm
ISRAELI $

13 Map p90, E4

This tiny joint whips up some of the best falafels in the city. You can order them Green (traditional style), Harissa (with Tunisian spices) or Red (with roasted peppers). Whichever you

Top Tip

Lost Like a Local

It's perfectly acceptable to arm yourself with a map (or rely on your smartphone) to get around the West Village's charming-but-challenging side streets. Even some locals have a tricky time finding their way. Just remember that 4th St makes a diagonal turn north – breaking away from the usual east–west street grid – and you'll quickly become a Village pro.

choose, you'll get them stuffed into pita bread with creamy tahini sauce and a generous dose of Israeli salad. (📞212-691-1287; www.taimfalafel.com; 222 Waverly Pl, btwn Perry & W 11th Sts; sandwiches $7-8; ⏱11am-10pm; 🚇1/2/3, A/C/E to 14th St)

Jeffrey's Grocery

MODERN AMERICAN $$

14 🍴 Map p90, E4

A West Village classic, Jeffrey's is a lively eating and drinking spot that hits all the right notes. Seafood is the focus: there's an oyster bar and beautifully executed seafood selections such as razor clams with caviar and dill, whole roasted dorade with curry, and seafood platters to share. Meat dishes come in the shape of roasted chicken with Jerusalem artichoke, and a humble but juicy pastrami burger. (📞646-398-7630; http://jeffreysgrocery.com; 172 Waverly Pl, at Christopher St; mains $25-

39; ⏱8am-11pm Mon-Fri, from 9:30am Sat & Sun; 🚇1 to Christopher St-Sheridan Sq)

Heath

SUPPER CLUB $$

15 🍴 Map p90, B1

The creators of hit interactive theater piece *Sleep No More* operate this atmospheric restaurant next door to their warehouse venue. Like the fictional McKittrick Hotel in the drama, the Heath is set in another place and time (vaguely Britain, 1920s), with suspenders-wearing barkeeps, period furnishings and (fake) smoke wafting over the dining room, as a jazz band performs on stage. (📞212-564-1622; http://mckittrickhotel.com/theheath; 542 W 27th St, btwn Tenth & Eleventh Aves; mains $23-39; ⏱6-11pm Wed & Thu, to 2am Fri & Sat, 11:30am-4:30pm Sat & Sun; 🚇C/E to 23rd St)

Rosemary's

ITALIAN $$

16 🍴 Map p90, E4

One of the West Village's hottest restaurants, Rosemary's serves high-end Italian fare that more than lives up to the hype. In a vaguely farmhouse-like setting, diners tuck into generous portions of housemade pastas, rich salads, and cheese and *salumi* (cured meat) boards. Current favorites include the *acqua pazza* (seafood stew) and smoked lamb with roasted vegetables. (📞212-647-1818; http://rosemarysnyc.com; 18 Greenwich Ave, at W 10th St; mains $15-32; ⏱8am-midnight Mon-Fri, from 10am Sat & Sun; 🚇1 to Christopher St-Sheridan Sq)

Schooner *Adirondack II* on the Hudson River (p94)

Morandi   ITALIAN $$

17  Map p90, E4

Run by celebrated restaurateur Keith McNally, Morandi is a warmly lit space where the hubbub of garrulous diners resounds amid brick walls, wide plank floors and rustic chandeliers. Squeeze into a table for the full-meal experience – hand-rolled spaghetti with lemon and Parmesan; meatballs with pine nuts and raisins; and grilled whole sea bream. (☏212-627-7575; www.morandiny.com; 211 Waverly Pl, btwn Seventh Ave & Charles St; mains $18-38; ☺8am-midnight Mon-Fri, from 10am Sat & Sun; ⓢ1 to Christopher St-Sheridan Sq)

Cookshop   MODERN AMERICAN $$

18 Map p90, C2

A brilliant brunching pit stop before (or after) tackling the verdant High Line across the street, Cookshop is a lively place that knows its niche and does it oh so well. Excellent service, eye-opening cocktails (good morning, bacon-infused BLT Mary!), a perfectly baked breadbasket and a selection of inventive egg mains make this a favorite in Chelsea on a Sunday afternoon. (☏212-924-4440; www.cookshopny. com; 156 Tenth Ave, btwn 19th & 20th Sts; mains brunch $14-20, lunch $16-24, dinner $22-38; ☺8am-11:30pm Mon-Fri, from 10am Sat, 10am-10pm Sun; ⓢL to 8th Ave; A/C/E to 23rd St)

Café Cluny
BISTRO $$

19 🍴 Map p90, D4

Café Cluny brings the charm of Paris to the West Village, with woven bistro-style bar chairs, light wooden upholstery, and a selection of *joie-de-vivre*-inducing platters such as wagyu sirloin *steak frites*, white-wine-braised hake, pasta with porcini and chanterelle ragout, fragrant cheese plates, mixed green salads and, for dessert, profiteroles or housemade biscotti. (📞212-255-6900; www.cafecluny.com; 284 W 12th St; mains lunch $15-32, dinner $29-35; ⏰8am-11pm Mon-Fri, 9am-4pm & 5:30-11pm Sat & Sun; 🚇L to 8th Ave; A/C/E, 1/2/3 to 14th St)

Blossom
VEGAN $$

20 🍴 Map p90, C2

This Chelsea veg oasis – with a sinful wine and chocolate bar attached – is a peaceful, romantic dining room that offers imaginative tofu, seitan and vegetable creations, some raw, all kosher. The stellar Autumn Sweet Potato Rolls have raw strips of the orange

---

Local Life
Eighth Avenue Brunch
If you're a dude looking to meet (or at least look at) other dudes, but the cruise-y bar scene isn't your style, then opt for the weekend brunch scene along Eighth Ave. You'll spot piles of friendly Chelsea boys drinking their hangovers off in tight T-shirts and even tighter jeans.

---

root wrapped around tangy strips of coconut, carrots and peppers, and will leave your taste buds reeling. (📞212-627-1144; www.blossomnyc.com; 187 Ninth Ave, btwn 21st & 22nd Sts; mains lunch $15-19, dinner $20-25; ⏰noon-2:45pm & 5-9:30pm; 🍴; 🚇C/E to 23rd St)

Blue Hill
AMERICAN $$$

21 🍴 Map p90, F4

A place for slow-food junkies with deep pockets, Blue Hill was an early crusader in the local-is-better movement. Gifted chef Dan Barber, who hails from a farm family in the Berkshires, Massachusetts, uses harvests from that land, as well as from farms in upstate New York, to create his widely praised fare. (📞212-539-1776; www.bluehillfarm.com; 75 Washington Pl, btwn Sixth Ave & Washington Sq W; prix-fixe menu $88-98; ⏰5-11pm; 🚇A/C/E, B/D/F/M to W 4th St-Washington Sq)

Foragers City Table
MODERN AMERICAN $$$

22 🍴 Map p90, D2

Owners of this excellent restaurant in Chelsea run a 28-acre farm in the Hudson Valley, from which much of their menu is sourced. The menu, which showcases seasonal hits, changes frequently. Recent temptations include squash soup with Jerusalem artichokes and black truffles, roasted chicken with polenta, heritage pork loin, and the season's harvest with toasted quinoa and a flavorful mix of vegetables. (📞212-243-8888; www.

foragerscitygrocer.com; 300 W 22nd St, cnr Eighth Ave; mains $25-36; ☺10:30am-2:30pm Sat & Sun, 5:30-10pm daily; 🖋; **S**C/E, 1 to 23rd St)

RedFarm
FUSION $$$

23 🍴 Map p90, D4

RedFarm transforms Chinese cooking into pure, delectable artistry at this small, buzzing space on Hudson St. Fresh crab and eggplant bruschetta, juicy rib steak (marinated overnight in papaya, ginger and soy) and pastrami egg rolls are among the many creative dishes that brilliantly blend East with West. Other hits include the spicy crispy beef, pan-fried lamb dumplings and the grilled jumbo shrimp red curry. (📞212-792-9700; www.redfarmnyc.com; 529 Hudson St, btwn 10th & Charles Sts; mains $22-46, dim sum $10-16; ☺11am-2:30pm Sat & Sun, 5-11pm daily; **S**A/C/E, B/D/F/M to W 4th St; 1 to Christopher St-Sheridan Sq)

Minetta Tavern
BISTRO $$$

24 🍴 Map p90, F5

Book in advance, or come early to snag a table on a weeknight, because Minetta Tavern is often packed to the rafters. The snug red-leather banquettes, dark-paneled walls with black-and-white photos, and glowing yellow bistro lamps will lure you in. The flavor-filled bistro fare – pan-seared marrow bones, roasted free-range chicken, mussels and foie gras – will have you wishing you lived upstairs. (📞212-475-3850; www.minetta

Eating at Chelsea Market

More than two dozen food vendors ply their temptations in the brick-walled corridors of this foodie haven (p92), including **Mokbar** (ramen with Korean accents), **Takumi Tacos** (mixing Japanese and Mexican ingredients), **Tuck Shop** (Aussie-style savory pies), **Bar Suzette** (crêpes), **Num Pang** (Cambodian sandwiches), **Ninth St Coffee** (perfect lattes), **Doughnuttery** (piping hot mini-doughnuts) and **L'Arte de Gelato** (rich ice cream).

tavernny.com; 113 MacDougal St; mains $22-36; ☺noon-3pm Wed-Sun, 5:30pm-midnight daily; **S**A/C/E, B/D/F/M to W 4th St)

Spotted Pig
PUB FOOD $$$

25 🍴 Map p90, D4

This Michelin-starred gastropub is a favorite with Villagers, and serves an upscale blend of hearty Italian and British dishes. Its two floors are bedecked with old-timey trinkets that give the whole place an air of relaxed elegance. No reservations are taken, so there is often a wait for a table. Lunch on weekdays is less crowded. (📞212-620-0393; www.thespottedpig.com; 314 W 11th St, at Greenwich St; mains lunch $17-26, dinner $22-36; ☺noon-2am Mon-Fri, from 11am Sat & Sun; 🖋🚻; **S**A/C/E to 14th St; L to 8th Ave)

Drinking

Employees Only
BAR

26 🍸 Map p90, D4

Duck behind the neon 'Psychic' sign to find this hidden hangout. The bar gets busier as the night wears on. Bartenders are ace mixologists, fizzing up crazy, addictive libations such as the Ginger Smash and the Mata Hari. Great for late-night drinking and eating, courtesy of the on-site restaurant that serves till 3:30am. (☑212-242-3021; www.employeesonlynyc.com; 510 Hudson St, near Christopher St; ☉6pm-4am; Ⓢ1 to Christopher St-Sheridan Sq)

Buvette
WINE BAR

27 🍸 Map p90, E5

The rustic-chic decor here (think delicate tin tiles and a swooshing marble counter) make it the perfect place for a glass of wine – no matter the time of day. For the full experience at this self-proclaimed *gastrotèque*, grab a seat at one of the surrounding tables, and nibble on small plates while enjoying the old-world wines (mostly from France and Italy). (☑212-255-3590; www.ilovebuvette.com; 42 Grove St, btwn Bedford & Bleecker Sts; ☉9am-2am; Ⓢ1 to Christopher St-Sheridan Sq; A/C/E, B/D/F/M to W 4th St)

Frying Pan
BAR

28 🍸 Map p90, A1

Salvaged from the bottom of the sea (or at least the Chesapeake Bay), the lightship *Frying Pan* and the two-tiered dockside bar where it's parked are fine go-to spots for a sundowner. On warm days, the rustic open-air space brings in the crowds, who come to laze on deck chairs and drink ice-cold beers ($7 for a microbrew; $25 for a pitcher). (☑212-989-6363; www.fryingpan.com; Pier 66, at W 26th St; ☉noon-midnight May-Oct; Ⓢ C/E to 23rd St)

Happiest Hour
COCKTAIL BAR

29 🍸 Map p90, E4

A super-cool, tiki-licious cocktail bar splashed with palm prints, '60s pop and playful mixed drinks. Below it sits serious sibling, Slowly Shirley, a subterranean temple to beautifully crafted, thoroughly researched libations. (☑212-243-2827; www.happiesthournyc.com; 121 W 10th St, btwn Greenwich St & Avenue of the Americas (Sixth Ave); ☉5pm-late Mon-Fri, from 2pm Sat & Sun; Ⓢ A/C/E, B/D/F/M to W 4th St; 1 to Christopher St-Sheridan Sq)

Jane Ballroom
LOUNGE

30 🍸 Map p90, C4

Inside the Jane Hotel, this spacious high-ceilinged lounge is an explosion of wild design: beneath an oversized disco ball is a mishmash of leather sofas and velour chairs, animal print fabrics, potted palms and various taxidermied creatures (a peacock, a ram's head over the flickering fireplace). (☑212-924-6700; www.thejanenyc.com; 113 Jane St, cnr West St; ☉5pm-2am Sun-Wed, to 4am Thu-Sat; Ⓢ L to 8th Ave; A/C/E, 1/2/3 to 14th St)

Dining at Spotted Pig (p99)

Bell Book & Candle BAR

31 Map p90, E4

Step down into this candelit gastro-pub for strong, inventive libations (try the canela margarita, with cinnamon-infused tequila) and hearty pub grub. A 20-something crowd gathers around the small, packed bar (for $1 oysters and happy-hour drink specials early in the night), though there's a lot more seating hidden in the back, with big booths ideal for larger groups. (☏212-414-2355; www.bbandcnyc.com; 141 W 10th St, btwn Waverley Pl & Greenwich Ave; ⏱5:30pm-2am Sun-Wed, to 4am Thu-Sat; ⑤A/B/C, B/D/F/M to W 4th St; 1 to Christopher St-Sheridan Sq)

Aria WINE BAR

32 Map p90, D4

In the western reaches of the Village, Aria is an inviting music-filled space, with a mix of brick and tile walls and rustic wood tables. There's a good selection of wines by the glass, particularly organic labels, with prices starting around $8 a (small) glass. Recommended *cicchetti* (bite-sized plates, good for sharing) include gorgonzola-stuffed dates, crab cakes and stewed calamari. (☏212-242-4233; 117 Perry St, btwn Greenwich & Hudson Sts; ⏱noon-midnight; ⑤1 to Christopher St-Sheridan Sq)

Understand

Gay in Greenwich Village

While the rough-and-ready Lower East Side had established quite a reputation for scandalous dancing halls, saloons and brothels by the 1890s, it was Greenwich Village that would ultimately play the leading role in NYC's long, illustrious queer history.

Village People

Writers and bohemians were already flocking to Greenwich Village in the early years of the 20th century. Their relatively unconventional attitudes were not lost on the day's 'inverts,' who flocked to the area to live a little more freely. A number of gay-owned businesses lined MacDougall St, among them the legendary Eve's Hangout at number 129. A tearoom run by Polish Jewish immigrant Eva Kotchever (Eve Addams), it was famous for two things: poetry readings and a sign on the door that read 'Men allowed but not welcome.'

Wowser Years

The relative transgression of the early 20th century was replaced with a new conservatism as the Great Depression, WWII and the Cold War took their toll. Conservatism was helped along by senator Joseph 'Joe' McCarthy, who declared that homosexuals in the State Department threatened America's security and children. Tougher policing aimed to eradicate queer visibility in the public sphere, forcing the scene further underground in the 1940s and '50s.

Gay Power

Resentment reached boiling point on June 28, 1969, when eight police officers raided the Stonewall Inn, a gay-friendly watering hole in Greenwich Village. Fed up with both the harassment and corrupt officers receiving payoffs from the bars' owners, the LGBT community began bombarding the officers with coins, bottles, bricks and chants of 'Gay power' and 'We shall overcome.' Police were also met by a line of high-kicking drag queens and the now legendary chant, 'We are the Stonewall girls, we wear our hair in curls, we wear no underwear, we show our pubic hair, we wear our dungarees, above our nelly knees...' Their collective anger and solidarity was a turning point, forming the catalyst for the modern gay rights movement.

Bathtub Gin COCKTAIL BAR

33 🚇 Map p90, D2

Amid New York City's obsession with speakeasy-styled hangouts, Bathtub Gin manages to poke its head above the crowd with its super-secret front door hidden on the wall of an unassuming cafe (the Stone Street Coffee Company). Once inside, chill seating, soft background beats and kindly staff make it a great place to sling back bespoke cocktails with friends. (☏646-559-1671; www.bathtubginnyc.com; 132 Ninth Ave, btwn 18th & 19th Sts; ☉6pm-1:30am Sun-Tue, to 3:30am Wed-Sat; **S**A/C/E to 14th St; L to 8th Ave; A/C/E to 23rd St)

Vin Sur Vingt WINE BAR

34 🚇 Map p90, E3

A cozy spot just off Seventh Ave's bustle, Vin Sur Vingt is a slender wine bar with a strip of bar seating and a quaint row of two-seat tables, perfect for a first date. Warning: if you come for a pre-dinner drink, you'll inevitably be charmed into staying through dinner as you munch on the excellent selection of bar bites. (☏212-924-4442; www.vinsur20nyc.com; 201 W 11th St, btwn Seventh Ave & Waverly Pl; ☉3pm-2am Mon-Fri, from 11:30am Sat & Sun; **S**1/2/3 to 14th St; 1/2 to Christopher St-Sheridan Sq; L to 8th Ave)

Little Branch COCKTAIL BAR

35 🚇 Map p90, E5

If it weren't for the doorman, you'd never guess that a charming drinking den lurked beyond the plain metal door positioned at this triangular intersection. When you get the go-ahead to enter, you'll find a basement bar that feels like a kickback to Prohibition times. Old-time jazz tunes waft overhead as locals clink glasses and sip inventive, artfully prepared cocktails. (☏212-929-4360; 20 Seventh Ave, at Leroy St; ☉7pm-3am; **S**1 to Houston St)

Highlands BAR

36 🚇 Map p90, E4

This handsome Scottish-inspired drinkery is a fine place to while away an evening. Exposed brick, a fireplace and a mix of animal heads, pheasant wallpaper, oil paintings and Edinburgh tartans on the walls contribute more than a touch of the old country. You'll find Scottish beers and spirits, plus haggis, Scotch eggs, shepherd's pie and other traditional bites rounding out the menu. (☏212-229-2670; www.highlands-nyc.com; 150 W 10th St; ☉5:30pm-1am Sun-Wed, to 2am Thu-Sat; **S**1 to Christopher St-Sheridan Sq)

Standard BAR

37 🚇 Map p90, C3

Rising on concrete stilts over the High Line, the Standard attracts an A-list crowd, with a chichi lounge and nightclub on the upper floors – the **Top of the Standard** (☏212-645-7600; http://standardhotels.com/high-line; ☉4pm-midnight Mon, to 9pm Tue-Sat, noon-midnight Sun) and **Le Bain** (☏212-645-7600; www.standardculture.com/lebain;

⏰4pm-midnight Mon, to 4am Tue-Thu, 2pm-4am Fri-Sun. There's also a grill, an eating-and-drinking plaza (that becomes a skating rink in winter) and an open-air beer garden with a classic German menu and frothy drafts. (📞877-550-4646, 212-645-4646; www.standardhotels.com; 848 Washington St, btwn 13th & Little W 12th Sts; 🚇1/2/3, A/C/E to 14th St; L to 8th Ave)

Cielo
CLUB

38 📍 Map p90, C3

This long-running club boasts a largely attitude-free crowd and an excellent sound system. Join dance-lovers on Deep Space Monday when DJ François K spins dub and underground beats. Other nights feature various DJs from Europe who mix entrancing, seductive sounds that pull everyone to their

Local Life
Marie's Crisis

Aging Broadway queens, wide-eyed out-of-town gay boys, giggly tourist girls and other miscellaneous fans of musical theater assemble around the piano at **Marie's Crisis** (Map p90, E4; 📞212-243-9323; 59 Grove St, btwn Seventh Ave & Bleecker St; ⏰4pm-4am; 🚇1 to Christopher St-Sheridan Sq), a one-time brothel, and take turns belting out campy numbers, often joined by the entire crowd. It's infectious, old-school fun, no matter how jaded you felt when you went in.

feet. (📞212-645-5700; www.cieloclub.com; 18 Little W 12th St; cover charge $15-25; ⏰10pm-5am Mon & Wed-Sat; 🚇A/C/E, L to 8th Ave-14th St)

Eagle NYC
GAY

39 📍 Map p90, B1

A bi-level club full of hot men in leather, the Eagle is the choice for out-and-proud fetishists. Its two levels, plus roof deck, offer plenty of room for dancing and drinking, which are done with abandon. Thursdays are Code nights, meaning everyone must meet the dress code (wear leather or nothing at all). (📞646-473-1866; www.eaglenyc.com; 554 W 28th St, btwn Tenth & Eleventh Aves; ⏰10pm-4am Mon-Fri, 5pm-4am Sat & Sun; 🚇C/E to 23rd St)

Entertainment

Smalls
JAZZ

40 📍 Map p90, E4

Living up to its name, this cramped but appealing basement jazz den offers a grab-bag collection of jazz acts who take the stage nightly. Cover for the evening is $20, with a come-and-go policy if you need to duck out for a bite. (📞212-252-5091; www.smallslive.com; 183 W 10th St; cover from 7:30pm-12:30am $20, after 12:30am $10; ⏰7:30pm-4am Mon-Thu, from 4pm Fri-Sun; 🚇1 to Christopher St-Sheridan Sq)

Duplex

Duplex CABARET

41 ⭐ Map p90, E4

Cabaret, karaoke and campy dance moves are par for the course at the legendary Duplex. Pictures of Joan Rivers line the walls, and the performers like to mimic her sassy form of self-deprecation, while getting in a few jokes about audience members as well. It's a fun and unpretentious place, and certainly not for the bashful. (☎212-255-5438; www.theduplex.com; 61 Christopher St; cover $5-15; ◷4pm-4am; Ⓢ1 to Christopher St-Sheridan Sq)

Village Vanguard JAZZ

42 ⭐ Map p90, E4

Possibly the city's most prestigious jazz club, the Vanguard has hosted literally every major star of the past 50 years. It started as a home to spoken-word performances and occasionally returns to its roots, but most of the time it's just big, bold jazz all night long. (☎212-255-4037; www.villagevanguard.com; 178 Seventh Ave, at 11th St; cover around $33; ◷7:30pm-12:30am; Ⓢ1/2/3 to 14th St)

Upright Citizens Brigade Theatre

COMEDY

43 ⭐ Map p90, D1

Pros of comedy sketches and outrageous improvisations reign at this popular 74-seat venue, which gets drop-ins from casting directors. Getting in is cheap, and so is the beer and wine. You may recognize pranksters on stage from late-night comedy shows. It's free on Sundays after 9:30pm and on Mondays after 11pm, featuring up-and-coming comics. You'll find quality shows happening nightly, from about 7:30pm, though the Sunday night Assscat Improv session is always a riot. (📞212-366-9176; www.ucbtheatre.com; 307 W 26th St, btwn Eighth & Ninth Aves; admission free-$10; ⏱7pm-midnight; Ⓢ C/E to 23rd St)

Sleep No More

THEATER

44 ⭐ Map p90, C1

One of the most immersive theater experiences ever conceived, *Sleep No More* is a loosely based retelling of *Macbeth* set inside a series of Chelsea warehouses that have been redesigned to look like an abandoned hotel. (www.sleepnomorenyc.com; McKittrick Hotel, 530 W 27th St; tickets from $91; ⏱7pm-midnight Mon-Sat; Ⓢ C/E to 23rd St)

Blue Note

JAZZ

45 ⭐ Map p90, F5

This is by far the most famous (and expensive) of the city's jazz clubs. Most shows are $30 at the bar or

$45 at a table, but can rise for the biggest jazz stars. There are also a few cheaper $20 shows, as well as jazz brunch on Sundays at 11:30am. Go on an off night, and be quiet – all attention is on the stage! (📞212-475-8592; www.bluenote.net; 131 W 3rd St, btwn Sixth Ave & MacDougal St; Ⓢ A/C/E, B/D/F/M to W 4th St-Washington Sq)

Mezzrow

JAZZ

46 ⭐ Map p90, E4

A new jazz bar opening in NYC is a rare thing, especially in the pricey West Village. All the more reason music fans should celebrate the arrival of this intimate basement jazz club, which opened its doors in 2014. It's run by the same folks behind nearby Smalls (p104), and admission (generally $20) gets you same-night admission to Smalls. (📞646-476-4346; www.mezzrow.com; 163 W 10th St, at Seventh Ave; ⏱7:30pm-12:30am Sun-Thu, to 2am Fri & Sat; Ⓢ 1 to Christopher St-Sheridan Sq)

Atlantic Theater Company

THEATER

47 ⭐ Map p90, D2

Founded by David Mamet and William H Macy in 1985, the Atlantic Theater is a pivotal anchor for the Off-Broadway community, hosting many Tony Award and Drama Desk winners over the last three decades. (📞212-691-5919; www.atlantictheater.org; 336 W 20th St, btwn Eighth & Ninth Aves; Ⓢ C/E to 23rd St; 1 to 18th St)

Jazz performance at Village Vanguard (p105)

IFC Center
CINEMA

48 ⭐ Map p90, E5

This art-house cinema in NYU-land has a solidly curated line-up of new indies, cult classics and foreign films. Catch shorts, documentaries, '80s revivals, director-focused series, weekend classics and frequent special series, such as cult favorites (*The Shining*, *Taxi Driver*, *Aliens*) at midnight. (📞212-924-7771; www.ifccenter.com; 323 Sixth Ave, at 3rd St; tickets $14; 🅂A/C/E, B/D/F/M to W 4th St-Washington Sq)

Le Poisson Rouge
LIVE MUSIC

49 ⭐ Map p90, F5

This high-concept art space hosts a highly eclectic line-up of live music,

with the likes of Deerhunter, Marc Ribot and Cibo Matto performing in past years. There's a lot of experimentation and cross-genre pollination between classical, folk music, opera and more. (📞212-505-3474; www.lepoissonrouge.com; 158 Bleecker St; 🅂A/C/E, B/D/F/M to W 4th St-Washington Sq)

Joyce Theater
DANCE

50 ⭐ Map p90, D2

A favorite among dance junkies thanks to its excellent sight lines and offbeat offerings, this is an intimate venue, seating 472 in a renovated cinema. Its focus is on traditional modern companies such as Pilobolus, Stephen Petronio Company and Parsons Dance as well as global stars, such as Dance Brazil, Ballet Hispanico and MalPaso Dance Company. (📞212-691-9740; www.joyce.org; 175 Eighth Ave; 🚇C/E to 23rd St; A/C/E to 8th Ave-14th St; 1 to 18th St)

Comedy Cellar

COMEDY

51 ⭐ Map p90, F5

A long-established basement comedy club in Greenwich Village, Comedy Cellar features mainstream material and a good list of regulars (Colin Quinn, *Saturday Night Live's* Darrell Hammond, and Wanda Sykes), plus an occasional high-profile drop-in like Dave Chappelle. Its success continues: Comedy Cellar now boasts another location around the corner on W 3rd St. (📞212-254-3480; www.comedycellar.com; 117 MacDougal St, btwn W 3rd St & Minetta Lane; cover $12-24; 🚇A/C/E, B/D/F/M to W 4th St-Washington Sq)

Angelika Film Center

CINEMA

52 ⭐ Map p90, G5

Angelika specializes in foreign and independent films and has some quirky charms (the rumble of the subway, long lines and occasionally bad sound). But its roomy cafe is a great place to meet and the beauty of its Stanford White–designed, beaux-arts building is undeniable. (📞212-995-2570; www.angelikafilmcenter.com; 18 W Houston St, at Mercer St; tickets $15; ♿; 🚇B/D/F/M to Broadway-Lafayette St)

Shopping

Strand Book Store

BOOKS

53 🔒 Map p90, G3

Book fiends (or even those who have casually skimmed one or two) shouldn't miss New York's most loved and famous bookstore. In operation since 1927, the Strand sells new, used and rare titles, spreading an incredible 18 miles of books (more than 2.5 million of them) among three labyrinthine floors. (📞212-473-1452; www.strandbooks.com; 828 Broadway, at 12th St; ⏰9:30am-10:30pm Mon-Sat, from 11am Sun; 🚇L, N/Q/R, 4/5/6 to 14th St-Union Sq)

Flat 128

ACCESSORIES

54 🔒 Map p90, E4

In a small, handsomely curated shop on tree-lined Christopher St, Flat 128 brings a dose of British craftiness to the Big Apple. You'll find rare, unusual jewelry (such as Alice Menter's metallic cuffs), vintage print cushion covers, vibrantly hued scarves by Age of Reason and a few curios (mini model of Battersea power station anyone?). (📞646-707-0673; http://flat128.com; 15 Christopher St, btwn Waverly Pl & Greenwich Ave; ⏰11am-7pm Mon-Sat, noon-6pm Sun; 🚇1 to Christopher St-Sheridan Sq)

Story

GIFTS

55 🔒 Map p90, C2

This high concept shop near the High Line functions like a gallery, showcasing new themes and products

Washington Square Park (p92)

every month or two. The 2000-sq-ft space covers all the bases from crafty jewelry and eye-catching accessories to lovely stationery, imagination-inspiring toys for kids, thick coffee-table books, environmentally friendly soaps and whimsical souvenirs. (http://thisisstory.com; 144 Tenth Ave, btwn 18th & 19th Sts; ⏰11am-8pm Mon-Fri, from 10am Sat & Sun; Ⓢ C/E to 23rd St; 1 to 18th St)

Personnel of New York
FASHION, ACCESSORIES

56 🔒 Map p90, E4

This small, delightful indie shop sells women's designer clothing that sport unique labels from the East and West Coasts, and beyond. Look

for easy-to-wear Sunja Link dresses, soft pullover sweaters by Ali Golden, statement-making jewelry by Marisa Mason, comfy canvas sneakers by Shoes Like Pottery, and couture pieces by Rodebjer. (📞212-924-0604; http://personnelofnewyork.com; 9 Greenwich Ave, btwn Christopher & W 10th Sts; ⏰11am-8pm Mon-Sat, noon-7pm Sun; Ⓢ A/C/E, B/D/F/M to W 4th St; 1 to Christopher St-Sheridan Sq)

Three Lives & Company
BOOKS

57 🔒 Map p90, E4

Your neighborhood bookstore extraordinaire, Three Lives & Company is a wondrous spot that's tended by a coterie of exceptionally well-read individuals. A trip here is not just a pleasure, it's an adventure into the magical world of words. (☎212-741-2069; www.threelives.com; 154 W 10th St, btwn Seventh Ave & Waverly Pl; ⏱noon-7pm Sun-Tue, 11am-8:30pm Wed-Sat; S1 to Christopher St-Sheridan Sq; A/C/E, B/D/F/M to W 4th St; 1/2/3 to 14th St)

Flight 001
ACCESSORIES

58 🔒 Map p90, E3

Travel is fun, sure – but getting travel gear is even more fun. Check out Flight 001's range of luggage and smaller bags by brands ranging from Bree to Rimowa, kitschy 'shemergency' kits (breath freshener, lip balm, stain remover etc), pin-up-girl flasks, brightly colored passport holders and leather luggage tags, travel guidebooks, toiletry cases and a range of mini toothpastes, eye masks, pillboxes and the like. (☎212-989-0001; www.flight001.com; 96 Greenwich Ave; ⏱11am-8pm Mon-Sat, noon-6pm Sun; SA/C/E to 14th St; L to 8th Ave)

McNulty's Tea & Coffee Co, Inc
FOOD & DRINK

59 🔒 Map p90, E4

Just down from a few sex shops, sweet McNulty's, with worn wooden floorboards, fragrant sacks of coffee beans and large glass jars of tea, flaunts a different era of Greenwich Village. It's been selling gourmet teas and coffees here since 1895. (☎212-242-5351; http://mcnultys.com; 109 Christopher St; ⏱10am-9pm Mon-Sat, 1-7pm Sun; S1 to Christopher St-Sheridan Sq)

Marc by Marc Jacobs
FASHION

60 🔒 Map p90, D4

With five small shops sprinkled around the West Village, Marc Jacobs has established a real presence in this well-heeled neighborhood. Large front windows allow easy peeking – assuming there's not a sale, during which you'll only see hordes of fawning shoppers. (☎212-924-0026; www.marcjacobs.com; 403 Bleecker St; ⏱11am-7pm Mon-Sat, noon-6pm Sun; SA/C/E to 14th St; L to 8th Ave)

Murray's Cheese
FOOD & DRINK

61 🔒 Map p90, E5

Founded in 1914, this is one of New York's best cheese shops. Owner Rob Kaufelt is known for his talent for sniffing out devastatingly delicious varieties from around the world. You'll find (and be able to taste) all manner of *fromage,* be it stinky, sweet or nutty, from European nations and from small farms in Vermont and upstate New York. (☎212-243-3289; www.murrayscheese.com; 254 Bleecker St, btwn Morton & Leroy Sts; ⏱8am-9pm Mon-Sat, 9am-7pm Sun; S1 to Christopher St-Sheridan Sq; A/C/E, B/D/F/V to W 4th St)

192 Books
BOOKS

62 🔒 Map p90, C2

Located right in the gallery district is this small indie bookstore, with sections on fiction, history, travel, art and criticism. Its rotating art exhibits are a special treat, during which the owners

Chelsea Market (p92)

organize special displays of books that relate thematically to the featured show or artist. Weekly book readings feature acclaimed (often NY-based) authors. (✆212-255-4022; www.192books.com; 192 Tenth Ave, btwn 21st & 22nd Sts; ⏱11am-7pm; Ⓢ C/E to 23rd St)

Housing Works Thrift Shop
VINTAGE

63 🅰 Map p90, E2

This shop, with its swank window displays, looks more boutique than thrift, but its selections of clothes, accessories, furniture, books and records are great value. All proceeds benefit the charity serving the city's HIV-positive and AIDS homeless communities.

There are 11 other branches around town. (✆718-838-5050; 143 W 17th St, btwn Sixth & Seventh Aves; ⏱10am-7pm Mon-Fri, to 6pm Sat, noon-6pm Sun; Ⓢ 1 to 18th St)

CO Bigelow Chemists
BEAUTY

64 🅰 Map p90, F4

The 'oldest apothecary in America' is now a slightly upscale fantasyland for the beauty-product obsessed, though there's still an actual pharmacy for prescriptions and standard drugstore items for sale on the premises, too. (✆212-533-2700; 414 Sixth Ave, btwn 8th & 9th Sts; ⏱7:30am-9pm Mon-Fri, 8:30am-7pm Sat, 8:30am-5:30pm Sun; Ⓢ 1 to Christopher St-Sheridan Sq; A/C/E, B/D/F/M to W 4th St-Washington Sq)

Explore

Union Square, Flatiron District & Gramercy

Wedged between the indie cool of the East Village and the corporate canyons of Midtown, this trio of neighborhoods is home to the eclectic crowds of Union Square, the triangular Flatiron Building and the verdant respite of Madison Square Park. It's also home to the private oasis of Gramercy Park.

The Sights in a Day

☀ Begin the day with coffee and croissants at **71 Irving Place** (p123). Stroll past **Gramercy Park** (p116), then walk to Union Square for New York's most vibrant people-watching playground: bankers, buskers, joggers, dog walkers and delivery bikers mix at this leafy crossroads. Time your visit with the **Union Square Green-market** (p118) for fresh produce and snacks plucked from upstate farms.

☀ Walk up scenic Broadway, stopping into **ABC Carpet & Home** (p124) to peruse gorgeously curated home decor from around the world. Continue the global roam at travel bookshop **Idlewild** (p124) – perfect for plotting your next big adventure. Take a break for lunch nearby at **Boqueria Flatiron** (p119).

☾ In the late afternoon, walk up to **Madison Square Park** (p116), a leafy oasis away from the urban bustle. Cross Broadway for mouthwatering gourmet goodies in **Eataly** (p117). You can nosh your way around the ground floor, or take the elevator up to **Birreria** (p122) for craft brews, and hearty fish and meat dishes. When you've had your fill, toast the night at **Raines Law Room** (p121) or beneath the tin ceilings of **Old Town Bar & Restaurant** (p121).

♥ Best of New York City

Eating
Eataly (p117)

Craft (p119)

Gramercy Tavern (p120)

Drinking
Raines Law Room (p121)

Old Town Bar & Restaurant (p121)

Flatiron Lounge (p122)

Pete's Tavern (p122)

Shopping
ABC Carpet & Home (p124)

Idlewild Books (p124)

DSW (p125)

Getting There

S Subway A slew of subway lines converge below Union Square, shuttling passengers up Manhattan's East Side on the 4/5/6 lines, straight across to Williamsburg on the L, or up and over to Queens on the N/Q/R lines.

🚌 Bus The M14A and M14D provide crosstown services along 14th St, while the M23 runs crosstown along 23rd St.

A W 34th St **B** E 34th St **C** **D**

34th St-
Herald Sq
Empire State
Building

W 33rd St
33rd St

W 32nd St (Korea Way)

KOREATOWN

W 31st St

E 34th St

E 33rd St

E 32nd St

E 31st St

0   400 m
0   0.2 miles

For reviews see
⊙	Sights	p115
❸	Eating	p116
⊕	Drinking	p121
★	Entertainment	p124
⛉	Shopping	p124

1

W 30th St

W 29th St
28th St ⑤

W 28th St

W 27th St
⊕ 21
W 26th St

E 30th St

E 29th St

28th St ⑤

**LITTLE
INDIA**

E 28th St

12 ❸
E 27th St

E 26th St

2

W 25th St

Madison
Square
Park
3 ⊙

E 25th St

W 24th St
6 ❸
9 ❸
8 ❸

W 23rd St
⑤
23rd St ⑤
23rd St

25 ★

E 24th St

E 23rd St

⊙ Flatiron
4 Building

**FLATIRON
DISTRICT**

W 21st St
22 ⊕
Theodore
Roosevelt ⊙ ❸ 15
W 20th St Birthplace 2 ❸ 14
27 ❸
⊕ 18

E 22nd St

GRAMERCY

16 ❸

5 Gramercy
⊙ Park
E 21st St

E 20th St

**GRAMERCY
PARK**

23 ⊕

E 19th St

3

⑤
23rd St

**UNION
SQUARE**

W 19th St
13 ❸ ⊕ 19
28 ⛉
W 18th St
31 ⛉

W 17th St
⊕ 17
W 16th St

W 15th St

**6th Ave-
14th St** ⑤

W 14th St

10 ❸⛉
30

❸ 11

⊕ 20

E 18th St

E 17th St

7 ❸
E 16th St

Union
Square
⊙ 1

26 ❸

14th St- ⑤
Union Sq
29 ⛉⛉
32

E 15th St

⊕ 24

E 14th St
1st Ave

Stuyvesant
Square

E 16th St

E 15th St

14th St-
Union Sq ⑤

W 13th St
E 13th St

4

W 12th St
E 12th St

W 11th St
E 11th St

E 13th St

E 12th St

E 11th St

**EAST
VILLAGE**

5

Sixth Ave (Avenue of the Americas)

Broadway

Fifth Ave

Madison Ave

Park Ave S

Lexington Ave

Third Ave

Second Ave

University Pl

Fourth Ave

Broadway

Irving Pl

Mt Carmel Pl

Union Square Greenmarket (p118)

Sights

Union Square SQUARE

1 ⊙ Map p114, B4

Union Square is like the Noah's Ark of New York, rescuing at least two of every kind from the curling seas of concrete. In fact, one would be hard-pressed to find a more eclectic cross-section of locals gathered in one public place: suited businessfolk gulping fresh air during their lunch breaks, dreadlocked loiterers tapping beats on their tabla, skateboarders flipping tricks on the southeastern stairs, rowdy college kids guzzling student-priced eats, and throngs of protesting masses chanting fervently for various causes. (www.unionsquarenyc .org; 17th St, btwn Broadway & Park Ave S; S 4/5/6, N/Q/R, L to 14th St-Union Sq)

Theodore Roosevelt Birthplace HISTORIC SITE

2 ⊙ Map p114, B4

Scheduled to reopen in 2016 after restoration work, this National Historic Site is a bit of a cheat, since the physical house where the 26th president was actually born was demolished in his own lifetime. But this building is a worthy reconstruction by his relatives, who joined it with another family residence next door. (☎ 212-260-1616; www .nps.gov/thrb; 28 E 20th St, btwn Broadway & Park Ave S; admission free; ⊙ 40min guided tours 10am, 11am, 1pm, 2pm, 3pm & 4pm Tue-Sat; Ⓢ N/R, 6 to 23rd St)

Madison Square Park PARK

3 Ⓞ Map p114, B3

This park defined the northern reaches of Manhattan until the island's population exploded after the Civil War. These days it's a much-welcome oasis from Manhattan's relentless pace, with a popular children's playground, dog-run area and Shake Shack burger joint. It's also one of the city's most cultured parks, with specially commissioned art installations and (in the warmer months) activities ranging from literary discussions to live music gigs. See the website for more information. (☏ 212-520-7600; www.madisonsquarepark.org; 23rd to 26th Sts, btwn Fifth & Madison Aves; ◷ 6am-midnight; ♿; Ⓢ N/R, F/M, 6 to 23rd St)

Flatiron Building HISTORIC BUILDING

4 Ⓞ Map p114, B3

Designed by Daniel Burnham and built in 1920, the 20-story Flatiron Building has a uniquely narrow triangular footprint that resembles the prow of a massive ship. It also features a traditional beaux art limestone and terra-cotta facade, built over a steel frame, that gets more complex and beautiful the longer you stare at it. Best viewed from the traffic island north of 23rd St between Broadway and Fifth Ave, this unique structure dominated the plaza back in the dawning skyscraper era of the early

1900s. (Broadway, cnr Fifth Ave & 23rd St; Ⓢ N/R, F/M, 6 to 23rd St)

Gramercy Park PARK

5 Ⓞ Map p114, C3

Romantic Gramercy Park was created by Samuel Ruggles in 1831 after he drained the area's swamp and laid out streets in an English style. You can't enter the private park, but peer through the gate and imagine tough guy James Cagney enjoying it – the Hollywood actor once resided at 34 Gramercy Park E. At 15 Gramercy Park S stands the **National Arts Club** (☏ 212-475-3424; www.nationalartsclub.org; 15 Gramercy Park S; drawing classes $15-25; Ⓢ N/R, 6 to 23rd St), whose members include Martin Scorsese, Uma Thurman and Ethan Hawke. (E 20th St, btwn Park & Third Aves; Ⓢ N/R, 6 to 23rd St)

Eating

Tacombi Café
El Presidente MEXICAN $

6 Ⓧ Map p114, A3

Channeling the cafes of Mexico City, pink-and-green Tacombi covers numerous bases, from juice and liquor bar to taco joint. Score a table, order a margarita and hop your way around a menu of Mexican street-food deliciousness. Top choices include *esquites* (grilled corn with *cotija* cheese and chipotle mayonnaise, served in a paper cup) and succulent *carnitas michoacan* (beer-marinated pork)

Understand
The Immortal Flatiron

The construction of the Flatiron Building (originally known as the Fuller Building) coincided with the proliferation of mass-produced picture postcards – the partnership was kismet. Even before its completion, there were images of the soon-to-be tallest tower circulating the globe, creating much wonder and excitement.

Publisher Frank Munsey was one of the building's first tenants. From his 18th-floor offices, he published *Munsey's Magazine,* which featured the work of short-story writer William Sydney Porter, whose pen name was 'O Henry'. His musings, the paintings of John Sloan and the photographs of Alfred Stieglitz best immortalized the Flatiron back in the day – along with a famous comment by actress Katharine Hepburn, who said in an interview that she'd like to be admired as much as the grand old building.

The ground floor of the building's 'prow' is now a glassed-in art space showcasing the work of guest artists. In 2013, the space featured a life-sized 3D-cutout replica of Edward Hopper's 1942 painting *Nighthawks*, its angular diner remarkably similar to the Flatiron's distinctive shape.

tacos. (☑212-242-3491; http://tacombi
.com; 30 W 24th St, btwn Fifth & Sixth Aves;
tacos $3.50-5.50, quesadillas $8-9; ⊙11am-
midnight Mon-Sat, to 10:30pm Sun; Ⓢ F/M,
N/R to 23rd St)

Republic   ASIAN $

7 ✖ Map p114, B4

Eat-and-go Republic feeds the masses with fresh 'n' tasty Asian staples. Slurp away on warming broth noodles, chomp on juicy pad Thai or keep it light with a green papaya and mango salad. Located right on Union Square, it's a handy spot for a cheap, uncomplicated, walk-in bite. (☑212-627-7172; www.thinknoodles.com; 37 Union Sq W; mains $13-16; ⊙11:30am-10:30pm; Ⓢ 4/5/6, N/Q/R, L to 14th St-Union Sq)

Shake Shack   BURGERS $

8 ✖ Map p114, B3

The flagship of chef Danny Meyer's gourmet burger chainlet, Shake Shack whips up hyper-fresh burgers, hand-cut fries and a rotating line-up of frozen custards. Veg-heads can dip into the crisp portobello burger. Lines are long, but worth it. (☑646-747-2606; www
.shakeshack.com; Madison Square Park, cnr 23rd St & Madison Ave; burgers $4.20-9.50; ⊙11am-11pm; Ⓢ N/R, F/M, 6 to 23rd St)

Eataly   ITALIAN $$

9 ✖ Map p114, A3

Mario Batali's sleek, sprawling temple to Italian gastronomy is a veritable wonderland. Feast on everything from vibrant *crudo* (raw fish) and *fritto misto* (tempura-style vegetables) to steamy pasta and pizza at the emporium's string of sit-down eateries. Alternatively, guzzle espresso at the bar and scour the countless counters and shelves for a DIY picnic hamper *nonna* would approve of. (www.eataly .com; 200 Fifth Ave, at 23rd St; ⏰8am-11pm; 🍴; S N/R, F/M, 6 to 23rd St)

Javelina
TEX-MEX $$

10 Map p114, C4

Guarded by a gang of cacti, easy, affable Javelina gives Tex-Mex some much-needed culinary cred. It's especially great for brunch, when prickly-

pear mimosas help wash down your peaches and cream French toast or the standout Red Headed Stranger breakfast taco – a hangover-busting combo of scrambled eggs, brisket, black beans avocado, cheese and piquant ranchero sauce. (☎212-539-0202; http://javelina texmex.com; 119 E 18th St, btwn Park Ave S & Irving Pl; tacos $12-16, dinner mains $19-23; ⏰11:30am-3:30pm & 5:30-11pm Mon-Thu, to 11:30pm Fri & Sat, to 10pm Sun; 🛜; S 4/5/6, N/Q/R, L to 14th St-Union Sq)

Bar Jamón
TAPAS $$

11 Map p114, C4

Around the corner from its big brother, Casa Mono, lies Mario Batali's fun, communal Bar Jamón. Sniff, swill and sip your way across Spain's wine terroirs while grazing on superb, Catalan-inspired tapas like pickled sardines, duck liver with apricots and *fuet catalán* (cured pork sausage) with lentils. (☎212-253-2773; http://casamononyc.com; 125 E 17th St, btwn Irving Pl & Third Ave; tapas $5-15; ⏰5pm-2am Mon-Fri, noon-2am Sat & Sun; S 4/5/6, N/Q/R, L to 14th St-Union Sq)

Dhaba
INDIAN $$

12 Map p114, C2

Murray Hill (aka Curry Hill) has no shortage of subcontinental bites, but funky Dhaba packs one serious flavor punch. Mouthwatering standouts include the crunchy, tangy *lasoni gobi* (fried cauliflower with tomato and spices) and the insanely flavorful *murgh bharta* (minced chicken cooked with smoked eggplant). (☎212-679-1284; www.dhabanyc.com; 108 Lexington

Metronome (p121) by Kristin Jones and Andrew Ginzel, Union Square

Ave, btwn 27th & 28th Sts; mains $11-24; ☺noon-midnight Mon-Thu, noon-1am Fri & Sat, 4-10pm Sun; 🖋; **S**6 to 28th St)

Boqueria Flatiron   TAPAS $$

13 🍽 Map p114, A4

A holy union between Spanish-style tapas and market-fresh fare, Boqueria woos the after-work crowd with a brilliant line up of small plates and larger *raciones*. Lick lips and fingers over the likes of garlicky shrimp with brandy and guindilla pepper, or bacon-wrapped dates stuffed with almonds and Valdeón blue cheese. A smooth selection of Spanish wines tops it all off. *¡Buen provecho!* (☎212-255-4160; www.boquerianyc.com; 53 W 19th St, btwn Fifth &

Sixth Aves; tapas $6-18; ☺noon-10:30pm Sun-Thu, to 11:30pm Fri & Sat; 🛜; **S**1 to 18th St, F/M, N/R to 23rd St)

Craft   NEW AMERICAN $$$

14 🍽 Map p114, B4

Humming, high-end Craft flies the flag for small, family-owned farms and food producers, their bounty transformed into pure, polished dishes. Whether nibbling on flawlessly charred braised octopus, pillowy scallops, or pumpkin mezzaluna pasta with sage, brown butter and Parmesan, expect every ingredient to sing with flavor. Book ahead Wednesday to Saturday or head in by 6pm or after 9:30pm. (☎212-780-0880; www.craftrestaurantsinc.com/

craft-new-york; 43 E 19th St, btwn Broadway & Park Ave S; lunch $15-35, dinner mains $31-45; ⏱5:30-10pm Sun-Thu, to 11pm Fri & Sat; 🛜; Ⓢ4/5/6, N/Q/R, L to 14th St-Union Sq)

Gramercy Tavern

MODERN AMERICAN $$$

15 ✕ Map p114, B4

Seasonal, local ingredients drive this perennial favorite, a vibrant, country-chic institution aglow with copper sconces, murals and dramatic floral arrangements. Choose from two spaces: the walk-in-only tavern and its à la carte menu, or the swankier dining room and its fancier prix-fixe and degustation feasts. Tavern highlights include a show-stopping duck meatloaf with mushrooms, chestnuts and brussels sprouts.

🅞 Local Life
Mad Sq Eats

Each spring and fall, foodies flock to tiny General Worth Sq – wedged between Fifth Ave and Broadway, opposite Madison Square Park – for **Mad Sq Eats** (Map p114, A3; www.madisonsquarepark.org/tag/mad-sq-eats; General Worth Sq; ⏱spring & fall; Ⓢ N/R, F/M, 6 to 23rd St), a month-long culinary pop-up market. Its 30 or so vendors include some of the city's hottest eateries, cooking up anything from proper pizza to brisket tacos using top local produce.

Desserts are suitably decadent and the wine list one of the city's best. (📞212-477-0777; www.gramercytavern.com; 42 E 20th St, btwn Broadway & Park Ave S; tavern mains $19-24, dining room 3-course menu $98, tasting menus $105-120; ⏱tavern noon-11pm Sun-Thu, to midnight Fri & Sat; dining room noon-2pm & 5:30-10pm Mon-Thu, to 11pm Fri, noon-1:30pm & 5:30-11pm Sat, 5:30-10pm Sun; 🛜🖊; Ⓢ N/R, 6 to 23rd St)

Maialino

ITALIAN $$$

16 ✕ Map p114, C3

Fans reserve tables up to four weeks in advance at this Danny Meyer classic, but the best seats in the house are at the walk-in bar, manned by sociable, knowledgeable staffers. Wherever you're plonked, take your taste buds on a Roman holiday, with Maialino's lip-smacking, rustic Italian fare created using produce from the nearby Union Square Greenmarket. (📞212-777-2410; www.maialinonyc.com; Gramercy Park Hotel, 2 Lexington Ave, at 21st St; mains lunch $21-34, dinner $27-42; ⏱7:30am-10:30pm Mon-Thu, to 11pm Fri, 10am-11pm Sat, 10am-10:30pm Sun; Ⓢ6, N/R to 23rd St)

ABC Kitchen

MODERN AMERICAN $$$

Looking part gallery, part rustic farmhouse, sustainable ABC Kitchen (see 27 🅐 Map p114, B4) is the culinary avatar of the chichi home goods department store ABC Carpet & Home (p124). Organic gets haute in dishes like tuna sashimi with ginger and mint, or crispy pork confit with smoked bacon marmalade and braised turnips. For a

Understand
Metronome

A walk around Union Square reveals almost a dozen notable pieces of art, such as Rob Pruitt's 10ft homage to Andy Warhol and the imposing equestrian statue of George Washington. But on the south side of the square sits a massive art installation that either earns confused stares or simply gets overlooked by passersby. A symbolic representation of the passage of time, *Metronome* has two parts: a digital clock with a puzzling display of numbers and a wand-like apparatus with smoke puffing out of concentric rings. We'll let you ponder the latter while we give you the skinny on what exactly the winking orange digits denote. The 14 numbers must be split into two groups of seven. The seven from the left tell the current time (hour, minute, second, tenth-of-a-second) and the seven from the right are meant to be read in reverse order: they represent the remaining amount of time in the day.

more casual bite, try the scrumptious whole-wheat pizzas. (☏212-475-5829; www.abckitchennyc.com; 35 E 18th St, at Broadway; pizzas $17-20, dinner mains $24-40; ☉noon-3pm & 5:30-10:30pm Mon-Wed, to 11pm Thu, to 11:30pm Fri, 11am-3pm & 5:30-11:30pm Sat, 11am-3pm & 5:30-10pm Sun; 🖉; ⑤4/5/6, N/Q/R, L to 14th St-Union Sq)

Drinking

Raines Law Room   COCKTAIL BAR

17 🍸 Map p114, A4

A sea of velvet drapes and overstuffed leather lounge chairs, the perfect amount of exposed brick, and expertly crafted cocktails using meticulously aged spirits – these guys are about as serious as a mortgage payment when it comes to amplified atmosphere. Reservations (recommended) are only possible Sunday to Tuesday. Whatever the night, style up for a taste of a far more sumptuous era. (www.raineslawroom.com; 48 W 17th St, btwn Fifth & Sixth Aves; ☉5pm-2am Mon-Wed, to 3am Thu-Sat, 7pm-1am Sun; ⑤F/M to 14th St, L to 6th Ave, 1 to 18th St)

Old Town Bar & Restaurant   BAR

18 🍸 Map p114, B4

It still looks like 1892 in here, with the original tile floors and tin ceilings – the Old Town is an 'old world' drinking-man's classic (and woman's: Madonna lit up at the bar here, when lighting up was still legal, in her 'Bad Girl' video). There are cocktails around, but most come for beers and a burger (from $12.50). (☏212-529-6732; www.oldtownbar.com; 45 E 18th St, btwn Broadway & Park Ave S; ☉11:30am-1am Mon-Fri, noon-2am Sat, 1pm-midnight Sun; ⑤4/5/6, N/Q/R, L to 14th St-Union Sq)

Flatiron Lounge

COCKTAIL BAR

19 Map p114, A4

Head through a dramatic archway and into a dark, swinging, deco-inspired fantasy of lipstick-red booths, racy jazz tunes and sassy grown-ups downing seasonal drinks. The Beijing Mule (Jasmine vodka, lime juice, ginger syrup and pomegranate molasses) is scrumptious, while the genial Flight of the Day (a trio of mini-sized cocktails) is head-spinning enlightenment. Happy hour cocktails go for $10 a pop (4pm to 6pm weekdays). (☏212-727-7741; www.flatironlounge.com; 37 W 19th St, btwn Fifth & Sixth Aves; ⏰4pm-2am Mon-Wed, to 3am Thu, to 4am Fri, 5pm-4am Sat, 5pm-2am Sun; 🛜; 🚇F/M, N/R, 6 to 6rd St)

Pete's Tavern

BAR

20 Map p114, C4

Adorned with its original 19th-century mirrors, pressed-tin ceiling and rosewood bar, this dark, atmospheric watering hole has all the earmarks of a New York classic. You can get a respectable prime-rib burger here and choose from 17 draft beers. The bar draws in everyone from post-theater couples and Irish expats to no-nonsense NYU students and the odd celebrity (see photos by the restrooms). (☏212-473-7676; www.petestavern.com; 129 E 18th St, at Irving Pl; ⏰11am-2am; 🚇4/5/6, N/Q/R, L to 14th St-Union Sq)

Birreria

BEER HALL

The crown jewel of Italian food emporium Eataly (p117) is its rooftop beer garden (see **9** Map p114, A3). A beer menu of encyclopedic proportions offers drinkers some of the best suds on the planet. If you're hungry, the signature beer-braised pork shoulder is your frosty one's soul mate. (☏212-937-8910; www.eataly.com; 200 Fifth Ave, at 23rd St; mains $17-37; ⏰11:30am-11pm Sun-Thu, to midnight Fri & Sat; 🚇N/R, F/M, 6 to 23rd St)

Flatiron Room

COCKTAIL BAR

21 Map p114, A2

Vintage wallpaper, a glittering chandelier and hand-painted coffer ceilings make for a suitably elegant scene at this grown-up drinking den, its artfully lit cabinets graced with rare whiskeys. Fine cocktails pair nicely with high-end sharing plates, from citrus-marinated olive tapenade to flatbread with guanciale and fig. Most nights also feature live music, including bluegrass and jazz. Reservations are highly recommended. (☏212-725-3860; www.theflatironroom.com; 37 W 26th St, btwn Sixth Ave & Broadway; ⏰4pm-2am Mon-Fri, 5pm-2am Sat, 5pm-midnight Sun; 🚇N/R to 28th St; F/M to 23rd St)

Toby's Estate

CAFE, COFFEE

22 Map p114, A3

Sydney-born, Williamsburg-roasting Toby's Estate is part of Manhattan's evolving artisanal coffee culture. Loaded with a custom-made Strada espresso machine, you'll find it tucked away in the Club Monaco store. Join coffee geeks for thick, rich brews, among them a geo-specific Flatiron Espresso Blend. Nibbles include pas-

Outdoor dining, Madison Square Park (p116)

tries and sandwiches from local baker-
ies. (☎646-559-0161; www.tobysestate.com;
160 Fifth Ave, btwn 20th & 21st Sts; ⏰7am-
9pm Mon-Fri, 8:30am-9pm Sat, 8:30am-8pm
Sun; ⓢN/R, F/M, 6 to 23rd St)

71 Irving Place   CAFE, COFFEE

23 🎯 Map p114, C4

From keyboard-tapping scribes to
gossiping friends and academics,
this bustling cafe is never short of a
crowd. Hand-picked beans are lovingly roasted on a farm in the Hudson
Valley (about 90 miles from NYC), and
served alongside tasty edibles such as
Balthazar-baked croissants, granola,
egg dishes, bagels and pressed sandwiches. (Irving Farm Coffee Company;

☎212-995-5252; www.irvingfarm.com; 71
Irving Pl, btwn 18th & 19th Sts; ⏰7am-10pm
Mon-Fri, 8am-10pm Sat & Sun; ⓢ4/5/6,
N/Q/R, L to 14th St-Union Sq)

Beauty Bar   BAR

24 🎯 Map p114, D5

A kitschy favorite since the mid-'90s,
this homage to old-fashioned beauty
parlors pulls in a cool local crowd
with its retro soundtrack, nostalgic
vibe and $10 manicures (with a free
Blue Rinse margarita thrown in) from
6pm to 11pm weekdays, and 3pm to
11pm at weekends. Nightly events
range from comedy to burlesque.
(☎212-539-1389; www.thebeautybar.com/
home-new-york; 231 E 14th St, btwn Second

& Third Aves; ⏱5pm-4am Mon-Fri, 2pm-4am Sat & Sun; Ⓢ L to 3rd Ave)

Entertainment

Peoples Improv Theater

COMEDY

25 ⭐ Map p114, C3

Aglow in red neon, this bustling comedy club serves up top-notch laughs at dirt-cheap prices. The string of nightly acts ranges from stand-up to sketch and musical comedy, playing in either the main stage theater or the basement lounge. PIT also runs courses, including three-hour, drop-in improv workshops at its Midtown venue, **Simple Studios** (☎212-273-9696; http://simplestudiosnyc.com; 134 W 29th St, btwn Sixth & Seventh Aves, Midtown West; Ⓢ1, N/R to 28th St). See the website for all classes and schedules. (PIT; ☎212-563-7488; www.thepit-nyc.com; 123 E 24th St, btwn Lexington & Park Aves; 🛜; Ⓢ6, N/R, F/M to 23rd St)

Irving Plaza

LIVE MUSIC

26 ⭐ Map p114, C4

Rocking since 1978, Irving Plaza has seen them all: the Ramones, Bob Dylan, U2, Pearl Jam, you name it. These days it's a great in-between stage for quirkier rock and pop acts – from indie chicks Sleater-Kinney to hard rockers Disturbed. There's a cozy floor around the stage, and good views from the mezzanine. (☎212-777-6817; www.irving plaza.com; 17 Irving Pl, at 15th St; Ⓢ4/5/6, N/Q/R, L to 14th St-Union Sq)

Shopping

ABC Carpet & Home

HOMEWARES

27 🔒 Map p114, B4

A mecca for home designers and decorators brainstorming ideas, this beautifully curated, seven-level temple to good taste heaves with all sorts of furnishings, small and large. Shop for easy-to-pack knickknacks, textiles and jewelry, as well as statement furniture, designer lighting, ceramics and antique carpets. Come Christmas season the shop is a joy to behold. (☎212-473-3000; www.abchome.com; 888 Broadway, at 19th St; ⏱10am-7pm Mon-Wed, Fri & Sat, to 8pm Thu, 11am-6:30pm Sun; Ⓢ4/5/6, N/Q/R, L to 14th St-Union Sq)

Idlewild Books

BOOKS

28 🔒 Map p114, A4

Named after JFK Airport's original moniker, this indie travel bookshop gets feet seriously itchy. Books are divided by region, and cover guidebooks as well as fiction, travelogues, history, cookbooks and other stimulating fare for delving into different corners of the world. The store also runs popular language classes in French, Italian, Spanish and German; see the website for details. (☎212-414-8888; www.idlewild books.com; 12 W 19th St, btwn Fifth & Sixth Aves; ⏱noon-7:30pm Mon-Thu, to 6pm Fri & Sat, to 5pm Sun; Ⓢ4/5/6, N/Q/R, L to 14th St-Union Sq)

DSW
SHOES

29 🛍 Map p114, B5

If your idea of paradise involves a great selection of cut-price kicks, make a beeline for this sprawling, unisex chain. Shoes range from formal to athletic, with no shortage of popular and higher-end labels. (📞212-674-2146; www. dsw.com; 4 Union Sq S, btwn University Pl & Broadway; ⏰10am-9:30pm Mon-Sat, to 8pm Sun; 🚇4/5/6, N/Q/R, L to 14th St-Union Sq)

Bedford Cheese Shop
FOOD

30 🛍 Map p114, C4

Whether you're after local, raw cow's-milk cheese washed in absinthe or garlic-infused goat's-milk cheese from Australia, chances are you'll find it among the 200-strong selection at this outpost of Brooklyn's most celebrated cheese vendor. Pair the cheesy goodness with artisanal charcuterie, deli treats, ready-to-eat sandwiches ($9 to $11), as well as a proud array of Made-in-Brooklyn edibles. (📞718-599-7588; www.bedfordcheeseshop.com; 67 Irving Pl, btwn 18th & 19th Sts; ⏰8am-9pm Mon-Sat, to 8pm Sun; 🚇4/5/6, N/Q/R, L to 14th St-Union Sq)

Books of Wonder
BOOKS

31 🛍 Map p114, A4

Devoted to children's and young-adult titles, this wonderful bookstore is a great place to take young ones on a rainy day, especially when a kids' author is giving a reading or a storyteller is on hand. There's an impressive range of NYC-themed picture books, as well as a section dedicated to rare and vintage children's books and limited-edition children's book artwork. (📞212-989-3270; www.booksofwonder.com; 18 W 18th St, btwn Fifth & Sixth Aves; ⏰10am-7pm Mon-Sat, 11am-6pm Sun; 👶; 🚇F/M to 14th St; L to 6th Ave)

Whole Foods
FOOD & DRINK

32 🛍 Map p114, B5

One of several locations of the popular, healthy food emporium, Whole Foods is an excellent place to fill the picnic hamper. Drool over endless rows of gorgeous produce, both organic and nonorganic, plus a butcher, a bakery, ready-to-eat dishes, a health and beauty section, and aisles packed with natural packaged goods. (📞212-673-5388; www.wholefoodsmarket.com; 4 Union Sq S, btwn University Place & Broadway; ⏰7am-11pm; 📶; 🚇4/5/6, N/Q/R, L to 14th St-Union Sq)

Explore

Midtown

Midtown is the NYC of postcards: Times Square and Broadway theaters, Grand Central Terminal, the Empire State and Chrysler Buildings, Fifth Ave and soaring canyons awash with yellow taxis and crowds. Cultural knockouts include MoMA, the New York Public Library and the Morgan Library & Museum, with hedonistic thrills beckoning on the food-packed, gay-friendly streets of hip Hell's Kitchen.

The Sights in a Day

Start the morning with art-gazing inside the hallowed **Museum of Modern Art** (p132). Grab a pick-me-up in the cafe and check out the sculpture garden before leaving for a stroll along Fifth Ave. Go window-shopping at **Bloomingdale's** (p153), **Barneys** (p152) and **Bergdorf Goodman** (p153). Check out **Rockefeller Center** (p136) and **St Patrick's Cathedral** (p138).

Head down to **Grand Central Terminal** (pictured left; p136) for glorious architecture. Pick up food at the sprawling market there, then take it over to **Bryant Park** (p146) for a picnic on the grass. After lunch, peak inside the grandiose **New York Public Library** (p137), and walk over to the **Empire State Building** (p130) – admire the panorama from the 86th floor.

After sundown, head to **Times Square** (p128) and take in the electrifying energy that resonates from this corner of Manhattan. See a blockbuster Broadway show, such as **Hamilton** (p148) or **Kinky Boots** (p148), followed by a dinner of Mediterranean extravagance at **Taboon** (p142). End the night in a classy cocktail den such as **Lantern's Keep** (p145) or at dive bar **Jimmy's Corner** (p147).

👁 Top Sights

Times Square (p128)

Empire State Building (p130)

Museum of Modern Art (p132)

💜 Best of New York City

Eating

Artisanal (p142)

Le Bernardin (p142)

ViceVersa (p140)

Totto Ramen (p140)

Drinking

Campbell Apartment (p144)

SixtyFive (p144)

Lantern's Keep (p145)

Entertainment

Hamilton (p148)

Kinky Boots (p148)

Book of Mormon (p149)

Getting There

🚇 **Subway** Times Sq-42nd St, Grand Central-42nd St and 34th St-Herald Sq.

🚌 **Bus** Useful for western and eastern extremes of Midtown. Routes include M11 (north on Tenth Ave and south on Ninth Ave) and M15 (north on First Ave and south on Second Ave). Crosstown buses run along 34th and 42nd Sts.

Top Sights
Times Square

Love it or hate it, the intersection of Broadway and Seventh Ave (better known as Times Square) is New York City's hyperactive heart. It's a restless, hypnotic torrent of glittering lights, bombastic billboards and raw urban energy. It's not hip, fashionable or in-the-know, and it couldn't care less. It's too busy pumping out iconic, mass-marketed NYC, from yellow cabs and golden arches to razzle-dazzle Broadway marquees.

⊙ Map p134, D4

www.timessquarenyc.org

Broadway, at Seventh Ave

S N/Q/R, S, 1/2/3, 7 to Times Sq-42nd St

Don't Miss

A Dramatic Transformation

Times Square wasn't always such a draw. The economic crash of the early 1970s led to a mass exodus of corporations from Times Square. Billboard niches went dark, stores shut and once grand hotels were converted into SRO (single-room occupancy) dives. While the adjoining Theater District survived, its respectable playhouses shared the streets with porn cinemas and strip clubs. That all changed with tough-talking Mayor Rudolph Giuliani, who, in the 1990s, boosted police numbers and lured a wave of 'respectable' retail chains, restaurants and attractions. By the new millennium, Times Square had gone from 'X-rated' to 'G-rated,' drawing almost 40 million visitors annually.

Broadway

New York's Theater District covers an area stretching roughly from 40th St to 54th St between Sixth and Eighth Aves, with dozens of Broadway and Off-Broadway theaters spanning blockbuster musicals to new and classic drama. Unless there's a specific show you're after, the best – and cheapest – way to score tickets in the area is at the TKTS Booth, where you can line up and get same-day discounted tickets for top Broadway and Off-Broadway shows. Smartphone users can download the free TKTS app, which shows real-time updates of what's available on that day.

Views From the TKTS Booth

The TKTS Booth is an attraction in itself, with its illuminated roof of 27 ruby-red steps rising a panoramic 16ft above 47th St. Needless to say, the view across Times Square from the top is a crowd pleaser, so good luck finding a spot to rest.

☑ Top Tips

▶ At the northwest corner of Broadway and 49th St, the Brill Building is arguably the most important generator of popular songs in the Western world. By 1962, more than 160 music businesses were based here, from songwriters and managers to promoters. It was a one-stop shop for artists, among them Carol King, Bob Dylan and Joni Mitchell.

✕ Take a Break

For panoramic views over the square, order a drink at Renaissance Hotel's **R Lounge** (☎212-261-5200; www.rloungetimessquare.com; Two Times Square, 714 Seventh Ave, at 48th St, Midtown West; ⊙5-11pm Mon, to 11:30pm Tue-Thu, to midnight Fri, 7:30am-midnight Sat, 7:30am-11pm Sun; ⑤N/Q/R to 49th St), which offers floor-to-ceiling vistas of the neon-lit spectacle below. It might not be the savviest spot for a sip in town, but with a view like this, who's judging?

Top Sights
Empire State Building

The Chrysler Building may be prettier and One World Trade Center and 432 Park Ave may be taller, but the Queen Bee of the New York skyline remains the Empire State Building. NYC's tallest star, it has enjoyed close-ups in around 100 films, from *King Kong* to *Independence Day*. And heading up to the top is as quintessential an experience as pastrami, rye and pickles at Katz's Delicatessen.

⊙ Map p134, E5

www.esbnyc.com

350 Fifth Ave, at 34th St

86th-fl observation deck adult/child $32/26, incl 102nd-fl observation deck $52/46

⊙8am-2am

Ⓢ B/D/F/M, N/Q/R to 34th St-Herald Sq

Don't Miss

Observation Decks

The Empire State Building has two observation decks. The open-air 86th-floor deck offers an alfresco experience, with coin-operated telescopes for close-up glimpses of the metropolis in action. Further up, the enclosed 102nd-floor deck puts you even higher. Needless to say, the views over the city's five boroughs (and five neighboring states, weather permitting) are quite simply exquisite. The views from both decks are especially spectacular at sunset, when the city dons its nighttime cloak in dusk's afterglow.

Light Shows

Since 1976, the building's top 30 floors have been floodlit in a spectrum of colors each night, reflecting seasonal and holiday hues. Famous combos include orange, white and green for St Patrick's Day; blue and white for Hanukkah; white, red and green for Christmas; and the rainbow colors for Gay Pride weekend in June. For a full rundown of the color schemes, check the website.

Astonishing Construction

The statistics are astounding: 10 million bricks, 60,000 tons of steel, 6400 windows and 328,000 sq ft of marble. Built on the original site of the Waldorf-Astoria, construction took a record-setting 410 days, using seven million hours of labor and costing a mere $41 million (nearly $650 million in today's reckoning). It might sound like a lot, but it fell well below its $50 million budget (just as well, given it went up during the Great Depression). Coming in at 102 stories, it's 1472ft from top to bottom.

☑ Top Tips

▶ Alas, the passage to heaven will involve a trip through purgatory: the queues to the top are notorious. Getting here very early or very late will help you avoid delays – as will buying your tickets online, ahead of time, where an extra $2 convenience fee is well worth the hassle.

▶ On the 86th floor between 9pm and 1am from Thursday to Saturday, the twinkling sea of lights below is accompanied by a live saxophone soundtrack (yes, requests are taken).

▶ The last elevators head up at 1:15am.

✕ Take a Break

Escape the maddening swarms of tourists, and stroll a few blocks east to fromage-loving Artisanal (p142), famed for its bistro dishes and swooning cheese selection. There's also the lively buzz of Koreatown, with abundant eating options along 32nd St, including peaceful Hangawi (p141).

Top Sights
Museum of Modern Art

MoMA boasts more A-listers than an Oscars after-party: Van Gogh, Matisse, Picasso, Warhol, Rothko, Pollock and Bourgeois. Since its founding in 1929, the museum has amassed almost 200,000 artworks, documenting the creative ideas and movements of the late 19th century through to those dominating today. For art buffs, it's Valhalla. For the uninitiated, it's a crash course in all that is addictive about art.

◉ Map p134, E2

☏ 212-708-9400

www.moma.org

11 W 53rd St, btwn Fifth & Sixth Aves

adult/child $25/free, 4-8pm Fri free

🕙10:30am-5:30pm Sat-Thu, to 8pm Fri

Ⓢ E, M to 5th Ave-53rd St

Don't Miss

Collection Highlights

MoMA's permanent collection spans four levels. Many of the big hitters are on the last two levels, so tackle the museum from the top down before fatigue sets in. Must-sees include Van Gogh's *Starry Night*, Cézanne's *The Bather*, Picasso's *Les Demoiselles d'Avignon*, and Henri Rousseau's *The Sleeping Gypsy*, not to mention iconic American works like Warhol's *Campbell's Soup Cans* and *Gold Marilyn Monroe*, Lichtenstein's equally poptastic *Girl with Ball*, and Hopper's haunting *House by the Railroad*.

Abby Aldrich Rockefeller Sculpture Garden

With architect Yoshio Taniguchi's acclaimed reconstruction of the museum in 2004 came the restoration of the Sculpture Garden to the original, larger vision of Philip Johnson's 1953 design. Johnson described the space as a 'sort of outdoor room,' and on warm, sunny days, it's hard not to think of it as a soothing alfresco lounge. Famous works include Aristide Maillol's *The River*, which sits among sculptures from greats including Matisse, Miró and Picasso. The Sculpture Garden is open free of charge from 9:30am to 10:15am daily, except in inclement weather and during maintenance.

Film Screenings

Not only a palace of visual art, MoMA screens an incredibly well-rounded selection of celluloid gems from its collection of over 22,000 films, including the works of the Maysles Brothers and every Pixar animation film ever produced. Expect anything from Academy Award–nominated documentary shorts and Hollywood classics to experimental works and international retrospectives. Best of all, your museum ticket will get you in for free.

☑ Top Tips

▶ To maximize your time and create a plan of attack, download the museum's free smartphone app from the website beforehand.

✕ Take a Break

MoMA has several on-site options. For communal tables and a casual vibe, nosh on Italian-inspired fare at **Cafe 2** (☎212-333-1299; sandwiches & salads $12-14, mains $19; ◷11am-5pm Sat-Thu, to 7:30pm Fri; 🛜). For table service, opt for **Terrace Five** (☎212-333-1288; mains $14-18; ◷11am-5pm Sat-Thu, to 7:30pm Fri; 🛜), which features an outdoor terrace overlooking the Sculpture Garden. If you're after high-end dining, book a table at the Michelin-starred **Modern** (☎212-333-1220; www.themodernnyc.com; 3-/4-course lunch $80/90, 4-course dinner $118; ◷restaurant noon-2pm & 5-10:30pm Mon-Fri, 5-10:30pm Sat, bar 11:30am-10:30pm Mon-Sat, to 9:30pm Sun).

E

44 🔒
5th Ave-
59th St

S

46 🔒
7th St

F

Lexington Ave-
59th St

S

45 🔒

59th St

S

E 61st St

G

Roosevelt Island
Tramway Station

E 60th St
Queensboro 59th St Bridge
E 59th St

E 58th St

H

1

seum of
dern Art
👁

47 🔒 Fifth Ave-
53rd St

kefeller
Plaza

👁

8 St Patrick's
👁 Cathedral

Rockefeller Center
p of the Rock

THE
AMOND
STRICT

22

42nd St

6
👁
New York
Public Library

26 ❂

Empire State
Building
👁 KOREATOWN

19
15 ✕

W 32nd St
(Korea Way)

Madison Ave

Fifth Ave

Park Ave

Vanderbilt Ave

51st St

S

Grand
Central
Terminal

E 44th St

E 43rd St
5th Ave

Grand
Central
Terminal

42nd St-
Grand Central

Madison Ave

Park Ave S

7
👁
Morgan
Library &
Museum

Lexington Ave

Lexington Ave

E 57th St

E 56th St

E 55th St

25

E 54th St
Lexington Ave-
53rd St

E 53rd St

E 52nd St

E 51st St

E 50th St

E 49th St

E 48th St

E 47th St

E 46th St

E 45th St

Third Ave

E 44th St

Chrysler
Building

5
👁

E 43rd St

E 42nd St

E 41st St

E 40th St

E 39th St

E 38th St

E 37th St

E 36th St

E 35th St

33rd St

S

17

38
⚑

E 34th St

E 33rd St

E 32nd St

E 31st St

Second Ave

Second Ave

MURRAY
HILL

First Ave

St Vartan
Park

Beekman
Pl

First Ave

Tudor City Pl

Sutton Pl

Franklin D Roosevelt Dr

10 United
👁 Nations

Franklin D Roosevelt Dr

East River

2

3

Queens-Midtown
Tunnel

4

East River

Franklin D Roosevelt Dr

5

Sights

Radio City
Music Hall
HISTORIC BUILDING

1 ⊚ Map p134, D2

This spectacular art-deco movie palace
was the brainchild of vaudeville producer Samuel Lionel 'Roxy' Rothafel.
Never one for understatement, Roxy
launched his venue on 23 December
1932 with an over-the-top extravaganza
that included camp dance troupe the
Roxyettes (mercifully renamed the
Rockettes). Guided tours (75 minutes)
of the sumptuous interiors include the
glorious auditorium, Witold Gordon's
classically inspired mural *History of
Cosmetics* in the Women's Downstairs
Lounge, and the *très* exclusive VIP
Roxy Suite. (www.radiocity.com; 1260 Sixth
Ave, at 51st St; tours adult/child $26.95/19.95;
⊙tours 10am-5pm; ♿; S B/D/F/M to 47th-
50th Sts-Rockefeller Center)

Rockefeller
Center
HISTORIC BUILDING

2 ⊚ Map p134, E2

This 22-acre 'city within a city'
debuted at the height of the Great Depression. Taking nine years to build,
it was America's first multiuse retail,
entertainment and office space –
a sprawl of 19 buildings (14 of which
are the original moderne structures).
Developer John D Rockefeller Jr may
have sweated over the $100 million
price tag, but it was worth it, the
center declared a National Landmark

in 1987. Highlights include the Top of
the Rock observation deck and **NBC
Studio Tours** (☎212-664-3700; www.
thetouratnbcstudios.com; 30 Rockefeller
Plaza, entrance at 1250 Sixth Ave; tours adult/
child $33/29, children under 6yr not admitted;
⊙8:30am-2pm Mon-Fri, to 5pm Sat & Sun).
(www.rockefellercenter.com; Fifth to Sixth
Aves & 48th to 51st Sts; S B/D/F/M to 47th-
50th Sts-Rockefeller Center)

Top of the Rock
VIEWPOINT

3 ⊚ Map p134, E2

Designed in homage to ocean liners
and first opened in 1933, this 70th-
floor, open-air observation deck sits
atop the GE Building, the tallest skyscraper at the Rockefeller Center. Top
of the Rock trumps the Empire State
Building on several levels: it's less
crowded, has wider observation decks
(both outdoor and indoor) and actually offers a view of the Empire State
Building itself. (☎212-698-2000; www
.topoftherocknyc.com; 30 Rockefeller Plaza,
at 49th St, entrance on W 50th St btwn Fifth
& Sixth Aves; adult/child $32/26, sunrise/
sunset combo $47/36; ⊙8am-midnight, last
elevator at 11pm; S B/D/F/M to 47th-50th
Sts-Rockefeller Center)

Grand Central
Terminal
HISTORIC BUILDING

4 ⊚ Map p134, F3

Completed in 1913, Grand Central
Terminal – more commonly, if techni-
cally incorrectly, called Grand Central
Station – is another of New York's
beaux-arts beauties. Adorned with

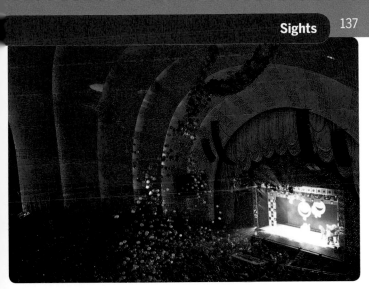

Radio City Music Hall

Tennessee marble floors and Italian marble ticket counters, its glorious main concourse is capped by a vaulted ceiling depicting the constellations. That these are presented backwards is no mistake: French painter Paul César Helleu wished to depict the stars from God's point of view, from the outside, looking in. (www.grandcentralterminal.com; 42nd St, at Park Ave, Midtown East; ☺5:30am-2am; ⒮S, 4/5/6, 7 to Grand Central-42nd St)

Chrysler Building   HISTORIC BUILDING

5 ◎ Map p134, F4

Designed by William Van Alen in 1930, the 77-floor Chrysler Building is prime-time architecture: a fusion of art-deco and Gothic aesthetics, adorned with steel eagles and topped by a spire that screams *Bride of Frankenstein*. The building was constructed as the headquarters for Walter P Chrysler and his automobile empire. Unable to compete on the production line with bigger rivals Ford and General Motors, Chrysler trumped them on the skyline and with one of Gotham's most beautiful lobbies. (405 Lexington Ave, at 42nd St, Midtown East; ☺lobby 8am-6pm Mon-Fri; ⒮S, 4/5/6, 7 to Grand Central-42nd St)

New York Public Library   HISTORIC BUILDING

6 ◎ Map p134, E4

Loyally guarded by 'Patience' and 'Fortitude' (the marble lions overlooking

Local Life
Roosevelt Island

Roosevelt Island, the tiny sliver of land that sits in the middle of the East River, makes a quick escape from Manhattan, and offers photogenic views of the city skyline. It's also the site of the Louis Kahn–designed **Franklin D Roosevelt Four Freedoms Park** (Map p134, H3; ☏212-204-8831; www.fdrfourfreedom spark.org; Roosevelt Island; admission free; ☺9am-7pm Wed-Mon Apr-Sep, to 5pm Wed-Mon Oct-Mar; ⑤F to Roosevelt Island; ﹫Roosevelt Island), which sits at the southern tip of the island. You can get here by subway (F line), but for the scenic journey take the Roosevelt Island tram, departing from Second Ave and 60th St.

Morgan Library & Museum
MUSEUM

7 ◉ Map p134, E4

Incorporating the mansion once owned by steel magnate JP Morgan, this sumptuous cultural center houses a phenomenal array of manuscripts, tapestries and books (with no fewer than three Gutenberg Bibles). Adorned with Italian and Dutch Renaissance artworks, Morgan's personal study is only trumped by his personal library (East Room), an extraordinary, vaulted space adorned with walnut bookcases, a 16th-century Dutch tapestry and zodiac-themed ceiling. The center's rotating exhibitions are often superb, as are its regular cultural events. (www.morganlibrary.org; 29 E 36th St, at Madison Ave, Midtown East; adult/child $18/12; ☺10:30am-5pm Tue-Thu, to 9pm Fri, 10am-6pm Sat, 11am-6pm Sun; ⑤6 to 33rd St)

St Patrick's Cathedral
CHURCH

8 ◉ Map p134, E2

Fresh from a major restoration, America's largest Catholic cathedral graces Fifth Ave with its Gothic Revival splendor. Built at a cost of nearly $2 million during the Civil War, the building did not originally include the two front spires; those were added in 1888. Step inside to appreciate the Louis Tiffany–designed altar and Charles Connick's stunning Rose Window, the latter gleaming above a 7000-pipe church organ. (www.saint patrickscathedral.org; Fifth Ave, btwn 50th & 51st Sts; ☺6:30am-8:45pm; ⑤B/D/F/M to

Fifth Ave), this beaux-arts show-off is one of NYC's best free attractions. When dedicated in 1911, New York's flagship library ranked as the largest marble structure ever built in the US, and to this day its Rose Main Reading Room steals the breath with its lavish, coffered ceiling. While the room may be closed for restoration until early 2017, it's only one of several glories, among them the DeWitt Wallace Periodical Room. (Stephen A Schwarzman Building; ☏917-275-6975; www.nypl.org; Fifth Ave, at 42nd St; admission free; ☺10am-6pm Mon & Thu-Sat, to 8pm Tue & Wed, 1-5pm Sun, guided tours 11am & 2pm Mon-Sat, 2pm Sun; ⑤B/D/F/M to 42nd St-Bryant Park; 7 to 5th Ave)

47th-50th Sts-Rockefeller Center; E/M to 5th Ave-53rd St)

Museum of Arts & Design   MUSEUM

9 ⊙ Map p134, C1

MAD offers four floors of superlative design and handicrafts, from blown glass and carved wood to elaborate metal jewelry. Its temporary exhibitions are top notch and innovative; one past show explored the art of scent. Usually on the first Sunday of the month, professional artists lead family-friendly explorations of the galleries, followed by hands-on workshops inspired by the current exhibitions. The museum gift shop sells some fantastic contemporary jewelry, while the 9th-floor restaurantbar **Robert** (☎212-299-7730; www. robertnyc.com; ☺11:30am-10pm Mon & Sun, to 11pm Tue, to midnight Wed-Sat) is perfect for panoramic cocktails. (MAD; www. madmuseum.org; 2 Columbus Circle, btwn Eighth Ave & Broadway; adult/child $16/free, by donation 6-9pm Thu; ☺10am-6pm Tue, Wed, Sat & Sun, to 9pm Thu & Fri; 🚻; Ⓢ A/C, B/D, 1 to 59th St-Columbus Circle)

United Nations   HISTORIC BUILDING

10 ⊙ Map p134, H3

Welcome to the headquarters of the UN, a worldwide organization overseeing international law, international security and human rights. While the Le Corbusier–designed Secretariat building is off-limits, one-hour guided tours do cover the recently restored General Assembly Hall, Security Council Chamber, Trusteeship Council Chamber and Economic and Social

---

Understand
A Brief History of Times Square

At the turn of last century, Times Square was known as Longacre Sq, an unremarkable intersection far from the city's commercial epicenter of Lower Manhattan. This changed with a deal between subway pioneer August Belmont and New York Times publisher Adolph Ochs. Heading construction of the city's first subway line (from Lower Manhattan to the Upper West Side and Harlem), Belmont realized that a business hub along 42nd St would maximize profit and patronage on the route. He then approached Ochs, who had recently turned around the fortunes of the *New York Times,* arguing that moving the newspaper's operations to the intersection of Broadway and 42nd St would be a win-win for Ochs. Not only would an in-house subway station mean faster distribution of the newspaper, but the influx of commuters to the square would mean more sales right outside its headquarters. Belmont even convinced New York Mayor George B McClellan Jr to rename the square in honor of the broadsheet.

Council (ECOSOC) Chamber, as well as exhibitions about the UN's work and artworks given by member states. Weekday tours must be booked online and photo ID is required to enter the site. (☎212-963-4475; http://visit.un.org; visitors' gate First Ave at 46th St, Midtown East; guided tour adult/child $20/11, children under 5yr not admitted, grounds access Sat & Sun free; ⊗tours 9am-4:30pm Mon-Fri, visitor center also open 10am-4:30pm Sat & Sun; Ⓢ S, 4/5/6, 7 to Grand Central-42nd St)

Eating

Totto Ramen
JAPANESE $

11 ✕ Map p134, C2

There might be another two branches in Midtown, but purists know that neither beats the tiny 20-seat original. Write your name and the number of guests on the clipboard and wait your turn. Your reward: extraordinary ramen. Skip the chicken and go for the pork, which sings in dishes like miso ramen (with fermented soybean paste, egg, scallion, bean sprouts, onion and homemade chili paste). (☎212-582-0052; www.tottoramen.com; 366 W 52nd St, btwn Eighth & Ninth Aves, Midtown West; ramen from $10; ⊗noon-4:30pm & 5:30pm-midnight Mon-Sat, 4-11pm Sun; Ⓢ C/E to 50th St)

Burger Joint
BURGERS $

12 ✕ Map p134, D1

With only a small neon burger as your clue, this speakeasy-style burger hut lurks behind the lobby curtain in the Le Parker Meridien hotel. Though it might not be as 'hip' or as 'secret' as it once was, it still delivers the same winning formula of graffiti-strewn walls, retro booths and attitude-loaded staff slapping up beef 'n' patty brilliance. (☎212-708-7414; www.burgerjointny.com; Le Parker Meridien, 119 W 56th St, btwn Sixth & Seventh Aves, Midtown West; burgers from $8.50; ⊗11am-11:30pm Sun-Thu, to midnight Fri & Sat; Ⓢ F to 57th St)

El Margon
CUBAN $

13 ✕ Map p134, D3

It's still 1973 at this ever-packed Cuban lunch counter, where orange Laminex and greasy goodness never went out of style. Go for gold with its legendary cubano sandwich (a pressed panino jammed with rich roast pork, salami, cheese, pickles, mojo and mayo). It's obscenely good. (☎212-354-5013; www.margonnyc.com; 136 W 46th St, btwn Sixth & Seventh Aves, Midtown West; sandwiches $4-8, mains from $10; ⊗6am-5pm Mon-Fri, from 7am Sat; Ⓢ B/D/F/M to 47th-50th Sts-Rockefeller Center)

ViceVersa
ITALIAN $$

14 ✕ Map p134, C2

ViceVersa is the quintessential Italian: suave and sophisticated, affable and scrumptious. Scan the menu for refined, cross-regional dishes like arancini with black truffle and fontina cheese. For a celebrated classic, order the *casoncelli alla bergamasca* (ravioli-like pasta filled with minced veal, raisins and amaretto cookies and

Hearst Tower (p143)

seasoned with sage, butter, pancetta and Grana Padano), a nod to chef Stefano Terzi's Lombard heritage. (📞212-399-9291; www.viceversanyc.com; 325 W 51st St, btwn Eighth & Ninth Aves, Midtown West; 2-course lunch $25, dinner mains $24-32; ⏱noon-2:30pm & 4:30-11pm Mon-Fri, 4:30-11pm Sat, 11:30am-3pm & 4:30-10pm Sun; 🚇C/E to 50th St)

Hangawi KOREAN $$

15 ✗ Map p134, E5

Meat-free Korean is the draw at high-achieving Hangawi. Leave your shoes at the entrance and slip into a soothing, Zen-like space of meditative music, soft low seating and clean, complex dishes. Show-stoppers include

the leek pancakes and a seductively smooth tofu claypot in ginger sauce. (📞212-213-0077; www.hangawirestaurant.com; 12 E 32nd St, btwn Fifth & Madison Aves; mains lunch $11-30, dinner $19-30; ⏱noon-2:30pm & 5:30-10:15pm Mon-Fri, 1-10:30pm Sat, 5-9:30pm Sun; 🍴; 🚇B/D/F/M, N/Q/R to 34th St-Herald Sq)

Danji KOREAN $$

16 ✗ Map p134, C2

Young-gun Hooni Kim woos palates with his Korean creations, served in a snug, slinky, whitewashed space. The simpler lunch menu includes *bibim-bap* (a traditional Korean rice dish), while the more expansive dinner list offers small, medium and large plates.

Thankfully, both lunch and dinner menus offer Danji's cult-status *bulgogi* beef sliders, made with heavenly, butter-grilled buns. Head in early or wait. (☎212-586-2880; www.danjinyc.com; 346 W 52nd St, btwn Eighth & Ninth Aves, Midtown West; dishes $13-26; ☺noon-2:30pm & 5-11pm Mon-Thu, noon-2:30pm & 5pm-midnight Fri, 5pm-midnight Sat; ⑤C/E to 50th St)

Artisanal

FRENCH $$$

 17 Map p134, F5

Artisanal is Valhalla for *fromage* fiends. From spicy Italian Canestrato to pungent French Livarot, you'll find over 200 varieties of cheese at what is a modern take on an old Parisian bistro. Experiment with a cheese-and-wine flight or throw caution to the wind with one of a string of fondues. Beyond them is a cast of bistro standbys, from onion soup *gratinée* (with a three-cheese blend, naturally) to bouillabaisse. (☎212-725-8585; www.artisanalbistro.com; 2 Park Ave S, btwn 32nd & 33rd Sts, Midtown East; mains $24-50 ; ☺10am-midnight Mon-Fri, from 9am Sat & Sun; ✎; ⑤6 to 33rd St)

Le Bernardin

SEAFOOD $$$

18 Map p134, D2

The interiors may have been subtly sexed-up for a 'younger clientele' (the stunning storm-themed triptych is by Brooklyn artist Ran Ortner), but triple Michelin-starred Le Bernardin remains a luxe, fine-dining holy grail. At the helm is French-born celebrity chef Éric Ripert, whose deceptively simple-looking seafood often borders on the transcendental. (☎212-554-1515; www.le-bernardin.com; 155 W 51st St, btwn Sixth & Seventh Aves, Midtown West; prix fixe lunch/dinner $80/140, tasting menus $170-205; ☺noon-2:30pm & 5:15-10:30pm Mon-Thu, to 11pm Fri, 5:15-11pm Sat; ⑤1 to 50th St; B/D, E to 7th Ave)

NoMad

NEW AMERICAN $$$

19 Map p134, E5

Sharing the same name as the 'It kid' hotel it inhabits, NoMad has become one of Manhattan's culinary highlights. Carved up into a series of distinctly different spaces – including a see-and-be-seen Atrium, an elegant Parlour and a snacks-only Library – the restaurant serves delicacies ranging from roasted quail with plums, kale and chanterelle, to suckling pig confit with pears and bitter greens. (☎212-796-1500; www.thenomadhotel.com; NoMad Hotel, 1170 Broadway, at 28th St; 2-course lunch prix fixe $29, dinner mains $23-41; ☺noon-2pm & 5:30-10:30pm Mon-Thu, to 11pm Fri, 11am-2:30pm & 5:30-11pm Sat, 11am-2:30pm & 5:30-10pm Sun; ⑤N/R, 6 to 28th St; F/M to 23rd St)

Taboon

MEDITERRANEAN $$$

20 Map p134, B2

Taboon is Arabic for stone oven, and it's the first thing you'll see when stepping through the curtain into this warm, casually chic hot spot. Join urbane theater-goers and Hell's Kitchen muscle boys for Med-inspired dishes like sizzling shrimp with garlic and lemon or truffle-oil-drizzled egg burek

Understand
Midtown Skyscrapers

Midtown's skyline is more than just the Empire State and Chrysler Buildings; it has enough modernist and postmodern beauties to satisfy the wildest of high-rise dreams. Celebrate all things phallic with three of Midtown's finest.

Lever House

Upon its debut, 21-story **Lever House** (390 Park Ave, btwn 53rd & 54th Sts, Midtown East; **S** E, M to 5th Ave-53rd St) was at the height of the cutting-edge, with only the UN Secretariat Building also boasting an innovative glass skin. The building's form was equally bold: two counter-posed rectangular shapes consisting of a slender tower atop a low-rise base. The open courtyard features marble benches by Japanese-American sculptor Isamu Noguchi, while the lobby exhibits contemporary art commissioned for the space.

Hearst Tower

Foster & Partners' **Hearst Tower** (949 Eighth Ave, btwn 56th & 57th Sts, Midtown West; **S** A/C, B/D, 1 to 59th St-Columbus Circle) is hands down one of New York's most creative works of contemporary architecture. Its diagonal grid of trusses evokes a jagged glass-and-steel honeycomb, best appreciated up close and from an angle. The tower rises above the hollowed-out core of John Urban's 1928 cast-stone Hearst Magazine Building, itself originally envisioned as a skyscraper. In the lobby you'll find *Riverlines*, a mural by Richard Long.

Bank of America Tower

The crystal-shaped **Bank of America Tower** (Sixth Ave, btwn 42nd & 43rd Sts; **S** B/D/F/M to 42nd St-Bryant Park) is lauded for its enviable green credentials. The stats are impressive: a clean-burning, on-site cogeneration plant provides around 65% of the tower's annual electricity requirements; CO_2-detecting air filters channel filtered air where needed; and the destination-dispatch elevators are designed to avoid empty car trips. Designed by Cook & Fox Architects, the 58-floor role model was awarded 'Best Tall Building in America' by the Council on Tall Buildings & Urban Habitat awards in 2010.

(soft-poached egg in crispy phyllo dough). Reservations recommended... as are the oven-fresh breads. (📞212-713-0271; www.taboononline.com; 773 Tenth Ave, at 52nd St, Midtown West; meze dishes $11-20, mains $26-38; ⏱5-11pm Mon-Fri, to 11:30pm Sat, 11am-3:30pm & 5-10pm Sun; ⑤C/E to 50th St)

John Dory Oyster Bar
SEAFOOD $$$

21 🍴 Map p134, E5

Anchored to the **Ace Hotel** (📞212-679-2222; www.acehotel.com/newyork; 20 W 29th St, btwn Broadway & Fifth Ave, Midtown West; r from $329; ❄🏂; ⑤N/R to 28th St) lobby, John Dory is a fine spot to sip some bubbles and slurp on an oyster or three. Top billing goes to happy hour (5pm to 7pm weekdays, noon to 3pm

---

Local Life
Koreatown

For kimchi and karaoke, it's hard to beat **Koreatown** (Map p134, E5; 31st to 36th Sts & Broadway to Fifth Ave; ⑤B/D/F/M, N/Q/R to 34th St-Herald Sq). Mainly concentrated on 32nd St, with some spillover into the surrounding streets both south and north of this strip, it's a Seoulful mix of Korean-owned restaurants, shops, salons and spas. Authentic BBQ is available around the clock at many of the all-night spots on 32nd St, some with microphones, video screens and 'Manic Monday' at the ready.

---

on weekends), when both oysters and clams beckon at $2 a pop (minimum of six). (📞212-792-9000; www.thejohndory.com; 1196 Broadway, at 29th St; plates $10-38; ⏱noon-midnight; ⑤N/R to 28th St)

Drinking

Campbell Apartment
COCKTAIL BAR

Party like it's 1928! This sublime, deliciously buttoned-up gem in Grand Central (see 4 ◎ Map p134, F3) was once the office of a '20s railroad magnate fond of Euro eccentricities: think Florentine-style carpets, decorative wooden ceiling beams and a soaring leaded glass window. Suitably tucked away from the hordes, reach it from the lift beside the Oyster Bar or the stairs to the West Balcony. (📞212-953-0409; www.hospitalityholdings.com; Grand Central Terminal, 15 Vanderbilt Ave, at 43rd St; ⏱noon-1am Mon-Thu, to 2am Fri & Sat, to midnight Sun; ⑤S, 4/5/6, 7 to Grand Central-42nd St)

SixtyFive
COCKTAIL BAR

Not to be missed, sophisticated Sixty-Five (see 2 ◎ Map p134, E2) sits on level 65 of the GE Building at Rockefeller Center. Dress well (no sportswear or guests under 21) and arrive by 5pm for a seat with a multi-million-dollar view. Even if you don't score a table on the balcony or by the window, head outside to soak up that sweeping New York panorama. (📞212-632-5000; www.rainbowroom.com; 30 Rockefeller Plaza, entrance on W 49th St; ⏱5pm-midnight Mon-

Bryant Park (p146)

Fri; [S] B/D/F/M to 47th-50th Sts-Rockefeller Center)

Lantern's Keep
COCKTAIL BAR

22 🚇 Map p134, E3

Can you keep a secret? If so, cross the lobby of the **Iroquois Hotel** (☎212-840-3080; www.iroquoisny.com; r from $509; ❄️ 🛜) and slip into this dark, intimate cocktail salon. Its specialty is classic drinks, shaken and stirred by passionate, personable mixologists. If you're feeling spicy, request a Gordon's Breakfast, a fiery mélange of gin, Worcestershire sauce, hot sauce, muddled lime and cucumber, salt and pepper. Reservations are recommended. (☎212-453-4287; www.thelanternskeep. com; Iroquois Hotel, 49 W 44th St, btwn Fifth & Sixth Aves, Midtown West; ⏲5-11:30pm Mon-Fri, 7pm-12:30am Sat; [S] B/D/F/M to 42nd St-Bryant Park)

Waylon
BAR

23 🚇 Map p134, B2

Slip on your spurs, partner: there's a honky-tonk in Hell's! Celebrate Dixie at this saloon-style watering hole, where the jukebox keeps good folk dancing to Tim McGraw's broken heart, where the barkeeps pour American whiskeys and tequila, and where the bar bites include Texan-style Frito pie and country-fried steak sandwiches. For live country-and-western sounds, head in on Thursdays between

Q Local Life
Bryant Park

European coffee kiosks, alfresco chess games, summer film screenings (Monday nights), a carousel, and ice-skating and a holiday market in winter: it's hard to believe that this **leafy oasis** (Map p134, E4; ☎212-768-4242; www.bryantpark. org; 42nd St, btwn Fifth & Sixth Aves; ⊙7am-midnight Mon-Fri, to 11pm Sat & Sun Jun-Sep, shorter hours rest of year; §B/D/F/M to 42nd St-Bryant Park; 7 to 5th Ave) was dubbed 'Needle Park' in the '80s. Nestled behind the beaux-arts New York Public Library building, it's a delightful spot for a little time out from the Midtown madness.

8pm and 11pm. (☎212-265-0010; www. thewaylon.com; 736 Tenth Ave, at 50th St, Midtown West; ⊙2pm-4am Mon-Fri, from noon Sat & Sun; §C/E to 50th St)

Rum House   COCKTAIL BAR
24 ⓠ Map p134, C3

This sultry, revamped slice of old New York is revered for its cognoscenti rums and whiskeys. Savor them straight up or mixed in impeccable cocktails like a classic Dark & Stormy (rum, ginger beer and lime). Adding to the magic is nightly live music, spanning solo piano tunes to jaunty jazz trios and sentimental torch divas. (☎646-490-6924; www.therumhousenyc. com; 228 W 47th St, btwn Broadway & Eighth Ave, Midtown West; ⊙1pm-4am; §N/Q/R to 49th St)

PJ Clarke's   BAR
25 ⓠ Map p134, F2

A bastion of old New York, this lovingly worn wooden saloon has been straddling the scene since 1884; Buddy Holly proposed to his fiancée here and Ol' Blue Eyes pretty much owned table 20. Choose a jukebox tune, order the knockout burger and settle in with a come-one-and-all crowd of collar-and-tie colleagues, college students and nostalgia-craving urbanites. (☎212-317-1616; www.pjclarkes. com; 915 Third Ave, at 55th St, Midtown East; ⊙11:30am-4am; §E, M to Lexington Ave-53rd St)

Top of the Strand   COCKTAIL BAR
26 ⓠ Map p134, E4

For that 'Oh my God, I'm in New York' feeling, head to the rooftop bar of the **Strand** (☎212-448-1024; www.thestrand-nyc.com; r from $224; ❄️ 🛜) hotel, order a martini (extra dirty) and drop your jaw (discreetly). Top of the Strand sports comfy cabana-style seating, a refreshingly mixed-age crowd and a sliding glass roof, and its view of the Empire State Building is simply unforgettable. (www.topofthestrand.com; Strand Hotel, 33 W 37th St, btwn Fifth & Sixth Aves, Midtown East; ⊙5pm-midnight Mon & Sun, to 1am Tue-Sat; §B/D/F/M, N/Q/R to 34th St-Herald Sq)

Jimmy's Corner

27 🚇 Map p134, D3   BAR

This welcoming, completely unpretentious dive off Times Square is run by an old boxing trainer – as if you wouldn't guess by all the framed photos of boxing greats (and lesser-known fighters, too). The jukebox covers Stax to Miles Davis (plus Lionel Richie's most regretful moments), kept low enough for post-work gangs to chat away. (☎212-221-9510; 140 W 44th St, btwn Sixth & Seventh Aves, Midtown West; ⊗11am-4am Mon-Fri, from 12:30pm Sat, from 3pm Sun; Ⓢ N/Q/R, 1/2/3, 7 to 42nd St-Times Sq; B/D/F/M to 42nd St-Bryant Park)

Russian Vodka Room

28 🚇 Map p134, C2   BAR

Long for Mother Russia at this swank, affable drinking hole, pouring a head-spinning list of flavored vodkas, from cranberry to horseradish. When the room starts spinning, slow it down with stoic grub like borscht, *pirozhki* (stuffed buns), smoked fish and schnitzel. (☎212-307-5835; www.russianvodkaroom.com; 265 W 52nd St, btwn Eighth Ave & Broadway, Midtown West; ⊗4pm-2am Mon-Thu, to 4am Fri & Sat; Ⓢ C/E to 50th St)

Rudy's Bar & Grill

29 🚇 Map p134, B3   BAR

The big pantless pig in a red jacket out front marks Hell's Kitchen's best divey mingler, with cheap pitchers of Rudy's two beers, half-circle booths covered in red duct tape, and free hot

Atlas, by Lee Lawrie, at the Rockefeller Center (p136)

dogs. A mix of folks come to flirt or watch muted Knicks games as classic rock plays. (☎646-707-0890; www.rudysbarnyc.com; 627 Ninth Ave, at 44th St, Midtown West; ⊗8am-4am Mon-Sat, noon-4am Sun; Ⓢ A/C/E to 42nd St-Port Authority Bus Terminal)

Industry

30 🚇 Map p134, C2   GAY

What was once a parking garage is now one of the hottest gay bars in Hell's Kitchen – a slick 4000-sq-ft watering hole with handsome lounge areas, a pool table and a stage for top-notch drag divas. Head in between 4pm and 9pm for the two-for-one drinks special or squeeze in later to party with the eye-candy party hordes. Cash only. (☏646-476-2747; www.industry-bar.com; 355 W 52nd St, btwn Eighth & Ninth Aves, Midtown West; ◷4pm-4am; ⑤C/E, 1 to 50th St)

Entertainment

Hamilton

THEATER

31 ⭐ Map p134, C3

Lin-Manuel Miranda's acclaimed new musical is Broadway's hottest ticket, using contemporary hip-hop beats to recount the story of America's founding father, Alexander Hamilton. Inspired by Ron Chernow's biography *Alexander Hamilton*, the musical has won a swath of awards, including Outstanding Musical at the Drama Desk Awards and Best Musical at the New York Drama Critics' Circle Awards. (Richard Rodgers Theatre; ☏tickets 877-250-2929; www.hamiltonbroadway.com; 226 W 46th St, btwn Seventh & Eighth Aves, Midtown West; ⑤N/Q/R to 49th St)

Kinky Boots

THEATER

32 ⭐ Map p134, C3

Adapted from a 2005 British indie film, Harvey Fierstein and Cyndi Lauper's smash hit tells the story of a doomed English shoe factory unexpectedly saved by Lola, a business-

---

Understand
TV Tapings

If you want to be part of a live studio audience for a TV taping, NYC is the place to do it. For more show ticket details, visit the websites of individual TV stations, or try www.tvtickets.com.

Saturday Night Live Known for being difficult to get into. Try your luck in the fall lottery by sending an email to snltickets@nbcuni.com in August. Or line up by 7am on the day of the show on the 48th St side of Rockefeller Plaza for standby tickets.

The Late Show with Stephen Colbert Tickets for this hugely popular late-night show are available online, but they commonly sell out on the day of their release. Check *The Late Show*'s official Twitter account (@colbertlateshow) and Facebook page for release date announcements, usually made one to two months in advance.

Last Week Tonight with John Oliver Tickets to the news recap show of this biting British comedian are available at www.lastweektickets.com up to 2½ weeks in advance of taping dates.

savvy drag queen. Its solid characters and electrifying energy have not been lost on critics, the musical winning six Tony Awards, including Best Musical in 2013. (Hirschfeld Theatre; ☑ tickets 212-239-6200; www.kinkybootsthemusical. com; 302 W 45th St, btwn Eighth & Ninth Aves, Midtown West; S A/C/E to 42nd St-Port Authority Bus Terminal)

Book of Mormon THEATER

33 ⭐ Map p134, C3

Subversive, obscene and ridiculously hilarious, this cutting musical satire is the work of *South Park* creators Trey Parker and Matt Stone and *Avenue Q* composer Robert Lopez. Winner of nine Tony Awards, it tells the story of two naive Mormons on a mission to 'save' a Ugandan village. (Eugene O'Neill Theatre; ☑ tickets 212-239-6200; www. bookofmormonbroadway.com; 230 W 49th St, btwn Broadway & Eighth Ave, Midtown West; S N/Q/R to 49th St; 1 to 50th St; C/E to 50th St)

Jazz at Lincoln Center JAZZ

Perched high atop the Time Warner Center, Jazz at Lincoln Center (see **52 ⓐ** Map p134, C1) consists of three state-of-the-art venues: the mid-sized Rose Theater; the panoramic, glass-backed Appel Room; and the intimate, atmospheric **Dizzy's Club Coca-Cola**. It's the last of these that you're most likely to visit given its nightly shows. The talent is often exceptional, as are the dazzling Central Park views. (☑ tickets to Dizzy's Club Coca-Cola 212-258-9595,

A saxophonist plays outside Carnegie Hall

tickets to Rose Theater & Appel Room 212-721-6500; www.jazz.org; Time Warner Center, Broadway, at 60th St, Midtown West; S A/C, B/D, 1 to 59th St-Columbus Circle)

Carnegie Hall LIVE MUSIC

34 ⭐ Map p134, D1

This legendary music hall may not be the world's biggest, nor grandest, but it's definitely one of the most acoustically blessed venues around. Opera, jazz and folk greats feature in the Isaac Stern Auditorium, with edgier jazz, pop, classical and world music in the hugely popular Zankel Hall. The intimate Weill Recital Hall hosts chamber-music concerts, debut performances and panel discussions. (☑ 212-247-7800; www.carnegiehall.org;

The Broadway of the 1920s was well known for lighthearted musicals, commonly fusing vaudeville and music hall traditions, and producing classic tunes such as George Gershwin's *Rhapsody in Blue* and Cole Porter's *Let's Misbehave*. At the same time, Midtown's Theater District was evolving as a platform for new American dramatists. One of the greatest was Eugene O'Neill. Born in Times Square at the long-gone Barrett Hotel (1500 Broadway) in 1888, the playwright debuted many of his works here, including Pulitzer Prize winners *Beyond the Horizon* and *Anna Christie*. O'Neill's success on Broadway paved the way for other American greats such as Tennessee Williams, Arthur Miller and Edward Albee. This surge of serious talent led to the establishment of the annual Tony Awards in 1947, Broadway's answer to Hollywood's Oscars.

W 57th St, at Seventh Ave, Midtown West; ⏱tours 11:30am, 12:30pm, 2pm & 3pm Mon-Fri, 11:30am & 12:30pm Sat, 12:30pm Sun Oct-Jun; Ⓢ N/Q/R to 57th St-7th Ave)

An American in Paris

THEATER

35 ⭐ Map p134, D3

Adapted from the 1951 film starring Gene Kelly, this elegant, critically acclaimed stage musical tells the story of an American ex-GI in postwar Paris, following his artistic dreams and falling head over heels for an alluring dancer. Packed with toe-tapping Gershwin tunes (including rarer numbers), it's directed by renowned English choreographer Christopher Wheeldon. (Palace Theatre; ☎212-730-8200, tickets 877-250-2929; www.anamericaninparisbroadway.com; 1564 Broadway, at 47th St, Midtown West; Ⓢ N/Q/R to 49th St)

Signature Theatre

THEATER

36 ⭐ Map p134, B4

Looking good in its Frank Gehry–designed home – complete with three theaters, bookshop and cafe – the Signature Theatre is devoted to the work of its playwrights-in-residence, both past and present. To date, featured dramatists have included Tony Kushner, Edward Albee, Athol Fugard and Kenneth Lonergan. Shows aside, the theater also runs talks with playwrights, directors, designers and actors. Aim to book performances one month in advance. (☎tickets 212-244-7529; www.signaturetheatre.org; 480 W 42nd St, btwn Ninth & Tenth Aves, Midtown West; Ⓢ A/C/E to 42nd St-Port Authority Bus Terminal)

Playwrights Horizons

THEATER

37 ⭐ Map p134, B4

An excellent place to catch what could be the next big thing, this veteran 'writers' theater' is dedicated to fostering contemporary American works. Notable past productions include Bruce Norris's Tony Award–winning *Clybourne Park,* as well as *I Am My Own Wife* and *Grey Gardens,* both of which moved on to Broadway. (☎212-279-4200; www.playwrightshorizons.org; 416 W 42nd St, btwn Ninth & Tenth Aves, Midtown West; §A/C/E to 42nd St-Port Authority Bus Terminal)

Jazz Standard   JAZZ

38 ⭐ Map p134, F5

One of the city's other great jazz clubs is the Jazz Standard. The service is impeccable. The food is great. There's no minimum and it's programmed by Seth Abramson, a guy who really knows his stuff. (☎212-576-2232; www.jazzstandard.com; 116 E 27th St, btwn Lexington & Park Aves; §6 to 28th St)

Matilda   THEATER

39 ⭐ Map p134, C3

Giddily subversive, this multi-award-winning musical is an adaptation of Roald Dahl's classic children's tale. Star of the show is a precocious five-year-old who uses wit, intellect and a little telekinesis to tackle parental neglect, unjust punishment, even the Russian mafia. (Shubert Theatre; ☎tickets 212-239-6200; http://us.matildathemusical.com; 225 W 44th St, btwn Seventh & Eighth Aves, Midtown West; ♿; §N/Q/R, S, 1/2/3, 7 to Times Sq-42nd St; A/C/E to 42nd St-Port Authority Bus Terminal)

Madison Square Garden   STADIUM

40 ⭐ Map p134, C5

NYC's major performance venue – part of the massive complex housing Penn Station and the Theater at Madison Square Garden – hosts big-arena performers, from Kanye West to Madonna. It's also a sports arena, with New York Knicks' and New York Rangers' games, as well as boxing and events like the Annual Westminster Kennel Club Dog Show. (www.thegarden.com; Seventh Ave, btwn 31st & 33rd Sts, Midtown West; §A/C/E, 1/2/3 to 34th St-Penn Station)

Birdland   JAZZ, CABARET

41 ⭐ Map p134, C3

This bird's got a slick look, not to mention the legend – its name dates

✅ Top Tip

Budget Broadway

Many of the hottest Broadway shows – including Hamilton (p148), Kinky Boots (p148) and Book of Mormon (p149) – run ticket lotteries, which can be entered at the theater 2½ hours before the performance. If your name is drawn, the show costs you less than $40. The bad news: tickets are limited and in high demand. Some shows (including those above) also offer online ticket lotteries. Visit show websites to try your luck.

from bebop legend Charlie Parker (aka 'Bird'), who headlined at the previous location on 52nd St, along with Miles, Monk and just about everyone else (you can see their photos on the walls). Covers run from $20 to $50 and the lineup is always stellar. (☑212-581-3080; www.birdlandjazz.com; 315 W 44th St, btwn Eighth & Ninth Aves, Midtown West; admission $20-50; ☺5pm-1am; ☎; ⑤A/C/E to 42nd St-Port Authority Bus Terminal)

Caroline's on Broadway
COMEDY

42 ⭐ Map p134, D2

You may recognize this big, bright, mainstream classic from comedy specials filmed here on location. It's a top spot to catch US comedy big guns and sitcom stars. (☑212-757-4100; www.carolines.com; 1626 Broadway, at 50th St, Midtown West; ⑤N/Q/R to 49th St; 1, C/E to 50th St)

Don't Tell Mama
CABARET

43 ⭐ Map p134, C3

Piano bar and cabaret venue extraordinaire, Don't Tell Mama is an unpretentious little spot that's been around for more than 30 years and has the talent to prove it. Its regular roster of performers aren't big names, but true lovers of cabaret who give each show their all. (☑212-757-0788; www.donttellmamanyc.com; 343 W 46th St, btwn Eighth & Ninth Aves, Midtown West; ☺4pm-3am Mon-Thu, to 4am Fri-Sun; ⑤N/Q/R, S, 1/2/3, 7 to Times Sq-42nd St)

Shopping

MoMA Design & Book Store
GIFTS, BOOKS

The flagship store at the Museum of Modern Art (see ◉ Map p134, E2) is a fab spot to souvenir shop in one fell swoop. Aside from stocking gorgeous books (from art and architecture tomes to pop culture readers and kids' picture books), you'll find art prints and posters, and one-of-a-kind knickknacks. For furniture, lighting, homewares, jewelry, bags and MUJI merchandise, head to the MoMA Design Store across the street. (☑212-708-9700; www.momastore.org; 11 W 53rd St, btwn Fifth & Sixth Aves; ☺9:30am-6:30pm Sat-Thu, to 9pm Fri; ⑤E, M to 5th Ave-53rd St)

Barneys
DEPARTMENT STORE

44 🅐 Map p134, E1

Serious fashionistas swipe their plastic at Barneys, respected for its spot-on collections of top-tier labels like Isabel Marant Étoile, Mr & Mrs Italy and Lanvin. For (slightly) less expensive deals geared to a younger market, shop street-chic labels on the 8th floor. Coveted threads aside, other in-store highlights include a popular basement cosmetics department and Genes, a futuristic cafe with touch-screen communal tables for online shopping. (www.barneys.com; 660 Madison Ave, at 61st St, Midtown East; ☺10am-8pm Mon-Fri, to 7pm Sat, 11am-7pm Sun; ⑤N/Q/R to 5th Ave-59th St)

Theatre-lined 42nd St

Bloomingdale's   DEPARTMENT STORE

45 🔒 Map p134, F1

Blockbuster Bloomie's is something like the Metropolitan Museum of Art of the shopping world: historic, sprawling, overwhelming and packed with bodies, but you'd be sorry to miss it. Raid the racks for clothes and shoes from a who's who of US and global designers, including a number of 'new-blood' collections. Refuel pit stops include a branch of cupcake heaven Magnolia Bakery. (📞212-705-2000; www.bloomingdales.com; 1000 Third Ave, at E 59th St, Midtown East; ⏲10am-8:30pm Mon & Tue, to 10pm Wed-Sat, to 9pm Sun; 🛜; 🆂4/5/6 to 59th St; N/Q/R to Lexington Ave-59th St)

Bergdorf Goodman   DEPARTMENT STORE

46 🔒 Map p134, E1

Not merely loved for its Christmas windows (the city's best), plush BG leads the fashion race, its fashion director Linda Fargo considered an Anna Wintour of sorts. A mainstay of ladies who lunch, its drawcards include exclusive collections of Tom Ford and Chanel shoes and a coveted women's shoe department. The men's store is across the street. (📞212-753-7300; www.bergdorfgoodman.com; 754 Fifth Ave, btwn 57th & 58th Sts; ⏲10am-8pm Mon-Sat, 11am-7pm Sun; 🆂N/Q/R to 5th Ave-59th St; F to 57th St)

Uniqlo FASHION

47 🔒 Map p134, E2

Uniqlo is Japan's answer to H&M and this is its showstopping 89,000-sq-ft flagship megastore. Grab a mesh bag at the entrance and let the elevators whoosh you up to the 3rd floor to begin your retail odyssey. The forte here is affordable, fashionable, quality basics, from T-shirts and undergarments to Japanese denim, cashmere sweaters and super-light, high-tech parkas. (📞877-486-4756; www.uniqlo.com; 666 Fifth Ave, at 53rd St; ⏰10am-9pm Mon-Sat, 11am-8pm Sun; 🚇E, M to 5th Ave-53rd St)

Nepenthes New York FASHION

48 🔒 Map p134, C4

Occupying an old sewing shop in the Garment District, this cult Japanese collective stocks edgy menswear from the likes of Engineered Garments and Needles, known for their quirky detailing and artisanal production value (think tweed lace-up hem pants). Accessories include bags and satchels, gloves, eyewear and footwear. (📞212-643-9540; www.nepenthesny.com; 307 W 38th St, btwn Eighth & Ninth Aves, Midtown West; ⏰noon-7pm Mon-Sat, to 5pm Sun; 🚇A/C/E to 42nd St-Port Authority Bus Terminal)

Hell's Kitchen Flea Market MARKET

49 🔒 Map p134, B4

This weekend flea lures both collectors and the common curious with its wonderful booty of vintage furnishings, accessories, clothing and unidentifiable objects from past eras. (📞212-243-5343; www.annexmarkets.com; 39th St, btwn Ninth & Tenth Aves, Midtown West; ⏰9am-5pm Sat & Sun; 🚇A/C/E to 42nd St)

B&H Photo Video ELECTRONICS

50 🔒 Map p134, C5

Visiting NYC's most popular camera shop is an experience in itself – it's massive and crowded, and bustling with black-clad (and tech-savvy) Hasidic Jewish salesmen. Your chosen item is dropped into a bucket, which then moves up and across the ceiling to the purchase area (which requires a second queue). (📞212-444-6615; www.bhphotovideo.com; 420 Ninth Ave, btwn 33rd & 34th Sts, Midtown West; ⏰9am-7pm Mon-Thu, to 2pm Fri, 10am-6pm Sun, closed Sat; 🚇A/C/E to 34th St-Penn Station)

Macy's DEPARTMENT STORE

51 🔒 Map p134, D5

Fresh from a much-needed facelift, the world's largest department store covers most bases, with fashion, furnishings, kitchenware, sheets, cafes, hair salons and even a branch of the Metropolitan Museum of Art gift store. It's more 'mid-priced' than 'exclusive,' with mainstream labels and big-name cosmetics. The store also houses a NYC Information Center (p245) with information desk and free city maps. (📞212-695-4400; www.macys.com; 151 W 34th St, at Broadway; ⏰9:30am-

Chrysler Building (p137)

10pm Mon & Wed-Fri, to 9:30pm Tue, 10am-10pm Sat, 11am-9pm Sun; **S**B/D/F/M, N/Q/R to 34th St-Herald Sq)

Time Warner Center   MALL

52 Map p134, C1

A great add-on to an adventure in Central Park, the swank Time Warner Center has a fine lineup of largely up-scale vendors including Coach, Eileen Fisher, Williams-Sonoma, True Religion, Sephora and J Crew. For salubrious picnic fare, visit the enormous **Whole Foods** (☏212-823-9600; www.wholefoodsmarket.com) in the basement. (☏212-823-6300; www.theshopsatcolumbuscircle.com; Time Warner Center, 10 Columbus Circle; ⊗10am-9pm Mon-Sat, 11am-7pm Sun; **S**A/C, B/D, 1 to 59th St-Columbus Circle)

Explore

Upper East Side

High-end boutiques line Madison Ave and sophisticated mansions run parallel along Fifth Ave, culminating in an architectural flourish called Museum Mile – one of the most cultured strips in the city, if not the world. It's here that you'll find the gigantic Metropolitan Museum of Art holding court with its learned siblings – Guggenheim, Whitney and Frick – in orbit.

The Sights in a Day

☀ Start the morning with a fine Viennese-style breakfast at **Café Sabarsky** (p170). Afterwards, head upstairs to the exquisite collections of the **Neue Galerie** (p166). Stroll up to the **Guggenheim Museum** (p162) for a look at its wild facade, then head to the magnificent **Metropolitan Museum of Art** (p158). Limit your art exploring to a couple of hours (there's much more to see today!). Cap off the visit with a drink in the rooftop garden.

☀ Have lunch at earth-friendly **Candle Cafe** (p169), then walk to the **Frick Collection** (p165) to explore its treasure trove of Old Masters set inside an opulent mansion. End the afternoon with window-shopping along Madison Ave, perhaps lingering at **Encore** (p175) for some secondhand designer clothing.

☾ In the evening, attend a book signing or a performance at the **92nd Street Y** (p172). Afterwards (assuming you've booked in advance), enjoy a sushi feast at **Tanoshi** (p170). While UES nightlife is limited, the scene has improved in recent years. New neighborhood favorite the **Daisy** (p171) is a great place to sample creative cocktails and inventive small plates.

◉ Top Sights

Metropolitan Museum of Art (p158)

Guggenheim Museum (p162)

♥ Best of New York City

Eating
Tanoshi (p170)

Boqueria (p168)

Up Thai (p168)

Candle Cafe (p169)

Beyoglu (p169)

Drinking
Uva (p171)

Daisy (p171)

Bondurants (p172)

Vinus & Marc (p172)

Getting There

S Subway The main subway lines in this neighborhood are the 4/5/6, traveling north–south on Lexington Ave. The new Second Ave line should be running by the time you read this.

🚌 Bus The M1, M2, M3 and M4 make the scenic drive down Fifth Ave beside Central Park. The M15 is handy for getting around the far eastern side, traveling up First Ave and down Second.

Top Sights
Metropolitan Museum of Art

This sprawling encyclopedic museum, founded in 1870, houses one of the biggest art collections in the world. Its permanent collection has more than two million individual objects, from Egyptian temples to American paintings. Known colloquially as 'The Met,' the museum attracts over six million visitors a year to its 17 acres of galleries – making it the largest single-site attraction in New York City.

◉ Map p164, A2

☎ 212-535-7710

www.metmuseum.org

1000 Fifth Ave, at 82nd St

suggested donation adult/child $25/free

🕒 10am-5:30pm Sun-Thu, to 9pm Fri & Sat

Ⓢ 4/5/6 to 86th St

Temple of Dendur

Don't Miss

Egyptian Art

The museum has an unrivaled collection of ancient Egyptian art, some of which dates back to the Paleolithic era. Located to the north of the Great Hall, the 39 Egyptian galleries open dramatically with one of the Met's prized pieces: the Mastaba Tomb of Perneb (c 2300 BC), an Old Kingdom burial chamber crafted from limestone. From here, a web of rooms is cluttered with funerary stele, carved reliefs and fragments of pyramids. (Don't miss the intriguing Models of Meketre, clay figurines meant to help in the afterlife, in Gallery 105.) These eventually lead to the Temple of Dendur (Gallery 131), a sandstone temple to the goddess Isis that resides in a sunny atrium gallery with a reflecting pool – a must-see for the first-time visitor.

Greek & Roman Art

The 27 galleries devoted to classical antiquity are another Met doozy. From the Great Hall, a passageway takes viewers through a barrel vaulted room flanked by the chiseled torsos of Greek figures. This spills right into one of the Met's loveliest spaces: the airy Roman sculpture court (Gallery 162), full of marble carvings of gods and historical figures. The statue of a bearded Hercules from AD 68–98, with a lion's skin draped about him, is particularly awe-inspiring.

European Paintings

On the museum's 2nd floor, the European galleries display a stunning collection of masterworks. This includes more than 1700 canvases from the roughly 500-year-period starting in the 13th century, with works by every important painter from Duccio to Rembrandt. In fact, everything here

☑ Top Tips

▶ Don't try to see the entire collection in one day. Pick a few collections and really immerse yourself.

▶ A desk inside the Great Hall has audio tours in several languages ($7); you can also access audio tours for free if you have a smartphone.

▶ Docents offer free guided tours of galleries. Check the website or info desk for details.

▶ Kids love the Egyptian, African and Oceania galleries (great masks) and the collection of medieval arms and armor. The Met hosts plenty of kid-centric happenings and distributes a special kids' museum brochure and map.

✕ Take a Break

The casual **Petrie Court Cafe** serves tasty salads, soups, pasta and hot sandwiches, plus wine and a good tea selection, in an airy setting with floor-to-ceiling windows overlooking Central Park.

is, literally, a masterpiece. In Gallery 621, are several Caravaggios, including the masterfully painted *The Denial of St Peter*. Gallery 611, to the west, is packed with Spanish treasures, including El Greco's famed *View of Toledo*. Continue south to Gallery 632 to see various Vermeers, including the *Young Woman with a Water Pitcher*. Nearby, in Gallery 634, gaze at several Rembrandts, including a 1660 self-portrait. And that's just the beginning. You could spend hours exploring these many powerful works.

Art of the Arab Lands

On the 2nd floor you'll find the Islamic galleries with 15 incredible rooms showcasing the museum's extensive collection of art from the Middle East and Central and South Asia. In addition to garments, secular decorative objects and manuscripts, you'll find gilded and enameled glassware (Gallery 452) and a magnificent 14th-century *mihrab* (prayer niche) lined with elaborately patterned polychrome tilework (Gallery 455). There is also a superb array of Ottoman

Armor of Henry II of France

A 14th-century *mihrab* (prayer niche)

American Wing

textiles (Gallery 459), a medieval-style
Moroccan court (Gallery 456) and an
18th-century room from Damascus
(Gallery 461).

American Wing
In the northwestern corner, the
American galleries showcase a wide
variety of decorative and fine art from
throughout US history. These include
everything from colonial portraiture
to Hudson River School masterpieces
to John Singer Sargent's unbearably
sexy *Madame X* (Gallery 771) – not to
mention Emanuel Leutze's massive
canvas of *Washington Crossing the
Delaware* (Gallery 760).

Roof Garden
One of the best spots in the entire
museum is the roof garden, which
features rotating sculpture installations by contemporary and 20th-
century artists. (Jeff Koons, Andy
Goldsworthy and Imran Qureshi have
all shown here.) But its best feature
are the views it offers of the city and
Central Park. It's also home to the
Roof Garden Café & Martini Bar, an
ideal spot for a drink – especially at
sunset. The roof garden is open from
April to October.

Top Sights
Guggenheim Museum

A sculpture in its own right, architect Frank Lloyd Wright's building almost overshadows the collection of 20th-century art that it houses. Completed in 1959, the inverted ziggurat structure was derided by some critics but hailed by others who welcomed it as a beloved architectural icon. Since it first opened, this unusual structure has appeared on countless postcards, TV programs and films.

👁 Map p164, A1

📞 212-423-3500

www.guggenheim.org

1071 Fifth Ave, at 89th St

adult/child $25/free

🕙10am-5:45pm Sun-Wed & Fri, to 7:45pm Sat, closed Thu

Ⓢ4/5/6 to 86th St

Exterior, Solomon R Guggenheim Museum, New York ©SRGF, NY

Don't Miss

Permanent Collection Galleries

Although the Museum of Modern Art has garnered a reputation in New York City for having a more robust collection of oeuvres, the Guggenheim is very much a heavy hitter as well, boasting a variety of art from the 20th and 21st centuries. Hanging on the whitewashed walls are works by the likes of Kandinsky, Picasso, Chagall, Jackson Pollock, Van Gogh, Monet, Magritte and Degas. Much of the Guggenheim's art is made up of several personal collections, including those of Justin Thannhauser, Peggy Guggenheim and the Robert Mapplethorpe Foundation, which generously bequeathed 200 photographs, making the museum the single-most important public repository of his work.

Exterior Views of the Facade

Wright made hundreds of sketches and pondered the use of various materials for the construction of the museum. At one point he considered using red marble for the exterior facade – a 1945 model sketch shows a pink building – but the color scheme was rejected. Like any development in New York City, the project took forever to come to fruition. Construction was delayed for almost 13 years due to budget constraints, the outbreak of WWII and outraged neighbors who weren't all that excited to see an architectural spaceship land in their midst. Construction was completed in 1959, after both Wright and Guggenheim had passed away.

☑ Top Tips

▶ The line to get into the museum can be brutal at any time of the year. You'll save a lot of time if you purchase your tickets in advance on the website.

▶ If you have a smart-phone, download the Guggenheim's free app, which has info on the building and the collections in five languages.

▶ Entry is by donation from 5:45pm to 7:45pm Saturdays.

✗ Take a Break

There are two good on-site food options: **Wright**, at ground level, a space-age eatery serving steamy risotto and classic cocktails, and **Cafe 3** on the 3rd floor, which offers sparkling views of Central Park and excellent coffee and light snacks.

A

7 Jewish Museum
8
Museum of the City of New York

B

E 93rd St
E 92nd St
E 91st St

C

D

400
0.2 mile

1

31
10 17
2
Cooper-Hewitt National Design Museum
5 National Academy Museum

24

25

Gracie Mansion 4

Guggenheim Museum

E 90th St
E 89th St
E 88th St
E 87th St

First Ave

27

Jacqueline Kennedy Onassis Reservoir

3 Neue Galerie

86th St

YORKVILLE

86th St

E 86th St

Carl Schurz Park

Metropolitan Museum of Art

33

Fifth Ave

Park Ave

Madison Ave

Lexington Ave

Third Ave

Second Ave

York Ave

East End Ave

22   23

E 85th St
E 84th St
E 83rd St
E 82nd St
E 81st St
E 80th St

2

12
32

26
29
16

East River

79th St Transverse

UPPER EAST SIDE

E 79th St
E 78th St

John Jay Park

Central Park

77th St

21

Franklin D Roosevelt Dr

East End Ave

28
34

E 77th St
E 76th St

13

18

3

19

15
11 14

30

Conservatory Water

72nd St Transverse

72nd St

20

E 75th St
E 74th St
E 73rd St

E 72nd St

The Mall

Asia Society & Museum

6

E 71st St
E 70th St
E 69th St

New York Hospital-Cornell Medical Center

Rockefeller University

Roosev Isla

1

Frick Collection

68th St-Hunter College

E 68th St
E 67th St
E 66th St

4

9
Temple Emanu-El

65th St Transverse

Lexington Ave-63rd St

E 65th St
E 64th St
E 63rd St
E 62nd St

For reviews see

5

5th Ave-59th St

Lexington Ave-59th St

59th St

E 61st St
E 60th St

Roosevelt Island Tramway Station

Ed Koch
Queensboro Bridge

Central Park South

The Pond

Central Park South

E 59th St

Top Sights   p158
Sights   p165
Eating   p167
Drinking   p171
Entertainment   p174
Shopping   p174

Exhibit at the Asia Society & Museum (p167)

Sights

Frick Collection
GALLERY

1 ◎ Map p164, A4

This spectacular art collection sits in a mansion built by prickly steel magnate Henry Clay Frick, one of the many such residences that made up Millionaires' Row. The museum has over a dozen splendid rooms that display masterpieces by Titian, Vermeer, Gilbert Stuart, El Greco and Goya. (☎212-288-0700; www.frick.org; 1 E 70th St, at Fifth Ave; admission $20, by donation 11am-1pm Sun, children under 10 not admitted; ◎10am-6pm Tue-Sat, 11am-5pm Sun; ⓢ6 to 68th St-Hunter College)

Cooper-Hewitt National Design Museum
MUSEUM

2 ◎ Map p164, A1

Part of the Smithsonian Institution in Washington, DC, this house of culture is the only museum in the country that's dedicated to both historic and contemporary design. The collection is housed in the 64-room mansion built by billionaire Andrew Carnegie in 1901. The 210,000-piece collection is exquisite, with artful displays spanning 3000 years spread across four floors of the building. An extensive three-year renovation, completed in 2014, brings novelty to its exhibitions with interactive touch screens and wild technology. (☎212-849-8400; www

Understand
Second Avenue Subway

Although it was first proposed back in the 1920s, it took nearly 100 years before the Second Ave subway line became a reality. After nine years and some $4.5 billion spent on construction, the first section should be open by early 2017. The line, an extension of the Q train, has stations on 72nd St, 86th St and 96th St. More stations are planned in the (distant) years ahead.

.cooperhewitt.org; 2 E 91st St, at Fifth Ave; adult/child/student $18/free/9, by donation 6-9pm Sat; ⌚10am-6pm Sun-Fri, to 9pm Sat; S4/5/6 to 86th St)

Neue Galerie

MUSEUM

3 👁 Map p164, A2

This restored Carrère and Hastings mansion from 1914 is a resplendent showcase for German and Austrian art, featuring works by Paul Klee, Ernst Ludwig Kirchner and Egon Schiele. In pride of place on the 2nd floor is Gustav Klimt's golden 1907 portrait of Adele Bloch-Bauer – which was acquired for the museum by cosmetics magnate Ronald Lauder for a whopping $135 million. (☎212-628-6200; www.neuegalerie.org; 1048 Fifth Ave, cnr E 86th St; admission $20, 6-8pm 1st Fri of the month free, children under 12yr not admitted; ⌚11am-6pm Thu-Mon; S4/5/6 to 86th St)

Gracie Mansion

HISTORIC BUILDING

4 👁 Map p164, D1

This Federal-style home served as the country residence of merchant Archibald Gracie in 1799. Since 1942, it has been where New York's mayors have lived – with the exception of Mayor Michael Bloomberg, who preferred his own plush, Upper East Side digs. The house has been added to and renovated over the years. To peer inside, you'll have to go online to reserve a spot on one of the 45-minute house tours held once a week (less frequently during the holiday season). (www.nyc.gov/gracie; East End Ave, at E 88th St; ⌚tours 10am, 11am, 2pm & 3pm Tue; S4/5/6 to 86th St)

National Academy Museum

GALLERY

5 👁 Map p164, A1

Co-founded by painter/inventor Samuel Morse in 1825, the National Academy Museum comprises an incredible permanent collection of paintings by figures such as Will Barnet, Thomas Hart Benton and George Bellows. (This includes some highly compelling self-portraits.) It's housed in a beaux-arts structure designed by Ogden Codman Jr and featuring a marble foyer and spiral staircase. (☎212-369-4880; www.nationalacademy.org; 1083 Fifth Ave, at 89th St; admission by donation; ⌚11am-6pm Wed-Sun; S4/5/6 to 86th St)

Asia Society & Museum
MUSEUM

6 ◉ Map p164, B4

Founded in 1956 by John D Rockefeller (an avid collector of Asian art), this cultural center hosts fascinating exhibits (pre-Revolutionary art of Iran, retrospectives of leading Chinese artists, block prints of Edo-era Japan), as well as Jain sculptures and Nepalese Buddhist paintings. There are daily tours (free with admission) at 2pm Tuesday through Sunday year-round and at 6:30pm Friday (excluding summer months). (☎212-288-6400; www. asiasociety.org; 725 Park Ave, at E 70th St; adult/child $12/free, 6-9pm Fri mid-Sep–Jun free; ☺11am-6pm Tue-Sun, to 9pm Fri mid-Sep–Jun; ⑤6 to 68th St-Hunter College)

Jewish Museum
MUSEUM

7 ◉ Map p164, A1

This New York City gem is tucked into a French-Gothic mansion from 1908, housing 30,000 items of Judaica, as well as sculpture, painting and decorative arts. It hosts excellent temporary exhibits, featuring retrospectives on influential figures such as Art Spiegelman, as well as world-class shows on the likes of Marc Chagall, Édouard Vuillard and Man Ray among other past luminaries. (☎212-423-3200; www.thejewishmuseum.org; 1109 Fifth Ave, btwn 92nd & 93rd Sts; adult/child $15/free, Sat free, by donation 5-8pm Thu; ☺11am-6pm Sat-Tue, to 8pm Thu, to 4pm Fri, closed Wed; ♿; ⑤6 to 96th St)

Museum of the City of New York
MUSEUM

8 ◉ Map p164, A1

Situated in a colonial Georgian-style mansion, this local museum focuses solely on New York City's past, present and future. Don't miss the 22-minute film *Timescapes* (on the 2nd floor), which charts NYC's growth from tiny native trading post to burgeoning metropolis. (☎212-534-1672; www.mcny. org; 1220 Fifth Ave, btwn 103rd & 104th Sts; suggested admission adult/child $14/free; ☺10am-6pm; ⑤6 to 103rd St)

Temple Emanu-El
SYNAGOGUE

9 ◉ Map p164, A4

Founded in 1845 as the first Reform synagogue in New York, this temple, completed in 1929, is now one of the largest Jewish houses of worship in the world. An imposing Romanesque structure, it is more than 175ft long and 100ft tall, with a brilliant, hand-painted ceiling with gold details. (☎212-744-1400; www.emanuelnyc.org; 1 E 65th St, cnr Fifth Ave; ☺10am-4:30pm Sun-Thu; ⑤6 to 68th St-Hunter College)

Eating

Earl's Beer & Cheese
AMERICAN $

10 ✕ Map p164, B1

Chef Corey Cova's tiny comfort-food outpost channels a hipster hunting vibe, complete with a giant mural of a deer in the woods and a mounted buck's head. Basic grilled cheese is a paradigm shifter, served with pork belly, fried egg and kimchi. There is also mac 'n' cheese (with goat's cheese and crispy rosemary) and tacos (featuring braised pork shoulder and *queso fresco*). (212-289-1581; www.earlsny.com; 1259 Park Ave, btwn 97th & 98th Sts; grilled cheese $8; 11am-midnight Sun-Thu, to 2am Fri & Sat; 6 to 96th St)

JG Melon
PUB FOOD $

11 Map p164, B3

JG's is a loud, old-school pub that has been serving juicy burgers on tea plates since 1972. It's a local favorite for both eating and drinking (the Bloody Marys are excellent) and it gets crowded in the after-work hours. (212-744-0585; 1291 Third Ave, at 74th St; mains $11-18; 11:30am-4am; 6 to 77th St)

Top Tip

In Search of Cheap Eats

The Upper East Side is ground zero for all things luxurious, especially the area that covers the blocks from 60th to 86th Sts between Park and Fifth Aves. As a general rule, if you're looking for eating and drinking spots that are easier on the wallet, head east of Lexington Ave. First, Second and Third Aves are lined with less pricey neighborhood spots.

William Greenberg Desserts
BAKERY $

12 Map p164, A2

Make a pit stop here for New York City's finest black-and-white cookies – soft vanilla discs dipped in white sugar and dark chocolate glazes. Takeout only. (212-861-1340; www.wmgreenbergdesserts.com; 1100 Madison Ave, btwn E 82nd & 83rd Sts; baked goods from $3; 8am-6:30pm Mon-Fri, to 6pm Sat, 10am-4pm Sun; ; 4/5/6 to 86th St)

Boqueria
SPANISH $$

13 Map p164, C3

This lively, much-loved tapas place brings a bit of downtown cool to the Upper East Side, with nicely spiced *patatas bravas,* tender slices of jamon ibérico and rich *pulpo a gallega* (grilled octopus). Head chef Marc Vidal, who hails from Barcelona, also creates an exquisite seafood paella. (212-343-2227; www.boquerianyc.com; 1460 Second Ave, btwn 76th & 77th Sts; tapas $6-16, paella for two $38-46; noon-11pm Mon-Fri, 11am-11pm Sat & Sun; 6 to 77th St)

Up Thai
THAI $$

14 Map p164, C3

Hands down the best Thai place in the Upper East Side, this narrow but artfully designed restaurant serves a mix of traditional and innovative recipes. Standouts here include creamy rich Tom Kah soup (with coconut broth and vegetables), pillowy steamed chive dumplings and crispy duck breast with tamarind sauce. (212-256-1199;

GOQONG/CONTRIBUTOR/GETTY IMAGES ©

Artifact displayed at the Jewish Museum (p167)

www.upthainyc.com; 1411 Second Ave, btwn 73rd & 74th Sts; mains $15-30; ⊙noon-10:30pm Sun-Thu, to 11:30pm Fri & Sat; ⊿; ⑤6 to 77th St)

Candle Cafe
VEGAN $$

15 ✖ Map p164, B3

The moneyed, yoga set piles into this attractive vegan cafe serving a long list of sandwiches, salads, comfort food and market-driven specials. The specialty here is the housemade seitan. There is a juice bar and a gluten-free menu. (⌕212-472-0970; www.candlecafe.com; 1307 Third Ave, btwn 74th & 75th Sts; mains $15-22; ⊙11:30am-10:30pm Mon-Sat, to 9:30pm Sun; ⊿; ⑤6 to 77th St)

Beyoglu
TURKISH $$

16 ✖ Map p164, B2

A longtime favorite of Mediterranean-craving Upper East Siders, Beyoglu whips up meze (appetizer) platters that are ideal for sharing. Morsels include creamy rich hummus, juicy lamb kebabs, tender grape leaves and lemon-scented char-grilled octopus. Beyoglu has an airy and comfy interior, although on sunny days you might prefer to head to one of the sidewalk tables in front. (⌕212-650-0850; 1431 Third Ave, at 81st St; mains $16-18, sharing plates $6-8; ⊙noon-10pm Sun-Thu, to 11pm Fri & Sat; ⊿; ⑤6 to 77th St, 4/5/6 to 86th St)

ABV

MODERN AMERICAN $$

17 ✖️ Map p164, B1

On the borderline of East Harlem, ABV draws a young, laid-back crowd who come for eclectic sharing plates (wild morels and ramps, chicken liver mousse), heartier mains (roasted Maine scallops, buttermilk-brined fried chicken), wine ($9 to $14 per glass) and craft beers. Tall ceilings and brick walls invite lingering, and it's not a bad spot to catch the game (Yankees, Mets, Giants etc). (☎212-722-8959; www.abvny.com; 1504 Lexington Ave, at 97th St; mains $17-24; ⏱5pm-midnight Mon-Fri, 11am-midnight Sat & Sun; 🛜; ⑤6 to 96th St)

Jones Wood Foundry

BRITISH $$

18 ✖️ Map p164, C3

Inside a narrow brick building that once housed an ironworks, the Jones Wood Foundry is a British-inspired gastropub serving first-rate beer-battered fish and chips, bangers and mash, lamb and rosemary pie and other hearty temptations. On warm days, grab a table on the enclosed courtyard patio. (☎212-249-2700; www.joneswoodfoundry.com; 401 E 76th St, btwn First & York Aves; mains lunch $16-20, dinner $19-26; ⏱11am-11pm; 🛜; ⑤6 to 77th St)

Via Quadronno

CAFE $$

19 ✖️ Map p164, A3

A little slice of Italy that looks like it's been airlifted into New York, this cozy cafe-bistro has exquisite coffee, as well as a mind-boggling selection of sandwiches – piled high with delectable ingredients like prosciutto and Camembert. There are soups, pastas and a very popular daily lasagna. (☎212-650-9880; www.viaquadronno.com; 25 E 73rd St, btwn Madison & Fifth Aves; sandwiches $8-15, mains $23-38; ⏱8am-11pm Mon-Fri, 9am-11pm Sat, 10am-9pm Sun; 🖋; ⑤6 to 77th St)

Café Sabarsky

AUSTRIAN $$

The lines get long at this popular cafe at the Neue Galerie (see **3** ◉ Map p164, A2), which evokes opulent turn-of-the-century Vienna. But the well-rendered Austrian specialties make the wait worth it. Expect crepes with smoked trout, goulash soup and roasted bratwurst. There's also a long list of specialty sweets, including a divine Sacher torte (dark chocolate cake with apricot confiture). (☎212-288-0665; www.kg-ny.com/cafe-sabarsky; 1048 Fifth Ave, cnr E 86th St; mains $18-30; ⏱9am-6pm Mon & Wed, to 9pm Thu-Sun; 🖋🚻; ⑤4/5/6 to 86th St)

Tanoshi

SUSHI $$$

20 ✖️ Map p164, D3

It's not easy to snag one of the 20 stools at Tanoshi, a wildly popular sushi spot. The setting may be humble, but the flavors are simply magnificent; dishes might include Hokkaido scallops, Atlantic shad, seared salmon belly or mouthwatering *uni* (sea urchin). Only sushi is on offer and only *omakase* – the chef's

Temple Emanu-El (p167)

selection of whatever is particularly outstanding that day. BYO beer, sake or whatnot. Reserve well in advance. (☎917-265-8254; www.tanoshisushinyc.com; 1372 York Ave, btwn 73rd & 74th Sts; chef's sushi selection around $80; ☺6-10:30pm Mon-Sat; ⓢ6 to 77th St)

Drinking

Uva   WINE BAR

21 🍷 Map p164, C3

Rustic brick walls, low-lit chandeliers and worn floorboards give the feel of an old European tavern at this lively eating and drinking spot. There are dozens of wines by the glass (from $9) plus wine flights (before 7pm), allow-

ing you to sample a range of varietals – both Old World (particularly Italian) and New. (☎212-472-4552; www.uvanyc. com; 1486 Second Ave, btwn 77th & 78th Sts; ☺4pm-1am Mon-Fri, 11am-4pm Sat & Sun; ⓢ6 to 77th St)

The Daisy   BAR

22 🍷 Map p164, C2

Billing itself as an 'agave gastropub,' the Daisy serves up mescal cocktails and creative Latin-inspired drinks (Michelada) and dishes (rice with duck) alongside bistro fare like duck-fat fries and grilled octopus. Unlike most other UES bars, there are no TVs or bros here – it's a laid-back, low-lit spot, with good grooves, skilled

bartenders and a friendly crowd.
(☎646-964-5756; 1641 Second Ave, at 85th
St; ◷4pm-1am Sun-Wed, to 2am Thu-Sat;
§4/5/6 to 86th St)

Bondurants   BAR

23 🍷 Map p164, C2

Ticking all the boxes, Bondurants is
a craft beer and bourbon bar with
creative cocktails and a winning pub
menu (Gruyère mac and cheese, applewood smoked wings, flame-seared
shishito peppers). It has a wraparound
bar, vintage fixtures and TVs for the
sports minded. (☎212-249-1509; http://
bondurantsnyc.com; 303 E 85th St, btwn First
& Second Aves; ◷4pm-2am Mon-Fri, 11am-
2am Sat & Sun; §4/5/6 to 86th St)

Vinus & Marc   LOUNGE

24 🍷 Map p164, C1

Red walls, gilt-edge mirrors, vintage
fixtures and a long dark-wood bar set

Q Local Life
92nd Street Y
In addition to its wide spectrum
of concerts, dance performances
and literary readings, the nonprofit **92nd Street Y** (Map p164, B1;
☎212-415-5500; www.92y.org; 1395
Lexington Ave, at 92nd St; 🚸; §6 to
96th St) hosts an excellent lecture
and conversation series. Playwright
Edward Albee, cellist Yo-Yo Ma, fun-
nyman Steve Martin and novelist
Salman Rushdie have all taken the
stage here.

the stage at this inviting new lounge
in Yorkville. The cocktails range from
elegant inventions like the spicy Baby
Vamp (tequila, mescal, strawberry
and habanero bitters) to Prohibition-
era classics such as the Scofflaw (rye
whiskey, dry vermouth and housemade grenadine). (☎646-692-9105; www.
vinusandmarc.com; 1825 Second Ave, btwn
94th & 95th Sts; ◷noon-2am Mon-Fri, 10am-
3am Sat, 10am-1am Sun; §6 to 96th St)

Drunken Munkey   LOUNGE

25 🍷 Map p164, C1

This playful lounge channels colonial-
era Bombay with vintage wallpaper, cricket-ball door handles and
jauntily attired waitstaff. The monkey
chandeliers may be pure whimsy, but
the craft cocktails and tasty curries
(small, meant for sharing) are serious
business. Gin, not surprisingly, is
the drink of choice. Try the Bramble
(Bombay gin, blackberry liqueur and
fresh lemon juice and blackberries).
(☎646-998-4600; www.drunkenmunkeynyc.
com; 338 E 92nd St, btwn First & Second Aves;
◷11am-2am Mon-Thu, to 3am Fri-Sun; §6
to 96th St)

The Penrose   BAR

26 🍷 Map p164, C2

The Penrose brings a dose of style to
the Upper East Side, with craft beers,
exposed brick walls, vintage mirrors,
floral wallpaper, reclaimed wood
details and friendly bartenders setting
the stage for a fine evening outing
among friends. (☎212-203-2751; www.
penrosebar.com; 1590 Second Ave, btwn 82nd

Courtyard at the Frick Collection (p165)

& 83rd Sts; ⊙noon-4am Mon-Fri, 10am-4am
Sat & Sun; **S**4/5/6 to 86th St)

Auction House   BAR

27 Ⓣ Map p164, C1

Dark maroon doors lead into a
candlelit hangout that's perfect for a
relaxing drink. Victorian-style couches
and fat, overstuffed easy chairs are
strewn about the wood-floored rooms.
Take your well-mixed cocktail to a seat
by the fireplace and admire the scene
reflected in the gilt-edged mirrors
propped up on the walls. (☏212-427-
4458; www.auctionhousenyc.com; 300 E 89th
St, at Second Ave; ⊙7:30pm-2am Sun-Thu, to
4am Fri & Sat; **S**4/5/6 to 86th St)

Bemelmans Bar   LOUNGE

28 Ⓣ Map p164, B3

Sink into a chocolate leather ban-
quette and take in the glorious 1940s
elegance of this fabled bar at the
Carlyle Hotel – the sort of place where
the waiters wear white jackets, a
baby grand is always tinkling and the
ceiling is 24-carat gold leaf. Note the
charming murals by Ludwig Bemel-
mans (famed creator of *Madeline*).
(☏212-744-1600; www.rosewoodhotels.com/
en/the-carlyle-new-york; Carlyle Hotel, 35 E
76th St, at Madison Ave; ⊙noon-1am; **S**6 to
77th St)

Entertainment

Comic Strip Live
COMEDY

29 ⭐ Map p164, C2

Chris Rock, Adam Sandler, Jerry Seinfeld and Eddie Murphy have all performed at this club. Not recently, but you're sure to find somebody stealing their acts here most nights. Reservations required. (☏212-861-9386; www.comicstriplive.com; 1568 Second Ave, btwn 81st & 82nd Sts; cover charge $15-30, plus 2-drink min; ⏰shows 8:30pm Sun-Thu, 8:30pm, 10:30pm & 12:30am Fri, 8pm, 10:30pm & 12:30am Sat; Ⓢ4/5/6 to 86th St)

Frick Collection
CLASSICAL MUSIC

Once a month the opulent Frick Collection mansion-museum (see **1** ⏺ Map p164, A4) hosts a Sunday concert that brings world-renowned performers such as cellist Yehuda Hanani and violinist Thomas Zehetmair. (☏212-288-0700; www.frick.org; 1 E 70th St, at Fifth Ave; admission $40; Ⓢ6 to 68th St-Hunter College)

Café Carlyle
JAZZ

This swanky spot at the Carlyle Hotel (see **28** 🛏 Map p164, B3) draws top-shelf talent, including Woody Allen, who plays his clarinet here with the Eddy Davis New Orleans Jazz Band on Monday at 8:45pm (September through May). Bring bucks: the cover doesn't include food or drinks. (☏212-744-1600; www.thecarlyle.com/dining/cafe_carlyle; Carlyle Hotel, 35 E 76th St, at Madison Ave; cover $110-185; Ⓢ6 to 77th St)

Shopping

Marimekko
CLOTHING

30 🔒 Map p164, B4

This adorable store sells beautiful clothing and accessories adorned with colorful prints for which the Finnish designer is famed. Aside from dresses, skirts and tops, there's much eye candy here, including towels, umbrellas, bags, pillows, scarves, hats and fabric (designers may go weak in the knees). (☏212-628-8400; http://kiitos marimekko.com; 1262 Third Ave, btwn 72nd & 73rd Sts; ⏰10am-7pm Mon-Sat, noon-5pm Sun; Ⓢ6 to 68th St)

Blue Tree
FASHION, HOMEWARES

31 🔒 Map p164, B1

This charming (and expensive) little boutique, owned by actress Phoebe Cates Kline (of *Fast Times at Ridgemont High*) sells a dainty array of women's clothing, cashmere scarves, Lucite objects, whimsical accessories and quirky home design. (☏212-369-2583; www.bluetreenyc.com; 1283 Madison Ave, btwn 91st & 92nd Sts; ⏰10am-6pm Mon-Fri, 11am-6pm Sat; Ⓢ4/5/6 to 86th St)

Crawford Doyle Booksellers
BOOKS

32 🔒 Map p164, A2

This genteel bookstore invites browsing, with stacks devoted to art, literature and the history of New York – not to mention plenty of first editions. A wonderful place to while away a chilly

PANORAMIC IMAGES / GETTY IMAGES ©

Storefronts, Madison Ave

afternoon. (☏212-288-6300; http://craw
forddoyle.com; 1082 Madison Ave, btwn 81st &
82nd Sts; ⊙10am-6pm Mon-Sat, noon-5pm
Sun; ⑤6 to 77th St)

Encore   CLOTHING

33 🔒 Map p164, A2

An exclusive consignment store has
been emptying out Upper East Side
closets since the 1950s. (Jacqueline
Kennedy Onassis used to sell her
clothes here.) Expect to find a gently
worn selection of name brands such
as Louboutin, Fendi and Dior. Prices
are high but infinitely better than
retail. (☏212-879-2850; www.encoreresale.
com; 1132 Madison Ave, btwn 84th & 85th Sts;

⊙10:30am-6:30pm Mon-Sat, noon-6pm Sun;
⑤4/5/6 to 86th St)

Zitomer   BEAUTY

34 🔒 Map p164, B3

This multistory retro pharmacy
carries a treasure trove worth of high-
end, all-natural skincare products,
including brands like Kiehl's, Clarins,
Kneipp, Mustela and Ahava (made
from rejuvenating Dead Sea minerals).
On the 3rd floor, you can browse kids'
clothing and toys. (☏212-737-5560; www.
zitomer.com; 969 Madison Ave, btwn 75th &
76th Sts; ⊙9am-8pm Mon-Fri, to 7pm Sat,
10am-6pm Sun; ⑤6 to 77th St)

Explore

Upper West Side & Central Park

New York's antidote to the endless stretches of concrete, Central Park is a verdant escape from honking horns and sunless sidewalks. The Upper West Side lines the park with inspired residential towers, each one higher than the next. This area is most notably home to Lincoln Center, largely considered to hold the greatest concentration of performance spaces in town.

The Sights in a Day

☼ Start off with eggs and smoked fish at Jewish legend **Barney Greengrass** (p188). Afterwards, walk to the river and enjoy a scenic morning stroll down along **Riverside Park** (p185). Around 79th St, head inland to the **American Museum of Natural History** (p184) for a glimpse of the great marvels of millennia past. Afterwards, walk over to **Zabar's** (p179) to assemble a first-rate picnic.

☼ Spend the afternoon exploring **Central Park** (p178). Find a shaded spot on the edge of the lake for a picnic; get lost in the Ramble; stroll the elm-lined Mall; and watch buskers performing around Bethesda Fountain. For a pick-me-up, grab a coffee and a pastry at **Le Pain Quotidien** (p187).

☾ As the shadows grow long in Central Park, walk over to **Lincoln Center** (p184), New York's most celebrated destination for the performing arts. Catch an opera, a ballet or a symphony, then have a late-evening dinner of modern American cuisine at the always-lively bistro the **Smith** (p188). For a nightcap, check out the classy drinking den of the **Manhattan Cricket Club** (p189).

◉ Top Sights
Central Park (p178)

♥ Best of New York City

Eating
Barney Greengrass (p188)

Dovetail (p188)

Jacob's Pickles (p188)

Drinking
Manhattan Cricket Club (p189)

West End Hall (p190)

Entertainment
Metropolitan Opera House (p191)

New York City Ballet (p191)

Smoke (p192)

Getting There

⑤ Subway The 1/2/3 lines are good for destinations along Broadway and points west, while B and C trains are best for points of interest in and access to Central Park.

🚍 Bus M104 runs north–south along Broadway; M10 plies the scenic ride along the western edge of the park. Crosstown buses at 66th, 72nd, 79th, 86th and 96th Sts run through the park to the Upper East Side.

Top Sights
Central Park

Comprising more than 800 acres of picturesque meadows, ponds and woods, it might be tempting to think that Central Park represents Manhattan in its raw state. It does not. Designed by Frederick Law Olmsted and Calvert Vaux, the park is the result of serious engineering: thousands of workers shifted 10 million cartloads of soil to transform swamp and rocky outcroppings into the 'people's park' of today.

◉ Map p182, D5

www.centralparknyc.org

59th & 110th Sts, btwn Central Park West & Fifth Ave

⊙ 6am-1am

👬

Bethesda Fountain

Don't Miss

Bethesda Terrace & the Mall

The arched walkways of Bethesda Terrace, crowned by the magnificent Bethesda Fountain (at the level of 72nd St), have long been a gathering area for New Yorkers of all flavors. To the south is the Mall (featured in countless movies), a promenade shrouded in mature North American elms. The southern stretch, known as Literary Walk, is flanked by statues of famous authors.

Strawberry Fields

This tear-shaped **garden** (www.centralparknyc.org; Central Park, at 72nd St on the west side; ♿; §A/C, B to 72nd St) serves as a memorial to former Beatle John Lennon. The garden is composed of a grove of stately elms and a tiled mosaic that reads, simply, 'Imagine.'

Central Park Zoo

Officially known as Central Park Wildlife Center (no one calls it that), this small **zoo** (☎212-439-6500; www.centralparkzoo.com; Central Park, 64th St, at Fifth Ave; adult/child $12/7; ⏰10am-5:30pm May-Oct, to 4:30pm Nov-Apr; ♿; §N/Q/R to 5th Ave-59th St) is home to penguins, snow leopards, dart poison frogs and red pandas. Feeding times in the sea lion and penguin tanks make for a rowdy spectacle. (Check the website for times.) The attached **Tisch Children's Zoo** (www.centralparkzoo.com/animals-and-exhibits/exhibits/tisch-childrens-zoo.aspx; Central Park, at 65th & Fifth Ave; adult/child $12/7; ⏰10am-5:30pm May-Oct, to 4:30pm Nov-Apr; §N/Q/R to 5th Ave-59th St), a petting zoo, has alpacas and mini-Nubian goats and is perfect for small children.

☑ Top Tips

▶ Free and custom walking tours are available via the **Central Park Conservancy** (☎212-310-6600; www.centralparknyc.org/tours; 14 E 60th St; §N/Q/R to 5th Ave-59th St), a nonprofit organization that supports park maintenance.

▶ You can hire bikes at Loeb Boathouse or at the southwest entrance to the park, opposite Columbus Circle.

✗ Take a Break

Consider packing a picnic from the assortment of gourmet goodies at **Zabar's** (☎212-787-2000; www.zabars.com; 2245 Broadway, at 80th St; ⏰8am-7:30pm Mon-Fri, to 8pm Sat, 9am-6pm Sun; §1 to 79th St) or Whole Foods (p155), both a short hop from the park. Inside the park you can dine alfresco at casual Le Pain Quotidien (p187), or class things up a bit with a meal in the elegant Loeb Boathouse (p189).

Conservatory Water & Alice in Wonderland

North of the zoo at the level of 74th St is Conservatory Water, where model sailboats drift lazily and kids scramble about on a toadstool-studded statue of Alice in Wonderland. There are Saturday **story hours** (www.hcastorycenter. org) at 11am from June to September at the Hans Christian Andersen statue to the west of the water.

Great Lawn

The Great Lawn is a massive emerald carpet at the center of the park and is surrounded by ball fields and London plane trees. (This is where Simon & Garfunkel played their famous 1981 concert.) Immediately to the southeast is Delacorte Theater, home to an annual Shakespeare in the Park festival, as well as Belvedere Castle, a bird-watching lookout.

The Ramble

Further south is the leafy Ramble, a popular birding destination. On the southeastern end is the Loeb Boathouse (p186), home to a waterside restaurant that offers rowboat and bicycle rentals.

Jacqueline Kennedy Onassis Reservoir

The reservoir takes up almost the entire width of the park at the level of 90th St and serves as a gorgeous reflecting pool for the city skyline. It is surrounded by a 1.58-mile track that draws legions of joggers in the warmer months. Nearby, at Fifth Ave and 90th St, is a statue of New York City Marathon founder Fred Lebow, peering at his watch.

Conservatory Garden

If you want a little peace and quiet (as in, no runners, cyclists or buskers), the 6 acre Conservatory Garden serves as one of the park's official quiet zones. And it's beautiful, to boot: bursting with crabapple trees, meandering boxwood and, in the spring, lots of flowers. It's located at 105th St off Fifth Ave. Otherwise, you can catch maximum calm (and max bird life) in all areas of the park just after dawn.

Understand
Central Park

In the 1850s, the area now graced by Central Park was occupied by pig farms, a garbage dump, a bone-boiling operation and an African American village. It took thousands of laborers to shift 10 million cartloads of soil to transform swamp and rocky outcroppings into what is today the 'people's park'. Featuring more than 24,000 trees, 136 acres of woodland, 21 playgrounds and seven bodies of water, this giant green lung attracts more than 40 million visitors a year.

North Woods & Blockhouse

The North Woods, on the west side between 106th and 110th Sts, is home to the park's oldest structure, the Blockhouse, a military fortification from the War of 1812.

Summer Happenings in Central Park

During the warm months, Central Park is home to countless cultural events, many of which are free. The two most popular are: Shakespeare in the Park, which is managed by the **Public Theater** (www.publictheater. org), and **SummerStage** (www.summer stage.org; Rumsey Playfield, Central Park, access via Fifth Ave & 69th St; admission free; ⏱ Jun-Aug; ⑤ 6 to 68th St-Hunter College), a series of free concerts. Check out the websites for more information.

Metropolitan Museum of Art

E 79th St
Madison Ave
E 72nd St
E 65th St
5th Ave
E 59th St
Fifth Ave
5th Ave–59th St [S]
Central Park South
E 72nd St

Park

Great Lawn

81st St
Belvedere Castle ⦿ 6
79th St Transverse [S]
Turtle Pond

⦿ 8
Loeb Boathouse
Bow Bridge
Boathouse

The Ramble

The Lake

Cherry Hill
72nd St Transverse

Central Dr

The Mall
Sheep Meadow
Literary Walk

65th St Transverse

The Pond

Wollman Skating Rink
⦿ 7
Central Park Dr

Central Park South

Central Park West [S]
Central Park West
72nd St [S]

✗13
West Dr
West Dr

81st St ⦿ 30
Museum of Natural History [S]
American Museum of Natural History
⦿ 2
New-York Historical Society
⦿ 4
72nd St

W 81st St ⦿ 31
W 83rd St ⦿ 21
W 82nd St ✗9 ✗10
W 81st St ✗23
79th St [S]
⦿ 33
✗19
28 ★
18 ✗
11 ✗
W 80th St
W 79th St
W 78th St
W 77th St
W 76th St
W 75th St
W 74th St
W 73rd St
W 72nd St
W 71st St
W 70th St
W 69th St
W 68th St
W 67th St
W 66th St
W 65th St
W 64th St
W 63rd St
W 61st St
W 60th St
W 59th St

Columbus Ave

Broadway [S]

American Folk Art Museum
⦿ 3
✗16
W 66th St
24 ★
26 ⦿
⦿ 1 ★ 17
★ 25
Lincoln Center
Fordham University
66th St–Lincoln Center [S]

Columbus Circle [S]

Amsterdam Ave

West End Ave

Freedom Pl

Riverside Dr
West Side Hwy
⦿ 3

500 m
0.25 miles

For reviews see	
⦿ Top Sights	p178
⦿ Sights	p184
✗ Eating	p186
⦿ Drinking	p189
★ Entertainment	p191
🛍 Shopping	p194

5
6
7
8

A   B   C   D   E

Sights

Lincoln Center   CULTURAL CENTER

1 ◉ Map p182, C8

This stark arrangement of gleaming modernist temples contains some of Manhattan's most important performance spaces: Avery Fisher Hall (home to the New York Philharmonic), David H Koch Theater (site of the New York City ballet), and the iconic Metropolitan Opera House, whose interior walls are dressed with brightly saturated murals by painter Marc Chagall. Various other venues are tucked in and around the 16-acre campus, including a theater, two film-screening centers and the renowned Juilliard School. (☏212-875-5456, tours 212-875-5350; www.lincolncenter.org; Columbus Ave, btwn 62nd & 66th Sts; public plazas free, tours adult/student $18/15; ♿; Ⓢ1 to 66th St-Lincoln Center)

American Museum of Natural History   MUSEUM

2 ◉ Map p182, C5

Founded in 1869 this classic museum contains a veritable wonderland of more than 30 million artifacts, including lots of menacing dinosaur skeletons, as well as the Rose Center for Earth & Space, with its cutting-edge planetarium. From September through May, the museum is home to the Butterfly Conservatory, a glass-house featuring 500-plus butterflies from all over the world. (☏212-769-5100; www.amnh.org; Central Park West, at 79th St; suggested donation adult/child $22/12.50; ◷10am-5:45pm, Rose Center to 8:45pm Fri; ♿; Ⓢ B, C to 81st St-Museum of Natural History; 1 to 79th St)

American Folk Art Museum   MUSEUM

3 ◉ Map p182, C7

This tiny institution contains a couple of centuries' worth of folk and outsider art treasures, including pieces by Henry Darger (known for his girl-filled battlescapes) and Martín Ramírez (producer of hallucinatory *caballeros* on horseback). There is also an array of wood carvings, paintings, hand-tinted photographs and decorative objects. On Wednesday there are guitar concerts, and there's free music on Friday. (☏212-595-9533; www.folkart museum.org; 2 Lincoln Sq, Columbus Ave, at 66th St; admission free; ◷11:30am-7pm Tue-Thu & Sat, noon-7:30pm Fri, noon-6pm Sun; Ⓢ1 to 66th St-Lincoln Center)

New-York Historical Society   MUSEUM

4 ◉ Map p182, C6

As the antiquated hyphenation in its name implies, the Historical Society is the city's oldest museum, founded in 1804 to preserve the city's historical and cultural artifacts. Its collection of more than 60,000 objects is quirky and fascinating and includes everything from George Washington's inauguration chair to a 19th-century

Blue whale exhibit, American Museum of Natural History

Tiffany ice-cream dish (gilded, of course). (www.nyhistory.org; 170 Central Park West, at 77th St; adult/child $20/6, by donation 6-8pm Fri, library free; ⊙10am-6pm Tue-Thu & Sat, to 8pm Fri, 11am-5pm Sun; **S** B, C to 81st St-Museum of Natural History)

Riverside Park   PARK

5 ◉ Map p182, B1

A classic beauty designed by Central Park creators Frederick Law Olmsted and Calvert Vaux, this waterside spot, running north on the Upper West Side and banked by the Hudson River from 59th to 158th Sts, is lusciously leafy. Plenty of bike paths and playgrounds make it a family favorite. (☎212-870-3070; www.riversideparknyc.org; Riverside Dr, btwn 68th & 155th Sts; ⊙6am-1am; ⓡ; **S**1/2/3 to any stop btwn 66th & 157th Sts)

Belvedere
Castle   BIRD-WATCHING

6 ◉ Map p182, D5

For a DIY bird-watching expedition with the kids, borrow a 'Discovery Kit' at Belvedere Castle in Central Park. It comes with binoculars, a bird book, colored pencils and paper – a perfect way to get the kids excited about birds. Picture ID is required. (☎212-772-0288; Central Park, at 79th St; admission free; ⊙10am-5pm; ⓡ; **S**1/2/3, B, C to 72nd St)

STU99/GETTY IMAGES ©

Wollman Skating Rink

Wollman Skating Rink   SKATING

7 👁 Map p182, D8

Larger than the Rockefeller Center skating rink, and allowing all-day skating, this rink is at the southeastern edge of Central Park and offers nice views. Cash only. (📞212-439-6900; www.wollmanskatingrink.com; Central Park, btwn 62nd & 63rd Sts; adult Mon-Thu/Fri-Sun $11/18, child $6, skate rentals $8, lock rental $5, spectator fee $5; ⊙10am-2:30pm Mon & Tue, to 10pm Wed-Sat, to 9pm Sun Nov-Mar; 👤; 🅂F to 57 St; N/Q/R to 5th Ave-59th St)

Loeb Boathouse   KAYAKING, CYCLING

8 👁 Map p182, E6

Central Park's boathouse has a fleet of 100 rowboats as well as a Venetian-style gondola that seats up to six if you'd rather someone else do the paddling. Bicycles are also available, weather permitting. Rentals require ID and a credit card, and helmets are included. (📞212-517-2233; www.thecentral parkboathouse.com; Central Park, btwn 74th & 75th Sts; boating per hr $15, bike rental per hr $9-15; ⊙10am-6pm Apr-Nov; 👤; 🅂B, C to 72nd St; 6 to 77th St)

Eating

Peacefood Cafe   VEGAN $

9 🍴 Map p182, C5

This bright and airy vegan haven dishes up a popular fried seitan panino (served on homemade focaccia and topped with cashew cheese, arugula, tomatoes and pesto), as well as pizzas, roasted vegetable plates and an excellent quinoa salad. There are daily raw specials, energy-fueling juices and rich desserts. Healthy and good – for you, the animals and the environment. (212-362-2266; www.peacefoodcafe.com; 460 Amsterdam Ave, at 82nd St; mains $12-18; 10am-10pm; ; S1 to 79th St)

Jin Ramen
JAPANESE $

10 Map p182, C5

This buzzing little joint off Amsterdam Ave serves up delectable bowls of piping hot ramen. *Tonkotsu* (pork broth) ramen is a favorite though vegetarians also have options. Don't neglect the appetizers: *shishito* peppers, pork buns and *hijiki* salad. The mix of rustic wood elements, exposed bulbs and red industrial fixtures give the place a cozy vibe. (646-657-0755; www.jinramen.com; 462 Amsterdam Ave, btwn 82nd & 83rd Sts; mains $12-16; 11:30am-3:30pm & 5-11pm Mon-Sat, to 10pm Sun; ; S1 to 79th St)

Birdbath Bakery
BAKERY $

11 Map p182, C6

Aside from the lack of seating inside, it's hard to find fault with this delightful cafe. The menu changes daily and features excellent sandwiches, vitamin-rich juices and salads (try the chicken, kale and corn salad). The bakery items are outstanding. Birdbath also has an ecofriendly ethos implemented through the use

of green building materials, recycled woods, and deliveries made on bicycle. (646-722-6562; http://thecitybakery.com/birdbath-bakery; 274 Columbus Ave, at 72nd St; mains $10-14; 8am-7pm; ; S1/2/3, B, C to 72nd St)

Tum & Yum
THAI $

12 Map p182, C2

This small neighborhood Thai eatery whips up excellent curries, crispy roast duck and steaming bowls of rich Tom Yum shrimp soup – best washed down with fresh coconut juice or a sweet Thai iced coffee. The rustic all-wooden interior makes a cozy retreat when the weather sours. (212-222-1998; www.tumyumnyc.com; 917 Columbus Ave, at 105th St; mains $10-19; 11am-11pm; SB, C to 103rd St)

Le Pain Quotidien
SANDWICHES $

13 Map p182, D7

Fresh salads and tartines (open-faced sandwiches) are to be found inside the airy Mineral Springs Pavilion, or outside if you are lucky enough to snag a terrace seat. Other Le Pain treats include beautiful berry tarts, draft beer and big cups (bowls, really) of café au lait (plus free wi-fi). You can also hit the takeout window and have a picnic on Sheep Meadow, just a few steps away. (646-233-3768; www.lepainquotidien.com; Mineral Springs Pavilion, Central Park, off West Dr; mains $12-17, pastries $4-5; 7am-8pm Mon-Thu, to 9pm Fri-Sun; ; SB, C to 72nd St)

Barney Greengrass

DELI **$$**

14 Map p182, C4

The self-proclaimed 'King of Sturgeon,' Barney Greengrass serves up the same heaping dishes of eggs and salty lox, luxuriant caviar, and melt-in-your-mouth chocolate babkas that first made it famous when it opened a century ago. Pop in to fuel up in the morning or for a quick lunch; there are rickety tables set amid the crowded produce aisles. (☏212-724-4707; www.barneygreengrass.com; 541 Amsterdam Ave, at 86th St; mains $12-22; ◷8:30am-4pm Tue-Fri, to 5pm Sat & Sun; ⓢ1 to 86th St)

Jacob's Pickles

AMERICAN **$$**

15 Map p182, C5

Jacob's elevates the humble pickle to exalted status at this inviting and warmly lit eatery on a restaurant-lined stretch of Amsterdam Ave. Aside from briny cukes and other preserves, you'll find heaping portions of upscale comfort food, such as catfish tacos, wine-braised turkey leg dinner, and mushroom mac and cheese. The biscuits are top notch. (☏212-470-5566; www.jacobspickles.com; 509 Amsterdam Ave, btwn 84th & 85th Sts; mains $15-26; ◷10am-2am Mon-Thu, to 4am Fri, 9am-4am Sat, to 2am Sun; ⓢ1 to 86th St)

The Smith

MODERN AMERICAN **$$**

16 Map p182, C8

On a restaurant-lined strip across from Lincoln Center, this always buzzing bistro serves up high-end comfort food with seasonal accents. Braised short ribs with butternut squash, pastrami spiced salmon with roasted cauliflower, and chicken pot pie are a few recent selections. There's also a raw bar and myriad drink selections. On warm days, there's open-air seating in front. (☏212-496-5700; http://thesmithrestaurant.com; 1900 Broadway, btwn 63rd & 64th Sts; mains $17-44; ◷7:30am-midnight Mon-Fri, from 9am Sat & Sun; ⓢ1, A/C, B/D to 59th St-Columbus Circle)

PJ Clarke's

AMERICAN **$$**

17 Map p182, C8

Across the street from Lincoln Center, this spot has red-checked tablecloths, a buttoned-down crowd, friendly bartenders and a solid menu. If you're in a rush, belly up to the bar for a Black Angus burger and a Brooklyn Lager. A raw bar offers fresh Long Island Little Neck and Cherry Stone clams, as well as jumbo shrimp cocktails. (☏212-957-9700; www.pjclarkes.com; 44 W 63rd St, cnr Broadway; burgers $13-16, mains $20-26; ◷11:30am-2am; ⓢ1 to 66th St-Lincoln Center)

Dovetail

MODERN AMERICAN **$$$**

18 Map p182, C6

This Michelin-starred restaurant showcases its Zen-like beauty in both its decor (exposed brick, bare tables) and its delectable seasonal menus. Think: striped bass with sunchokes and burgundy truffle, and venison with bacon, golden beets and foraged greens. Each evening there are two

Rowboaters in Central Park with Belvedere Castle (p185) in the background

seven-course tasting menus: one for omnivores ($135) and one for vegetarians ($108). (☑212-362-3800; www. dovetailnyc.com; 103 W 77th St, cnr Columbus Ave; tasting menu $58-135; ⏱5:30-10pm Mon-Thu, to 11pm Fri & Sat, 5-10pm Sun; ✐; ⑤A/C, B to 81st St-Museum of Natural History; 1 to 79th St)

Loeb Boathouse   AMERICAN $$$

Perched on the northeastern tip of the Central Park Lake, the Loeb Boathouse (see ❽ ⊙ Map p182, E6), with its views of the Midtown skyline in the distance, provides one of New York's most idyllic spots for a meal. That said, what you're paying for is the setting. While the food is generally good (the crab cakes are the stand-

out), we've often found the service to be indifferent. (☑212-517-2233; www. thecentralparkboathouse.com; Central Park Lake, Central Park, at 74th St; mains $25-36; ⏱noon-4pm Mon-Fri, 9:30am-4pm Sat & Sun year-round, 6pm-9:30pm daily Apr-Nov; ⑤A/C, B to 72nd St; 6 to 77th St)

Drinking

Manhattan Cricket Club   COCKTAIL LOUNGE

19 🍸 Map p182, C5

Situated above an Australian **bistro** (☑646-823-9251; www.burkeandwillsny. com; mains lunch $19-26, dinner $20-45; ⏱noon-3pm & 5:30-11pm Mon-Fri, from 11am

Sat & Sun), this elegant drinking lounge is modeled on the classy Anglo-Aussie cricket clubs of the early 1900s. Sepia-toned photos of batsmen adorn the gold brocaded walls, while mahogany bookshelves and Chesterfield sofas create a fine setting for quaffing well-made – but pricey – cocktails. The Manhattan Cricket Club is a guaranteed date-pleaser. (☏646-823-9252; www.mccnewyork.com; 226 W 79th St, btwn Amsterdam Ave & Broadway; ⏰6pm-2am; ⑤1 to 79th St)

West End Hall BEER GARDEN

20 ⬤ Map p182, B1

Beer drinkers of the UWS have much to celebrate with the arrival of this grand beer hall that showcases craft brews from around Belgium, Germany, the US and beyond. There are roughly 20 drafts on rotation along with another 30 bottle choices, most of which go nicely with the meaty menu of sausages, schnitzel, pork sliders and an excellent truffle burger. (☏212-662-7200; www.westendhall. com; 2756 Broadway, btwn 105th & 106th Sts; ⏰4pm-1am Mon-Fri, from 11am Sat & Sun; ⑤1 to 103rd St)

Joe's BAR

21 ⬤ Map p182, C5

Joe's brings a bit of Brooklyn to the Upper West Side, with a changing lineup of craft beers, creative cocktails and moustached barkeeps. Exposed brick walls and wide plank floors give an old-fashioned jauntiness to the place, and the long wooden bar is a fine place to nosh on juicy burgers. (☏646-918-6510; http://joesbarnyc.com; 480 Amsterdam Ave, btwn 83rd & 84th Sts; ⏰4pm-4am Mon-Fri, from noon Sat & Sun; ⑤1 to 86th St)

Earth Cafe CAFE

22 ⬤ Map p182, B3

This charming neighborhood cafe fairly beckons you inside with its cheery, sunny interior of whitewashed brick walls and the scent of fresh-roasted coffee beans lingering in the air. Order an expertly poured almond latte, take a seat beside the oversized world map and watch the city glide past. (☏917-363-8867; 2850 Broadway, at 97th St; ⏰7am-11pm Mon-Fri, from 8am Sat & Sun; ⑨; ⑤1/2/3 to 96th St)

Dead Poet BAR

23 ⬤ Map p182, C5

This skinny, mahogany-paneled pub has been a neighborhood favorite for more than a decade. Join the mix of locals and students nursing pints of Guinness. There are also cocktails named after dead poets, including a Walt Whitman Long Island iced tea ($11) and a Pablo Neruda spiced rum sangria ($9). Which is funny, because we always pegged Neruda as a pisco sour kind of guy. (☏212-595-5670; www. thedeadpoet.com; 450 Amsterdam Ave, btwn 81st & 82nd Sts; ⏰noon-4am; ⑤1 to 79th St)

New York Philharmonic (p192) in concert

Entertainment

Metropolitan Opera House

OPERA

New York's premier opera company, the Metropolitan Opera is based at the Lincoln Center (see **1** ⊙ Map p182, C8) and is the place to see classics such as *Carmen*, *Madame Butterfly* and *Macbeth*, not to mention Wagner's *Ring Cycle*. The Opera also hosts premieres and revivals of more contemporary works, such as Peter Sellars' *Nixon in China*. The season runs from September to April. (✆tickets 212-362-6000, tours 212-769-7028; www.metopera.org; Lincoln Center, 64th St, at Columbus Ave; **S** 1 to 66th St-Lincoln Center)

New York City Ballet

DANCE

24 ✪ Map p182, C8

This prestigious ballet company was first directed by renowned Russian-born choreographer George Balanchine back in the 1940s. Today, the company has 90 dancers and is the largest ballet organization in the US, performing 23 weeks a year at Lincoln Center's David H Koch Theater. During the holidays the troop is best known for its annual production of *The Nutcracker*. (✆212-496-0600; www.nycballet.com; David H Koch Theater, Lincoln Center, Columbus Ave, at 62nd St; ♿; **S** 1 to 66th St-Lincoln Center)

Smoke

JAZZ

25 ⭐ Map p182, B1

This swank but laid-back lounge – where you'll get good stage views from plush sofas – brings out old-timers and local faves, such as George Coleman and Wynton Marsalis. Most nights there's a $10 cover, plus a $20 to $30 food and drink minimum spend. On Sundays there's a soulful jazz brunch from 11am to 4pm. Purchase tickets online for weekend shows. (📞212-864-6662; www.smokejazz.com; 2751 Broadway, btwn 105th & 106th Sts; ⏱5:30pm-3am Mon-Sat, 11am-3am Sun; 🚇1 to 103rd St)

Film Society of Lincoln Center

CINEMA

The Film Society is one of New York's cinematic gems, providing an invaluable platform for a wide gamut of documentary, feature, independent, foreign and avant-garde art pictures. Films screen in one of two facilities at Lincoln Center (see **1** ◎ Map p182, C8): the **Elinor Bunin Munroe Film Center** (📞212-875-5232; www.filmlinc.com; Lincoln Center, 144 W 65th St; 🚇1 to 66 St-Lincoln Center), a more intimate, experimental venue, or the **Walter Reade Theater** (📞212-875-5601; www.filmlinc.com; Lincoln Center, 165 W 65th St; 🚇1 to 66th St-Lincoln Center), with wonderfully wide, screening-room–style seats. (📞212-875-5610; www.filmlinc.com; 🚇1 to 66th St-Lincoln Center)

New York Philharmonic

CLASSICAL MUSIC

26 ⭐ Map p182, C8

The oldest professional orchestra in the US (dating back to 1842) holds its season every year at Avery Fisher Hall. Directed by Alan Gilbert, the son of two Philharmonic musicians, the orchestra plays a mix of classics (Tchaikovsky, Mahler, Haydn) and contemporary works, as well as concerts geared toward children. (📞212-875-5656; www.nyphil.org; Avery Fisher Hall, Lincoln Center, cnr Columbus Ave & 65th St; ♿; 🚇1 to 66 St-Lincoln Center)

Symphony Space

LIVE MUSIC

27 ⭐ Map p182, B3

Symphony Space is a multidisciplinary gem supported by the local community. It often hosts three-day series that are dedicated to one musician, and has an affinity for world music, theater, film, dance and literature (with appearances by acclaimed writers). (📞212-864-5400; www.symphonyspace.org; 2537 Broadway, btwn 94th & 95th Sts; 🚇1/2/3 to 96th St)

Beacon Theatre

LIVE MUSIC

28 ⭐ Map p182, C6

This historic 1929 theater is a perfect medium-size venue with 2600 seats (not a terrible one in the house) and a constant flow of popular acts from Nick Cave to Bryan Adams. A recent restoration has left the gilded

Understand
New York City on Page & Screen

New York City, more than any other place in the world, has been the setting of countless works of literature, television and film. From critical commentary on class and race to the lighter foibles of falling in love, New York's stories are not just entertainment; they are carefully placed tiles in the city's diverse mosaic of tales. In the lists below, you'll find some of our favorite movies and books that take place in – and are inspired by – this most wild and whimsical city.

Books
The Amazing Adventures of Kavalier & Clay (Michael Chabon, 2000) Beloved Pulitzer-winning novel that touches upon Brooklyn, escapism and the nuclear family.

A Tree Grows in Brooklyn (Betty Smith, 1943) An Irish-American family living in the Williamsburg tenements at the beginning of the 20th century.

Down These Mean Streets (Piri Thomas, 1967) Memoirs of tough times growing up in Spanish Harlem.

Invisible Man (Ralph Ellison, 1952) Poignant prose exploring the situation of African Americans in the early 20th century.

The Age of Innocence (Edith Wharton, 1920) Tales and trials of NYC's social elite in the late 1800s.

Films
Annie Hall (1977) Oscar-winning romantic comedy by the king of New York neuroses, Woody Allen.

Manhattan (1979) Allen's at it again with tales of twisted love set among NYC's concrete landscape.

Taxi Driver (1976) Scorsese's tale of a troubled taxi driver and Vietnam vet.

West Side Story (1961) A modern-day Romeo and Juliet set on the gang-ridden streets of New York.

Precious (2009) An unflinching tale of an obese, abused Harlem teenager determined to rise above her circumstances.

interiors – a mix of Greek, Roman, Renaissance and rococo design elements – totally sparkling. ([📞]212-465-6500; www.beacontheatre.com; 2124 Broadway, btwn 74th & 75th Sts; [S]1/2/3 to 72nd St)

Shopping

Shishi
CLOTHING

29 [🏠] Map p182, B3

A welcome addition to a fashion-challenged hood, Shishi is a delightful boutique stocking an ever-changing selection of stylish but affordable apparel. Recent finds include felt hats, elegant sweaters, eye-catching jewelry and soft flannels. It's a fun place to browse – the chandelier and vintage

◯ Local Life
Greenflea

Browsing this friendly, well-stocked **flea market** (Map p182, C6; [📞]212-239-3025; www.greenfleamarkets.com; 100 W 77th St, near Columbus Ave; [🕙]10am-5:30pm Sun; [S]B, C to 81st St-Museum of Natural History; 1 to 79th St), one of the oldest open-air shopping spots in the city, is a perfect activity for a lazy Upper West Side Sunday morning. You'll find a little bit of everything here, including vintage and contemporary furnishings, antique maps, custom eyewear, hand-woven scarves, handmade jewelry and so much more.

nude prints on the wall remind you this is no TJ Maxx. The friendly young staff offer helpful guidance. ([📞]646-692-4510; http://shishiboutique.com; 2488 Broadway, btwn 92nd & 93rd Sts; [🕙]11am-8pm Mon-Sat, to 7pm Sun; [S]1/2/3 to 96th St)

Unique Boutique
VINTAGE

30 [🏠] Map p182, C5

A first-rate vintage store on the Upper West Side is something of a rarity, so it's worth stopping in if you need to freshen up your wardrobe. The prices are excellent, though the sheer quantity of clothing means you'll have to dig. Aside from designer labels and friendly staff, you'll also find an extensive collection of CDs and books (hardbacks for a buck). (487 Columbus Ave, btwn 83rd & 84th Sts; [🕙]10am-8pm; [S]B, C to 86th St)

Magpie
CRAFTS

31 [🏠] Map p182, C5

When you're short of gift ideas, stop in this charming little outpost, where you'll find a wide range of eco-friendly objects. Elegant stationery, beeswax candles, hand-painted mugs, organic cotton scarves, recycled resin necklaces, hand-dyed felt journals and wooden earth puzzles are a few things that may catch your eye. Most products are fair-trade, made of sustainable materials or are locally designed and made. ([📞]646-998-3002; http://magpienewyork.com; 488 Amsterdam Ave, btwn 83rd & 84th Sts; [🕙]11am-7pm Tue-Sat, to 6pm Sun; [S]1 to 86th St)

Lincoln Center (p184)

West Side Kids TOYS

32 Map p182, C5

A great place to pick up a gift for that little someone special, no matter their age. Stocks lots of hands-on activities and fun but educational games, as well as puzzles, mini musical instruments, science kits (carnivorous creations? indeed), magic sets, snap circuits, old-fashioned wooden trains and building kits. (212-496-7282; www.westsidekidsnyc.com; 498 Amsterdam Ave; 10am-7pm Mon-Sat, 11am-6pm Sun; S 1 to 86th St)

Westsider Books BOOKS

33 Map p182, B5

This great little shop is packed to the gills with rare and used books, including a good selection of fiction and illustrated tomes. There are first editions and a smattering of vintage vinyl. (212-362-0706; www.westsiderbooks.com; 2246 Broadway, btwn 80th & 81st Sts; 10am-10pm; S 1 to 79th St)

Local Life
Harlem

Harlem: the neighborhood where Cab Calloway crooned; where Ralph Ellison penned *Invisible Man,* his epic novel on truth and intolerance; and where acclaimed artist Romare Bearden pieced together his first collages. Simultaneously vibrant and effusive, brooding and melancholy, Harlem is the deepest recess of New York's soul.

Getting There

Harlem is 5 miles north of Midtown.

S Take the A/D one stop from Columbus Circle. The 2/3 takes 15 minutes to reach Harlem from Times Square.

The M10 follows the west side of Central Park up into Harlem.

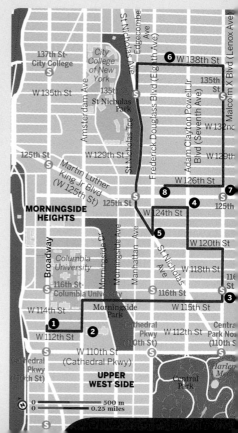

❶ Tom's Restaurant

Rev your engine with a cup o' joe and a side of nostalgia at **Tom's Restaurant** (☏212-864-6137; www.tomsrestaurant. net; 2880 Broadway, at 112th St; mains $7-13; ⏱6am-1:30am Sun-Thu, 24hr Fri & Sat; Ⓢ1 to 110th St), whose exterior earned stardom in the TV comedy *Seinfeld*.

❷ Come to Jesus

The **Cathedral Church of St John the Divine** (☏tours 212-316-7540; www.stjohndivine.org; 1047 Amsterdam Ave, at W 112th St, Morningside Heights; suggested donation $10, highlights tour $12, vertical tour $20; ⏱7:30am-6pm, highlights tour 11am & 2pm Mon, 11am & 1pm Tue-Sat, 1pm on selected Sun, vertical tour noon Wed & Fri, noon & 2pm Sat; Ⓢ B, C, 1 to 110th St-Cathedral Pkwy), with its Byzantine-style facade, is the largest place of worship in the United States.

❸ Malcolm Shabazz Harlem Market

Trawl the semi-enclosed **Malcolm Shabazz Harlem Market** (52 W 116th St, btwn Malcolm X Blvd & Fifth Ave, Harlem; admission free; ⏱10am-9pm; 🚻; Ⓢ2/3 to 116th St) for African jewelry, textiles, drums, leather goods and oils.

❹ Studio Museum in Harlem

It might be small, but the **Studio Museum in Harlem** (☏212-864-4500; www.studiomuseum.org; 144 W 125th St, at Adam Clayton Powell Jr Blvd, Harlem; suggested donation $7, Sun free; ⏱noon-9pm Thu & Fri, 10am-6pm Sat, noon-6pm Sun; Ⓢ2/3 to 125th St) plays a vital role in the promotion of African American art.

❺ Flamekeepers Hat Club

Harlem's Gilded Age lives on at **Flamekeepers Hat Club** (☏212-531-3542; www.flamekeepershatclub.com; 273 W 121st St, at St Nicholas Ave; ⏱noon-7pm Sun-Wed, to 8pm Thu & Fri, to 9pm Sat; ⓈA/C, B/D to 125th St), a friendly corner boutique lined with elegant hats.

❻ Strivers' Row

On 138th and 139th Sts, **Strivers' Row** (W 138th & W 139th Sts, btwn Frederick Douglass & Adam Clayton Powell Jr Blvds, Harlem; Ⓢ B, C to 135th St) is graced with 1890s townhouses. The area earned its nickname in the 1920s when aspiring African Americans first moved here.

❼ Red Rooster

Taste the 'new Harlem' at **Red Rooster** (☏212-792-9001; www.redroosterharlem. com; 310 Malcolm X Blvd, btwn 125th & 126th Sts, Harlem; mains $18-30; ⏱11:30am-10:30pm Mon-Thu, to 11:30pm Fri, 10am-11:30pm Sat, 10am-10pm Sun; Ⓢ2/3 to 125th St), where upscale comfort food meets global influences.

❽ Apollo Theater

End at the **Apollo Theater** (☏212-531-5300, tours 212-531-5337; www.apollotheater. org; 253 W 125th St, btwn Frederick Douglass & Adam Clayton Powell Jr Blvds, Harlem; tickets from $15; Ⓢ A/C, B/D to 125th St), the famed concert hall where legends are born. Wednesday's Amateur Night draws notorious crowds.

Local Life
South Brooklyn

Getting There

Fort Greene is roughly 6 miles southeast of Times Square.

S For Fort Greene, take the B, Q/R to DeKalb or the 2/3, 4/5 to Nevins St. Gowanus is near the D, N/R at Union St.

This 4-mile walk takes in some of Brooklyn's most fascinating neighborhoods, where new restaurants, shops, bars and cafes are rapidly changing the urban landscape. Along the way, you'll stroll through leafy neighborhoods, past brownstone-lined streets and across two pretty parks. To hit the flea markets and greenmarket, do this walk on a Saturday.

❶ Fort Greene Park

Leafy, 30-acre **Fort Greene Park** (www.
fortgreenepark.org; btwn Myrtle & DeKalb Aves
& Washington Park & Edward's St, Fort Greene;
☺6am-1am; 👪; Ⓢ B, Q/R to DeKalb Ave) is a
leisurely spot to kick off the day. Climb
the hill to the Prison Ship Martyr's
Monument for Manhattan views.

❷ Smooch

The pretty neighborhood surrounding
the park is also called Fort Greene.
Stroll along DeKalb Ave, Fort Greene's
main thoroughfare, and stop for coffee
at **Smooch** (☏718-624-4075; 264 Carlton
Ave, btwn DeKalb & Willoughby Aves, Fort
Greene; ☺8am-9pm Mon-Wed, to 10pm Thu-
Sun; Ⓢ C to Lafayette Ave; G to Fulton St).

❸ Unique Finds

On the grounds of a school, the
Brooklyn Flea Market (www.brooklynflea.
com; 176 Lafayette Ave, btwn Clermont &
Vanderbilt Aves, Fort Greene; ☺10am-5pm
Sat Apr-Oct; 👪; Ⓢ G to Clinton-Washington
Aves) hosts more than 150 vendors
selling antiques, vintage clothes and
enticing snacks.

❹ Vanderbilt

Crossing Atlantic Ave you arrive in
Prospect Heights, another charming
'hood. Vanderbilt Ave is the main
drag, home to culinary hot spots such
as **Cooklyn** (☏347-915-0721; http://
cooklyn-nyc.com; 659 Vanderbilt Ave, btwn
Prospect & Park Pl, Prospect Heights; mains
$18-29; ☺5:30-11pm Mon-Thu, to midnight Fri
& Sat, to 10pm Sun; Ⓢ B, Q to 7th Ave; 2/3 to
Grand Army Plaza).

❺ Grand Army Plaza

Continue down to **Grand Army Plaza**
(Prospect Park, Prospect Park West & Flatbush
Ave; ☺6am-midnight; 👪; Ⓢ 2/3 to Grand
Army Plaza; B, Q to 7th Ave) and its mas-
sive arch. Just south, at the Prospect
Park entrance, is a popular Saturday
greenmarket.

❻ The Other Central Park

Prospect Park (☏718-965-8951; www.
prospectpark.org; Grand Army Plaza; ☺5am-
1am; Ⓢ 2/3 to Grand Army Plaza; F to 15th
St-Prospect Park) showcases many of the
same landscape features as Central
Park but with fewer crowds. Grassy
meadows, forested trails and a scenic
lake are the big draws.

❼ Hero's Supply

Strolling west out of the park, you
enter Park Slope, with its stately
brownstones. Fifth Ave is lined with
eye-catching shops, such as the curious **Brooklyn Superhero Supply Co**
(☏718-499-9884; www.superherosupplies.
com; 372 Fifth Ave, btwn 5th & 6th Sts, Park
Slope; ☺11am-5pm; 👪; Ⓢ R to 9th St; F, G
to 4th Ave).

❽ Lavender Lake

Gowanus, a once-industrial neighborhood, stretches west. Take the wood-
plank bridge on Carroll St to **Lavender
Lake** (☏347-799-2154; www.lavenderlake.
com; 383 Carroll St, btwn Nevins & Bond Sts,
Gowanus; ☺4pm-midnight Mon-Thu, to 2am
Fri, noon-2am Sat, noon-midnight Sun; Ⓢ F, G
to Carroll St; R to Union St), an enticing bar
with a backyard.

Local Life
Williamsburg

Getting There

Williamsburg is about 5 miles from Times Square.

S Take the L train to Bedford Ave, just one stop from Manhattan.

Williamsburg is essentially a college town without a college: it's New York's of-the-moment bohemian magnet, drawing slouchy, baby-faced artists, musicians, writers and graphic designers. Once a bastion of Latino working-class life, it's become a prominent dining and nightlife center. There's lots to explore, from vintage cocktail dens to colorful stores selling one-of-a-kind creations from Brooklyn's craftmakers.

1 Seeing Green

Offering fabulous Manhattan views, the **East River State Park** (www.nysparks.com/parks/155; Kent Ave, btwn 8th & 9th Sts, Williamsburg; ☻9am-dusk; 🚲; 🅂L to Bedford Ave) is an open green space that becomes a major draw in the summertime for picnicking and the occasional concert.

2 Homegrown Hops

Hearkening back to a time when the area was NYC's beer-brewing center, the **Brooklyn Brewery** (☎718-486-7422; www.brooklynbrewery.com; 79 N 11th St, btwn Berry St & Wythe Ave, Williamsburg; tours Sat & Sun free, Mon-Thu $12; ☻tours 5pm Mon-Thu, 1-5pm Sat, 1-4pm Sun, tasting room 6-11pm Fri, noon-8pm Sat, noon-6pm Sun; 🅂L to Bedford Ave) not only brews and serves tasty local suds, it also offers tours.

3 Hipster Garments

If you want to dress the part, stop in at **Buffalo Exchange** (☎718-384-6901; www.buffaloexchange.com; 504 Driggs Ave, at 9th St, Williamsburg; ☻11am-8pm Mon-Sat, noon-7pm Sun; 🅂L to Bedford Ave), a much-loved vintage shop.

4 Bodega Ephemera

For a glimpse of curious old objects from the days of yore, visit **City Reliquary** (☎718-782-4842; www.cityreliquary.org; 370 Metropolitan Ave, near Havemeyer St, Williamsburg; admission $5; ☻noon-6pm Thu-Sun; 🅂L to Lorimer Ave), which is packed with NYC relics, including exhibits on the 1939 World's Fair.

5 Latin American Detour

Fuego 718 (☎718-302-2913; http://fuego718.com; 249 Grand St, btwn Roebling St & Driggs Ave, Williamsburg; ☻noon-8pm; 🅂L to Bedford Ave) transports you south of the border with Day of the Dead boxes, colorful frames, and crafts from Mexico, Peru and beyond.

6 More Brooklyn Booze

Crank that time machine back one more notch at **Maison Premiere** (☎347-335-0446; www.maisonpremiere.com; 298 Bedford Ave, btwn S 1st & Grand Sts, Williamsburg; ☻4pm-2am Mon-Fri, from 11am Sat & Sun; 🅂L to Bedford Ave), which features bespoke cocktails, oysters and other treats.

7 Brooklyn Art Library

Browse sketchbooks from amateur artists around the world at this **space** (☎718-388-7941; www.sketchbookproject.com; 103 N 3rd St, btwn Berry St & Wythe Ave, Williamsburg; admission free; ☻10am-6pm Mon-Fri, 11am-7pm Sat & Sun; 🅂L to Bedford Ave). Or buy a blank book and add your work to the collection.

8 Brooklyn Oenology

Stop into friendly **Brooklyn Oenology** (☎718-599-1259; www.brooklynoenology.com; 209 Wythe Ave, btwn 3rd & 4th Sts, Williamsburg; ☻4-10pm Mon, 2-10pm Tue-Thu, to midnight Fri & Sat, noon-10pm Sun; 🅂L to Bedford Ave) to sample wines, whiskeys, beers ciders and other treats, all made in New York.

Top Sights
MoMA PS1

Getting There

MoMA PS1 is 3 miles straight east of Times Square, in Queens.

S Take the E or M to Court Sq-23rd St, or the 7 to Court Sq.

The smaller, hipper sibling of Manhattan's Museum of Modern Art, MoMA PS1 hunts down razor-sharp art and serves it up in an ex-school locale. Forget about lily ponds in gilded frames. Here you'll be peering at videos through floorboards and debating the meaning of nonstatic structures while staring through a hole in the wall. Nothing is predictable. Best of all, admission is free with your MoMA ticket.

Don't Miss

Roots, Radicals & PS1 Classics

In 1976 Alanna Heiss – a supporter of art in alternative spaces – took possession of an abandoned school building in Queens and invited artists such as Richard Serra, James Turrell and Keith Sonnier to create site-specific works. The end result was PS1's inaugural exhibition, Rooms. Surviving remnants include Richard Artschwager's oval-shaped wall 'blimps'; Alan Saret's light-channeling *The Hole at P.S.1, Fifth Solar Chthonic Wall Temple,* on the north wing's 3rd floor; Pipilotti Rist's video *Selfless in the Bath of Lava* (viewable through the lobby floorboards); and James Turrell's awe-inspiring *Meeting,* where the sky is the masterpiece.

Sunday Sessions

For a cultural treat, join the Sunday Sessions, on Sundays from September to May. Spanning lectures, film screenings, music performances an even architectural projects, the lineup has included experimental comedy, postindustrial noise jams and Latin art-house dance. One week you might catch a symphony debut, the next an architectural performance from Madrid. Upcoming events are listed on the MoMA PS1 website.

Summer 'Warm Up' Parties

On Saturdays in July to early September, from 3pm to 9pm, rock on at Warm Up, one of New York's coolest weekly music and culture events (admission online/at venue $18/20). It's a hit with everyone from verified hipsters to plugged-in music geeks, who spill into the MoMA PS1 courtyard to eat, drink and catch a stellar lineup of top bands, experimental music and DJs. It's like one big block party, albeit with better music and art than your usual neighborhood slap-up.

☏ 718-784-2084

www.momaps1.org

22-25 Jackson Ave, Long Island City

suggested donation adult/child $10/free, admission free with MoMA ticket

◷ noon-6pm Thu-Mon

Ⓢ E, M to 23rd St-Court Sq; G, 7 to Court Sq

☑ Top Tips

▶ Go online to see what exhibitions are on before heading out. Sometimes the museum has limited pieces on display, particularly between big shows.

▶ Stock up on MoMA exhibition catalogs, coffee-table tomes, art and design mags, CDs and new media at **Artbook** (☏ 718-433-1088; www.artbook.com/art bookps1.html), the MoMA PS1 bookstore.

✕ Take a Break

M Wells Dinette (☏ 718-786-1800; www.magasin wells.com; mains $9-29; ◷ noon-6pm Thu-Mon) gives regional ingredients a gutsy French-Canadian makeover.

The Best of
New York City

New York City's Best Walks

New York City's Best...

New York Public Library (p137)
SIEGFRIED LAYDA/GETTY IMAGES ©

Best Walks
Village Vibe

🏃 The Walk

Of all the neighborhoods in New York City, the West Village is easily the most walkable, its cobbled corners straying from the signature gridiron that unfurls across the rest of the island. An afternoon stroll is not to be missed; hidden landmarks and quaint cafes abound.

Start Commerce St; **S**1 to Christopher St–Sheridan Sq; 1 to Houston St

Finish Washington Sq Park; **S**A/C/E, B/D/F/M to W 4th St

Length 1 mile; one hour

✖ Take a Break

There are perhaps more cafes per acreage in the West Village than anywhere else in the world. Pause at any point during your stroll to slurp a latte street-side and enjoy the colorful crew of passing pedestrians: students, hipsters, moneyed professionals and celebrities hiding behind oversized sunglasses.

GARY LATHAM/LONELY PLANET ©

The Perry St brownstone featured in *Sex and the City*

❶ Cherry Lane Theatre

Start your walkabout at the **Cherry Lane Theater** at 38 Commerce St. Established in 1924, the small theater is the city's longest continuously running Off-Broadway establishment and was the center of the city's creative performance art moment during the 1940s.

❷ The Friends Apartment

Turn left and you'll see **90 Bedford St** on the corner of Grove St. You might recognize the apartment block as the fictitious home of the cast of *Friends* (sadly Central Perk was just a figment of the writers' imaginations).

❸ Carrie Bradshaw's Stoop

For another iconic TV landmark, wander up Bleecker and make a right, stopping at **66 Perry St**, which was used as the apartment of the city's it girl, Carrie Bradshaw, in *Sex and the City* (though in the show, her address was on the Upper East Side).

④ Christopher Park

Follow West 4th St until you reach **Christopher Park**, where two white, life-sized statues of same-sex couples (*Gay Liberation*, 1992) stand guard. On the north side of the green space is the legendary Stonewall Inn, where a clutch of fed-up drag queens and their supporters rioted for their civil rights in 1969, signaling the start of what would become the gay revolution.

⑤ Jefferson Market Library

Head toward Sixth Ave to find the **Jefferson Market Library** straddling a triangular plot of land at the intersection of several roads. The unmissable 'Ruskinian Gothic' spire was once a fire lookout tower. In the 1870s, it was used as a courthouse and today it houses a branch of the public library.

⑥ Café Wha?

Take in the flurry of passers-by on Sixth Ave,

then swing by **Café Wha?**, the notorious institution where many young musicians and comedians – like Bob Dylan and Richard Pryor – got their start.

⑦ Washington Square Park

Further down MacDougal St is **Washington Square Park** (p92), the Village's unofficial town square, which plays host to loitering students, buskers and a regular crowd of protestors chanting about various global and municipal injustices.

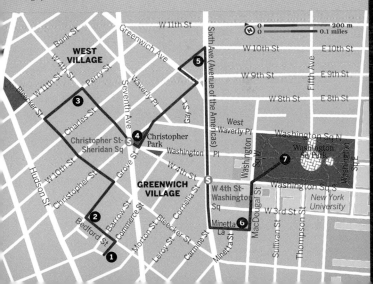

Best Walks
Iconic Architecture

🏃 The Walk

Midtown is home to some of New York's grandest monuments, with artful works of architecture soaring above the concrete canyons. This walk provides a mix of perspectives, from godlike views from up high to street-side exploring amid the raw energy of the whirling city.

Start Grand Central Terminal; ⑤4/5/6, 7 to Grand Central-42nd St

Finish Rockefeller Center; ⑤B/D/F/M to 47th-50th Sts-Rockefeller Center; N/Q/R to Herald Sq

Length 2 miles; three hours

🍴 Take a Break

Tucked within the highrises of Midtown, Koreatown has first-rate dining options, including noodle and dumpling joints, and fancier grilled barbecue spots. Vegetarians shouldn't miss **Hangawi** (p141). Koreatown's epicenter is 32nd St, between Broadway and Fifth Ave.

Prometheus, by Paul Manship, at the Rockefeller Center

❶ Grand Central Terminal

Start your Midtown saunter at beaux-arts marvel **Grand Central Terminal** (p136). Star-gaze at the Main Concourse ceiling; share sweet nothings at the Whispering Gallery; and pick up a gourmet treat at the Grand Central Market.

❷ Chrysler Building

Walk to 44th St and Third Ave for a view of the **Chrysler Building** (p137). Walk down Third Ave to 42nd St, turn right and slip into the Chrysler Building's sumptuous art-deco lobby.

❸ New York Public Library

At the corner of 42nd St and Fifth Ave stands the stately **New York Public Library** (p137). Step inside the library to peek at its spectacular Rose Reading Room.

❹ Bank of America Tower

Enjoy your market treat in neighboring **Bryant Park** (p146). While taking a rest, note the **Bank of America Tower** (p143) on the northwest corner of 42nd St and Sixth Ave. NYC's fourth-tallest building is also one of its most ecofriendly.

❺ St Patrick's Cathedral

Walk up Fifth Ave and admire the splendor of **St Patrick's Cathedral** (p138); its impressive rose window is the work of American artist Charles Connick.

❻ Rockefeller Center

Your last stop is **Rockefeller Center** (p136), a magnificent complex of art-deco skyscrapers and sculptures. Enter between 49th and 50th Sts to the main plaza to spot its golden statue of Prometheus.

❼ Top of the Rock

From the plaza, consider two options: either head to the 70th-floor of the GE Building for an unforgettable vista at the **Top of the Rock** (p136) observation deck, or, if it's after 5pm, head straight up to cocktail bar **SixtyFive** (p144), where you can toast while scanning the skyline.

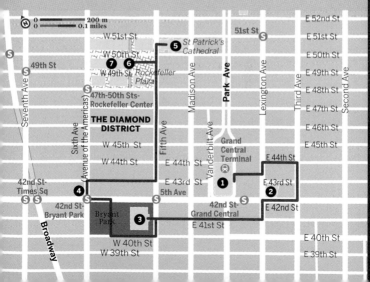

Best Walks
East Village Nostalgia

🏃 The Walk

Gentrification may be taming the beast, but few neighborhoods exude that old-school NYC cool like the East Village. For decades an epicenter of counterculture, its gritty streets sizzle with tales of drugs, drag and rocking punks. Countless cultural icons got their break here, from Patti Smith and the Ramones, to Blondie and Madonna. Times may have changed, but clues to the Village's halcyon days live on.

Start CBGB; **S** 6 to Bleecker St; F to 2nd Ave

Finish Tompkins Sq Park; **S** 6 to Astor Pl

Length 1.5 miles; 1½ hours

✗ Take a Break

The streets below 14th St and east of First Ave are packed with excellent snack-food spots, offering styles and flavors from around the world. It's a mixed bag, indeed, and perhaps one of the most emblematic of the city today.

Cooper Union

WIN-INITIATIVE/GETTY IMAGES ©

❶ CBGB

Start at the former **CBGB** (315 Bowery), a famous music venue that opened in 1973 and launched punk rock via the Ramones. Now a John Varvatos boutique, the fading wall posters and wild graffiti remain untouched.

❷ Joey Ramone Place

The corner to the north marks the block-long **Joey Ramone Place**, named in honor of the Ramones' singer, who succumbed to cancer in 2001.

❸ Cooper Union

Head north on the Bowery to Astor Pl. Turn right and head east through the square to **Cooper Union**, where in 1860 presidential hopeful Abraham Lincoln rocked a skeptical New York crowd with a rousing anti-slavery speech that ensured his candidacy.

❹ St Marks Place

Continue east on **St Marks Place** (p70), a block full of tattoo parlors and cheap eateries.

Number 23 was the site of the Electric Circus, where Andy Warhol staged his Exploding Plastic Inevitable multimedia shows in 1966.

5 Fillmore East

Head south down Second Ave to the site of the long-defunct **Fillmore East** (105 Second Ave), a 2000-seat live-music venue run by promoter Bill Graham from 1968 to 1971. In the '80s the space was transformed into the Saint – the legendary, 5000-sq-ft dance club that kicked off a joyous,

drug-laden, gay disco culture.

6 Physical Graffiti Cover

Head a block east to First Ave, turn left, rejoin St Marks Pl and turn right. The row of tenements is the site of Led Zeppelin's **Physical Graffiti** cover (96–98 St Marks Pl), where Mick and Keith sat in 1981 in the Stones' hilarious video for 'Waiting on a Friend.'

7 Tompkins Square Park

End your stroll at the infamous **Tompkins Square Park** (p69), where drag queens started the Wigstock summer festival at the bandshell where Jimi Hendrix played in the 1960s.

Best
Museums

The Met, MoMA and the Guggenheim are just the beginning of a dizzying list of art-world icons. You'll find museums devoted to everything from fin de siècle Vienna to immigrant life in the Lower East Side, and sprawling galleries filled with Japanese sculpture, postmodern American painting, Himalayan textiles and New York City lore.

SIWAN ASKAYO/LONELY PLANET ©

Cloisters Museum & Gardens

Planning Your Visit

Most museums close at least one day a week, usually Monday (though the Guggenheim shutters Thursdays). Many stay open late one or more nights a week – often a Thursday or Friday. You can save time at the most popular museums by purchasing tickets in advance online.

Galleries

Chelsea is home to the highest concentration of art galleries in the entire city – and the cluster continues to grow with each passing season. Most lie in the 20s, on the blocks between Tenth and Eleventh Aves. For a complete guide and map, pick up Art Info's *Gallery Guide,* available for free at most galleries, or visit http://chelseagallerymap. com. Wine-fueled openings for new shows are typically held on Thursday evenings, while most art houses tend to shutter their doors on Sundays and Mondays.

For Free

Many museums offer free or reduced admission once a week – check the museum websites to find out when. Although most of the city's gallery openings occur on Thursday, you'll find gratis events throughout the week.

Best Art Museums

MoMA Brilliantly curated galleries feature no shortage of iconic modern works. (p132)

Metropolitan Museum of Art Heavyweight of the Americas, the Met even comes with its own Egyptian temple. (p158)

Whitney Museum of American Art World-class contemporary shows in a grand new space designed by Renzo Piano. (p92)

Guggenheim Museum The architecture is the real star at this Frank Lloyd Wright creation. (p162)

New Museum of Contemporary Art A cutting-edge temple to

Lower East Side Tenement Museum

contemporary art in all its forms. (p68)

Best New York Museums

Lower East Side Tenement Museum Fascinating glimpse of life as an immigrant during the 19th and early 20th centuries. (p68)

Merchant's House Museum Step back in time at this perfectly preserved Federal home from well over a century ago. (p52)

Museum of the City of New York Details of the city's past abound in this refurbished Georgian mansion. (p167)

New York City Fire Museum Situated in an old firehouse, this museum recounts the story of New York's firemen and includes a haunting tribute to those who perished on September 11. (p54)

Best Lesser-Known Treasures

Frick Collection A Gilded Age mansion sparkling with Vermeers, El Grecos, Goyas, and a courtyard fountain. (p165)

Morgan Library & Museum Rare manuscripts, books, drawings and paintings in a lavish steel magnate's mansion. (p138)

Neue Galerie An exquisite collection in a former Rockefeller mansion. (p166)

Worth a Trip

Overlooking the Hudson River, the **Cloisters Museum & Gardens** (www.metmuseum.org/cloisters; Fort Tryon Park; suggested donation adult/child $25/free; ⊙10am-5pm; S A to 190th St) is a curious mishmash of European monasteries. Built in the 1930s to house the Metropolitan Museum of Art's medieval treasures, it also contains the beguiling 16th-century tapestry *The Hunt of the Unicorn*.

Best
Fine Dining

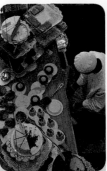

WALTER BIBIKOW/GETTY IMAGES ©

Tasting trends in New York City come and go, but there's one thing that will forever remain certain: fine dining never goes out of style. Sure, the culture of haute eats may have changed, but locals and visitors alike will never tire of dressing up to chow down. Defining the current scene is 'New American' cuisine and inventive new fusions, from Mexican-meets-Korean to Israeli-meets-Scottish.

Reservations

Popular restaurants abide by one of two rules: either they take reservations and you need to plan in advance (weeks or months early for the real treasures) or they only seat patrons on a first-come basis, in which case you should arrive when it opens. Last-minute cancellations do occur, so try your luck calling that hot spot restaurant around 4pm. Lunch is another option – many top dining rooms offer a midday prix fixe service.

Celebrity Chefs

In NYC, restaurateurs are often just as famous as their fare. It's not just buzz though – these taste masters really know their trade. Big-ticket names abound: Mario Batali has painted the town red with his spaghetti sauces, while Danny Meyer continues to break new ground with his ever-expanding, gratuity-free dining empire.

New American Cuisine

A gourmet spin on traditional comfort food, the 'New American' movement fuses classic favorites with market-fresh produce and seasonal ingredients. Many of the city's most critically acclaimed chow houses offer souped-up versions of family recipes – a tribute to Gotham's citizenry of immigrants.

☑ **Top Tips**

▶ New Yorkers are famous for offering their opinion on things, so why not capitalize on their taste-bud experiences by clicking through scores of websites catering to the discerning diner. Some of our favorite blog-style rags include Eater (www.ny.eater.com), New York Magazine (www.nymag.com) and Serious Eats (www.newyork.seriouseats.com).

Best High-End Restaurants

Le Bernardin This triple Michelin-star earner and New York's holy grail of fine dining is the domain of French meister Éric Ripert. (p142)

Bâtard Consistent brilliance from the hands of award-winning chef Markus Glocker. (p40)

Maialino Wildly popular Italian dining den facing Union Square from Danny Meyer. (p120)

Best Gourmet Groceries

Eataly Gorgeous food hall saluting the bustling markets of Italy. (p117)

Le District, Brookfield Place A sprawling gourmet emporium on the Hudson packed with Gallic larder essentials. (p39)

Dean & DeLuca Luxe SoHo grocer bursting with pantry fillers and delectable baked treats. (p49)

Best Buzzworthy Bites

Blue Hill A West Village classic using ingredients sourced straight from the associated farm upstate. (p98)

PETER PTSCHELINZEW/GETTY IMAGES ©

Fresh produce at Eataly

Degustation A tiny East Village eatery where you can watch the chefs create edible works of art. (p74)

Danji Wildly inventive 'Korean tapas' crafted by a young-gun pro. (p141)

Worth a Trip

Scores of Brooklyn restaurants beckon for a foodie pilgrimage. Try **Pok Pok** (www.pokpokpdx. com; 117 Columbia St, cnr Kane St, Columbia St Waterfront District; sharing plates $12-20; ⏱5:30-10pm Mon-Fri, from 10am Sat & Sun; ⒮F to Bergen St) for creative Thai cuisine and **River Café** (www. rivercafe.com; 1 Water St, Brooklyn Heights; dinner 3/6 courses $120/150, brunch $55; ⏱5:30-11:30pm daily, 11:30am-2:30pm Sat & Sun; ⓙ; ⒮A/C to High St) for haute cuisine and stunning views of Lower Manhattan.

Best
Local Eats

From inspired iterations of world cuisine to quintessentially local nibbles, New York City's dining scene is infinite, all-consuming and a proud testament to the kaleidoscope of citizens that call the city home. So go ahead, take a bite out of the Big Apple – we promise you won't be sorry.

SIVAN ASKAYO/LONELY PLANET ©

To Market, to Market

Don't let the concrete streets and buildings fool you – New York City has a thriving greens scene. At the top of your list should be the Chelsea Market (p92), packed with gourmet goodies of all kinds, stocked by both shops (where you can assemble picnics) and food stands (where you can eat on-site). Nearby is the new Gansevoort Market (p95), with its countless temptations. For picnics, head to the Union Square Greenmarket (p118), open four days a week. Check Grow NYC (www.grownyc.org/greenmarket) for a list of NYC's other 50-plus markets.

Food Trucks & Carts

Skip the bagel- and hot-dog-vending food carts. These days, there's a new mobile crew in town dishing up high-end treats and unique fusion fare. The trucks ply various routes, stopping in designated zones throughout the city – namely around Union Square, Midtown and the Financial District – so if you're looking for a particular grub wagon, it's best to follow them on Twitter. Among our favorites are **Red Hook Lobster Pound** (www.twitter.com/lobstertruckny), **Kimchi Taco** (www.twitter.com/kimchitruck), **Calexico Cart** (www.twitter.com/calexiconyc), **Souvlaki GR** (www.souvlakigr.com/location/food-truck) and **Van Leeuwen Ice Cream** (www.twitter.com/VLAIC).

☑ Top Tips

▶ Reserve a table at a number of restaurants around the city using **Open Table** (www.opentable.com).

Best for Old-School NYC

Katz's Delicatessen Try classic pastrami on rye at this New York stalwart and tourist haven on the Lower East Side. (www.katzsdelicatessen.com; 205 E Houston St, at Ludlow St)

Barney Greengrass Perfect plates of smoked salmon and sturgeon for more than 100 years in the Upper West Side. (p188)

El Margon An eclectic cast of regulars pile into this retro classic for

Gansevoort Market

Midtown's juiciest Cuban sandwiches. (p140)

Best Vegetarian

Hangawi Delicate Korean flavors define this soothing, Zen-like oasis, set snugly in the canyons of Midtown. (p141)

Candle Cafe Affluent vegans sip, sup and gossip at this Upper East Side favorite. (p169)

Peacefood Cafe A vegan oasis in the Upper West Side, famed for its fried seitan panini. (p186)

Best Quick Bites

Chelsea Market From tacos and pastries to gourmet ice cream, Manhattan's best-loved gourmet market is a foodie's Promised Land. (p92)

Taïm Outstanding falafel sandwiches in the West Village. (p95)

Spaghetti Incident Tasty, wallet-friendly pasta plates served in a hurry. (p70)

Xi'an Famous Foods Hands down, the best takeout Chinese counter in the city. (p55)

Tacombi Café El Presidente Mexican street food served in a festive spot near Madison Square Park. (p116)

Shake Shack American classics meet quality produce at Danny Meyer's citywide burger empire. (p117)

Gansevoort Market A mouthwatering spread of gourmet vendors. (p95)

Worth a Trip

Multicultural Queens spans all kitchens of the world, from Flushing's Chinese noodle houses – try **Hunan Kitchen of Grand Sichuan** (☎718-888-0553; 42-47 Main St, Flushing; mains $10-24; ⏰11am-12:30am; Ⓢ7 to Flushing-Main St) – to Astoria's Greek eats – try **Bahari** (☎718-204-8968; 31-14 Broadway, Astoria; oven dishes $9-15, grilled meats $12-29; ⏰noon-midnight; Ⓢ N/Q to Broadway).

Best **Drinking**

Considering that 'Manhattan' is thought to be a derivation of the Munsee word *manahactanienk* ('place of general inebriation'), it shouldn't be surprising that New York truly lives up to its nickname 'the city that never sleeps.' In fact, some 20 years after the city was founded, over a quarter of New Amsterdam's buildings were taverns. Sometimes it feels like things have barely changed.

Prohibition Chic

Here in the land where the term 'cocktail' was born, mixed drinks are still stirred with the utmost gravitas. Often, it's a case of history in a glass; New York's obsession with rediscovered recipes and Prohibition-era style showing no signs of abating.

Craft Beer

NYC's craft beer culture is increasingly dynamic, with an ever-expanding booty of breweries, bars and shops showcasing local artisan brews. Top local sud makers include Brooklyn Brewery, Six-point and SingleCut Beersmiths.

Coffee Culture

A boom in specialty coffee roasters is transforming New York's once-dismal caffeine culture. More locals are cluing-in on single-origin beans and different brewing techniques, with numerous roasters now offering cupping classes for curious drinkers. Many are transplants from A-list coffee cities, among them Portland's Stumptown, the Bay Area's Bluebottle, and Sydney's Toby's Estate. The antipodean influence is especially notable, with a growing number of top-notch cafes and roasters claiming Aussie roots.

SIVAN ASKAYO/LONELY PLANET ©

Best Cocktails

Death + Co Legendary cocktail den with wildly creative elixirs in the East Village. (p77)

Weather Up The place barkeeps go for a well-crafted drink in Tribeca. (p42)

Employees Only Award-winning barkeeps and arresting libations in the timeless West Village. (p100)

Maison Premiere A chemistry-lab-style bar full of syrups and essences that costume-clad barkeeps mix up and shake around. (p201)

Lantern's Keep Classic, elegant libations in a historic Midtown hotel. (p145)

Local bar scene in Brooklyn

Best Wine Selection

La Compagnie des Vins Surnaturels A love letter to Gallic wines, steps away from Little Italy. (p59)

Buvette Utterly charming wine bar tucked away in the West Village. (p100)

Immigrant Wonderful wines and service in a skinny East Village setting. (p76)

Best for Beer

Keg No 229 A veritable who's who of boutique American brews. (p42)

Brooklyn Brewery Hit the borough's most famous craft brewer for a tour and tasting. (p201)

West End Hall A new destination for craft brew fans in the Upper West Side. (p190)

Best for Spirits

Bar Goto Artfully concocted libations with Japanese roots (great sakes). (p75)

Rum House Unique, coveted rums – and a pianist to boot – in Midtown. (p146)

Mayahuel A sophisticated East Village temple to mescal and tequila. (p77)

Dead Rabbit NYC's finest collection of rare Irish whiskeys in the Financial District. (p40)

Best Dive Bars

Spring Lounge Soaks, ties and cool kids unite at this veteran Nolita rebel. (p59)

Jimmy's Corner Old boxing bar with a classic-rock jukebox. (p147)

Rudy's Bar & Grill Always a good time with cheap pitchers of beer and rock anthems in the background. (p147)

Frying Pan This ramshackle open-air spot on a pier jutting over the water is the perfect place for a sundowner. (p100)

Best
Entertainment

Hollywood may hold court when it comes to the motion picture, but it's NYC that reigns supreme over the pantheon of other arts. Actors, musicians, dancers and artists flock to the bright lights of the Big Apple like moths to a flame. It's like the old saying goes: if you can make it here, you can make it anywhere.

MATT MUNRO/LONELY PLANET ©

Comedy

A good laugh is easy to find in NYC, where comedians sharpen their stand-up chops, hoping to be scouted by a producer or agent. The best spots are downtown around Chelsea and Greenwich Village.

Dance

Dance fans are spoiled for choice in this town, home to both the New York City Ballet (p191) and the **American Ballet Theatre** (☏212-477-3030; www. abt.org; David Koch Theater, Lincoln Center, 64th St, at Columbus Ave; ⑤1 to 66th St-Lincoln Center), plus modern dance venue the Joyce Theater (p107). There are two major dance seasons: first in spring (March to May), then in late fall (October to December).

Live Music

NYC is the country's capital of live music and just about every taste is catered for – check out **New York Magazine** (www.nymag.com) and the **Village Voice** (www.villagevoice.com) for listings.

Theater

From the legendary hit factories of Broadway to the scruffy black-box theaters that dot downtown blocks, NYC boasts the full gamut of theater experiences. 'Off-Broadway' refers to theaters that are smaller in size, with less glitzy production budgets.

☑ Top Tips

▶ Good-value classical concerts can be scouted at various churches (oh the acoustics!) and smaller recital halls.

Best Broadway Shows

Book of Mormon
Uproariously brilliant Broadway musical appreciated citywide for its wit, charm and pitch-perfect performances. (p149)

Kinky Boots
A fun, sweet, feel-good tale of an old English shoe factory saved by a drag queen. Great costumes. (p148)

An American in Paris
Exuberant choreography, Gershwin tunes and a romantic Parisian setting. (p150)

Theater District at night

Best for Theater (Non-Broadway)

Playwrights Horizons
Catch what could be the next big thing to hit the stages of NYC. (p150)

Signature Theatre
A playwright-focused center showcasing the work of its writers-in-residence. (p150)

Flea Theater One of New York's top Off-Off-Broadway companies performs a regular rotation of theater. (p44)

Lincoln Center The mothership of the performing arts on the Upper West Side. (p184)

New York Theatre Workshop A showcase for cutting-edge works and an icon of the downtown arts scene. (p79)

Best for Laughs

Upright Citizens Brigade Theatre Improv at its finest by many who go on to star in *Saturday Night Live*. (p106)

Comedy Cellar Celebrity joke-tellers regularly plow through this basement club. (p108)

Best for Film

Angelika Film Center Foreign and independent films galore with a side of quirky charms. (p108)

Film Society of Lincoln Center One of NYC's cinematic gems and an invaluable platform for moving pictures. (p192)

Museum of Modern Art Midtown's MoMA screens everything from Hollywood classics to experimental works. (p132)

Film Forum A nonprofit downtown innovator with an excellent indie repertoire. (p60)

Best for Jazz

Village Vanguard Major jazz haven for more than 50 years. (p105)

Jazz at Lincoln Center Top talent in three state-of-the-art venues, including panoramic Dizzy's Club Coca-Cola. (p149)

Blue Note Famous worldwide for its rotating cast of visiting musicians. (p106)

Smalls Brick-lined basement jazz den with amazing jam sessions. (p104)

Birdland Sleek Midtown space that hosts big-band sounds, Afro-Cuban jazz and more. (p151)

Best
Nightlife & Clubbing

Trendy all-night lounges tucked behind the walls of a crumby Chinese restaurant, stadium-size discos thumping to DJ beats and rooftop after-parties as the sun rises. An alternate universe lurks between the cracks of everyday life and it welcomes savvy visitors just as much as the locals in the know.

DIVERSE IMAGES/GETTY IMAGES ©

Clubbing 101

New Yorkers are always looking for the next big thing, and thus the city's club scene changes faster than a New York minute. Promoters drag revelers around the city for weekly events held at all of the finest addresses, and when there's nothing on, it's time to hit the dance floor stalwarts. When clubbing it never hurts to plan ahead; having your name on a guest list can relieve unnecessary frustration and disappointment. If you're an uninitiated partier, dress the part. If you're fed the 'private party' line, try to bluff – chances are high that you've been bounced. Also, don't forget a wad of cash as many nightspots (even the swankiest ones) often refuse credit cards, and in-house ATMs scam a fortune in fees.

Best Clubs

Cielo An icon of the Meatpacking District, with Euro DJ talent and attitude-free dance fans. (p104)

Le Bain Sharp party people, skyline views and a plunge-pool-studded dance floor atop the Standard Hotel. (p103)

Berlin Yesteryear's free-spirited dance days live on at this underground East Village nightspot. (p75)

☑ Top Tips

While the NYC club scene may be fickle, there's no shortage of websites confirming what's hot and what's not.

▶ **New York Magazine** (www.nymag.com/nightlife) offers brilliantly curated nightlife options by those who know best.

▶ **Urbandaddy** (www.urbandaddy.com) delivers up-to-the-minute info and a handy 'hot right now' list.

▶ **Time Out** (www.timeout.com/new york/clubs-nightlife) serves up articles, reviews and on-the-ball listings of where to get your groove on.

Best
Festivals

It seems as though there's always some sort of celebration going on in NYC. National holidays, religious observances, arts festivals and just plain ol' weekends prompt parades, parties or street fairs.

JOE DRIVAS/GETTY IMAGES ©

Chinese New Year (www.explorechinatown. com) Fireworks and dancing dragons draw mobs of thrillseekers into the streets of Chinatown. Typically falls in late January or February.

St Patrick's Day Parade (☎718-793-1600; www.nyc stpatricksparade.org; ⏰Mar 17) Crowds line Fifth Ave for this parade of bagpipe blowers, sparkly floats and clusters of Irish-lovin' politicians.

Tribeca Film Festival (☎212-941-2400; www. tribecafilm.com; ⏰Apr) Robert De Niro's downtown film festival is an undisputed star of the indie movie circuit.

Cherry Blossom Festival (☎718-623-7200; www. bbg.org; ⏰late Apr) Japanese drumming, crafts, food and beautiful spring blooms in Brooklyn Botanic Garden.

NYC Pride (www.nycpride. org; ⏰Jun) Gay Pride culminates in a major march down Fifth Ave on the last Sunday of June.

HBO Bryant Park Summer Film Festival (www. bryantpark.org; ⏰mid-Jun–Aug) Midtown's Bryant Park hosts weekly outdoor screenings of classic Hollywood films.

Independence Day (www.macys.com; ⏰Jul 4) America's Independence Day is celebrated with fireworks and fanfare.

Shakespeare in the Park (www.publictheater. org) Pays tribute to the Bard, with free performances in Central Park.

Village Halloween Parade (www.halloween-nyc. com; Sixth Ave, from Spring St to 16th St; ⏰7-11pm Oct 31) Don a costume and join the parade or simply admire the wild outfits.

Thanksgiving Day Parade (www.macys.com; ⏰4th Thu in Nov) Massive helium-filled cartoons soar overhead, and high-school marching bands rattle their snares.

New York City Marathon (www.nycmarathon. org; ⏰Nov) Held in the first week of November, this 26-mile run draws thousands of athletes and just as many excited spectators.

Rockefeller Center Christmas Tree Lighting (www.rockefellercenter. com; ⏰Dec) The massive Christmas tree in Rockefeller Center gets bedecked with more than 25,000 lights.

New Year's Eve (www. timessquarenyc.org/nye) Times Square is the ultimate place to ring in the New Year.

Best
With Kids

New York City has loads of activities for young ones, including imaginative playgrounds and leafy parks where kids can run free, plus lots of kid-friendly attractions. While the Central Park Zoo, American Museum of Natural History and New York City Fire Museum are good places to start, the list of highs continues, from carousel rides and puppet shows, to market feasting and tram rides across the East River.

SIVAN ASKAYO/LONELY PLANET ©

Dining with Kids

Restaurants in the most touristy corners of the city are ready at a moment's notice to bust out the high chairs and kiddy menus. In general, however, dining venues are small – eating at popular joints sans reservation can often be more of a hassle with the little ones in tow. Early dinners can alleviate some of the stress, as most locals tend to take to their tables between 7:30pm and 9:30pm. In good weather, we recommend grabbing a blanket and food from one of the city's excellent grocers, and heading to Central Park or one of the many other green spaces for a picnic in the grass.

For Parents, Not For Parents

If you're hitting the Big Apple with kids, you can check for upcoming events online at **Time Out New York Kids** (www.timeoutnewyorkkids.com) and **Mommy Poppins** (www.mommypoppins.com). For an insight into New York aimed directly at kids, pick up a copy of Lonely Planet's *Not for Parents: New York*. Perfect for children aged eight and up, it opens up a world of intriguing stories and fascinating facts about New York people, places, history and culture.

Best Museums

American Museum of Natural History Dinosaurs, butterflies, a planetarium and IMAX films. My, oh my! (p184)

Metropolitan Museum of Art A fun trip back in time for the young ones – make sure to stop at the wondrous Egyptian Wing. (p158)

New York City Fire Museum Old-fashioned firefighting carriages, curious old-school uniforms, and amiable staff make this a winner for wide-eyed kids. (p54)

Best Shopping

West Side Kids A wide range of fun, hands-on toys and games for all ages. (p195)

Dinosaur Hill A petite, old-school toy shop

Brooklyn Bridge Park

packed with whimsical gifts, from shadow puppets and calligraphy sets to natural-fibre outfits for munchkins. (p83)

Books of Wonder
Storybooks, teen novels, NYC-themed gifts and in-house storytime make this rainy-day perfection. (p125)

Best Parks & Playgrounds

Central Park Row a boat, visit the zoo and say hello to the giant *Alice in Wonderland* statue, then hit Heckscher playground, the biggest and best of Central Park's 21 playgrounds. (p178)

The High Line NYC's celebrated elevated green space has food vendors, water features

(which kids can splash through) and great views, plus warm-weather family events, from story time to science and craft projects. (p86)

Hudson River Park Get indecisive over mini-golf near Moore St (Tribeca), a fun playground near West St (West Village), a carousel off W 22nd St, watery fun at W 23rd and 11th Ave or a science-themed play space near W 44th St. (p92)

Prospect Park Brooklyn's 585-acre Prospect Park has abundant amusement for kids, including a zoo, hands-on playthings at Lefferts Historic House and a new ice-skating rink that becomes a water park in summer. (p199)

Brooklyn Bridge Park
Come summer, hit the squeal-inducing water park on Pier 6 (bring swimsuits, all will get wet). Watered out, head further north for the grassy hills of Pier 1 and Jane's Carousel. (p233)

Best Food Outings

Seaport Smorgasburg
A great family spot; grab some snacks and head to the waterfront. (p38)

Chelsea Market Limitless temptations – assemble a picnic then munch in the nearby Hudson River Park or on the High Line. (p92)

Best
Shopping

You can blame the likes of Holly Golightly and Carrie Bradshaw for making it darned impossible not to associate New York City with diamonds for breakfast or designer labels for dinner – and the locals are all too happy to oblige. NYC isn't the world's fashion or technology capital, but private capital reigns supreme: there's no better place to shop till you drop.

SILVIA OTTE/GETTY IMAGES ©

Sample Sales

While clothing sales happen year-round – usually when seasons change and old stock must be moved out – sample sales are held frequently, mostly in the huge warehouses in the Fashion District of Midtown or in SoHo. While the original sample sale was a way for designers to get rid of one-of-a-kind prototypes that weren't quite up to snuff, most sample sales these days are for high-end labels to get rid of overstock at wonderfully deep discounts.

Flea Markets & Vintage Adventures

As much as New Yorkers gravitate towards all that's shiny and new, it can be infinitely fun to rifle through closets of unwanted wares and threads. The most popular flea market is the Brooklyn Flea (p199), housed in all sorts of spaces throughout the year. The East Village is the city's de facto neighborhood for secondhand, hipster-pulling stores.

Best Department Stores

Barneys Perfectly curated fashion labels lure serious New York fashionistas. (p152)

Bergdorf Goodman Exclusive labels, lunching ladies, and brilliant Christmas window installations. (p153)

Bloomingdale's A veritable museum to the world of shopping. (p153)

Century 21 A giant wonderland of cut-price fashion, kicks and more. (p43)

Macy's The legendary, block-long department store anchoring 34th St. (p154)

Barneys, Madison Ave

Best Fashion Boutiques

Opening Ceremony Head-turning, cutting-edge threads and kicks for the fashion avant-garde in SoHo. (p60)

Rag & Bone Beautiful tailoring and vintage inspiration define this homegrown unisex favorite. (p61)

Marc by Marc Jacobs A favorite both downtown and uptown, particularly at the West Village locations. (p110)

By Robert James Rugged menswear by a celebrated new local designer. (p81)

Best for Unique Souvenirs & Gifts

MoMA Design & Book Store Take home a piece of the Museum of Modern Art at its famous store, curated as beautifully as the museum itself. (p152)

Philip Williams Posters More than half a million original posters of all shapes and sizes hankering to be hung. (p44)

Obscura Antiques A curious haven for the historic and the macabre, from antique poison bottles to taxidermy critters. (p81)

MiN New York Hard-to-find perfumes and grooming products in an apothecary-like setting. (p49)

Shinola A super-cool boutique stocking design-savvy, American-made objects, from customized bags to watches. (p44)

Verameat Exquisite jewelry that treads the line between beauty and whimsy. (p82)

Best Bookstores

McNally Jackson Everyone's favorite indie bookstore has a slew of tomes and hosts a regular speaker series. (p49)

Strand Book Store New York's best-loved bookstore heaves with more than 18 miles of books. (p108)

Idlewild Books An inspiring place for travelers and daydreamers, with titles (both fiction and nonfiction) spanning the globe. (p124)

Best
For Free

From free concerts, theater and film screenings, to pay-what-you-wish nights at legendary museums, there's no shortage of ways to kick open the NYC treasure chest without spending a dime. Sometimes the best things in life *are* actually free!

SIEGFRIED LAYDA/GETTY IMAGES ©

Staten Island Ferry Hop on the free ferry bound for Staten Island for postcard-perfect views of Manhattan's southern edge. (p241)

Chelsea Galleries More than 300 galleries are open to the public along Manhattan's West 20s. (p88)

New Museum Ethereal tooth-white boxes house a serious stash of contemporary art that's (almost) free for visitors on Thursday evenings after 7pm; minimum suggested donation $2. (p68)

Central Park New York's giant backyard is yours for the taking, with acre after acre of tree-lined bliss. Go for a jog; relax on the lawn; or throw bread crumbs at the ducks in the pond. (p178)

The High Line The city's proudest achievement in urban renewal in the last decade, this catwalk of parkland is great for a stroll and skyline ogling. (p86)

New York Public Library This grand beaux-arts gem (aka the Stephen A Schwarzman Building) merits a visit for its sumptuous architecture and free exhibitions. (p137)

MoMA The glorious Museum of Modern Art is free from 4pm to 8pm on Fridays – be prepared for massive crowds and long lines. (p132)

National September 11 Memorial The largest artificial waterfalls in North America are a spectacular tribute to the victims of terrorism. (p26)

SummerStage Free summertime concerts and dance performances in Central Park. (p181)

Neue Galerie The gracious Neue is gratis from 6pm to 8pm on the first Friday of the month. It's well worth visiting this somewhat under-the-radar beauty on the Upper East Side. (p166)

Studio Museum in Harlem In the city's African American heart, this museum is free to browse on Sundays. (p197)

National Museum of the American Indian Beautiful textiles, objects and art are a vivid testament to Native American cultures at this gem. (p32)

American Folk Art Museum Exhibitions are small-scale but often feature fascinating outsider artists. (p184)

Frick Collection Gaze at works by European masters for a pay-as-you-wish donation on Sundays from 11am to 1pm. (p165)

Best
LGBT

With one of the largest disposable incomes of any demographic, queer New Yorkers seem to run the city, from the fashion runways and major music labels, to Wall St downtown. And now that same-sex couples can say 'I do,' it's never been more 'in' to be 'out.'

Weekdays are the New Weekend

In NYC, any night of the week is fair game to paint the town rouge – especially for the gay community. Wednesdays and Thursdays roar with a steady stream of parties, and locals love raging on Sundays (particularly in summer).

On the Pulse

Tons of websites are dedicated to the city's LGBT scene. Check out what's happening around town with **Next Magazine** (www.nextmagazine.com) or **Get Out!** (http://getoutmag.com). One of the best ways to dial into the party hotline is to follow the various goings-on of your favorite promoter.

Best for Classic NYC Gay

Marie's Crisis A one-time hooker hangout turned show-tune piano bar in the West Village. (p104)

Duplex Camp quips, smooth crooners and a riotously fun piano bar define this Village veteran. (p105)

Best Promoters

BoiParty (www.boiparty.com) Throws impressive weekly, monthly and annual dance parties.

The Saint at Large (www.saintatlarge.com) The team behind the annual Black Party, a massive circuit event held in March.

Daniel Nardicio (www.danielnardicio.com) Notorious party pro-

moter, famed for his often hedonistic events.

Josh Wood (www.joshwoodproductions.com) Well-established promoter increasingly known for gala events, celebrity guests and philanthropic causes.

Spank (www.spankartmag.com) Art-themed parties where thumping beats meet the downtown performance scene.

Best for Dancing Queens

Eagle NYC You'll find dancing, carousing and plenty of leather at this two-story club with a roof deck. (p104)

Industry As night deepens, this Hell's Kitchen hit turns from a buzzing bar and lounge into a thumping club. (p147)

Best
Architecture

New York's architectural history is a layer cake of ideas and styles. Colonial farmhouses and graceful Federal-style buildings are found alongside ornate beaux-arts palaces from the early 1900s. There are the revivals (Greek, Gothic, Romanesque and Renaissance) and the unadorned forms of the International style. For the architecture buff, it's a bonanza.

MITCHELL FUNK/GETTY IMAGES ©

City of Skyscrapers

By the time New York settled into the 20th century, elevators and steel-frame engineering had allowed the city to grow up – literally. This period saw a building boom of skyscrapers, starting with Cass Gilbert's neo-Gothic 57-story Woolworth Building (1913). To this day it remains one of the 50 tallest buildings in the US.

Others soon followed. In 1930, the Chrysler Building, the 77-story art-deco masterpiece designed by William Van Alen, became the world's tallest structure. The following year, the record was broken again by the Empire State Building, a clean-lined art-deco monolith crafted from Indiana limestone. Its spire was meant to be used as a mooring mast for dirigibles – an idea that made for good publicity, but which proved to be impractical and unfeasible.

A Starchitect's Canvas

NYC's heterogenous landscape lends itself well to the sketching pencils of some of the world's leading architectural personalities, or 'starchitects.' You'll find Frank O Gehry's rippling structures, SANAA's white-box exteriors and Renzo Piano's signature facade flip-flopping tucked between the city's glass towers and low-rise bricked behemoths.

Best Skyscrapers

Empire State Building Like a martini, a good steak and jazz, this Depression-era skyscraper never ever gets old. (p130)

Chrysler Building Manhattan's most elegant skyscraper boasts steel ornamentation inspired by the automobile, including gargoyles that are shaped like retro hood ornaments. (p137)

Flatiron Building This is New York's original flavor of skyscraper with 20 triangularly shaped floors tucked behind ornate brick. (p116)

One World Trade Center This blue, tapered monolith is now the tallest building in America and the Western Hemisphere. (p27)

St Patrick's Cathedral

Woolworth Building A neo-Gothic beauty now more than 100 years old. (p32)

Best Places of Worship

St Patrick's Cathedral A neo-Gothic wonder and the largest Catholic cathedral in America. (p138)

Grace Church Rescued from disrepair, it's now one of the daintiest structures in the city, complete with spires and ornate carvings. (p93)

Trinity Church Stunning stained glass accents what was once the tallest structure in New York. Don't miss the on-site cemetery. (p34)

Temple Emanu-el This imposing Romanesque synagogue on the Upper East Side has ceilings that are painted in gold. (p167)

Best Beaux-Arts Beauties

Grand Central Terminal Crowned by America's greatest monumental sculpture, *The Glory of Commerce,* this romantic ode to train travel also features a ballroom-like concourse capped by a celestial vaulted ceiling. (p136)

New York Public Library A vision in Vermont marble, this Midtown marvel takes civic architecture to elegant heights. (p137)

Best of the Rest

Whitney Museum of American Art A shimmering new masterpiece by Renzo Piano, set between the High Line and the Hudson. (p92)

New Museum of Contemporary Art SANAA's stacked-cube structure has a translucent aluminum exterior that is all kinds of sexy. (p68)

Guggenheim Museum Frank Lloyd Wright's inverted ziggurat structure is as quintessentially New York as Lady Liberty, yellow taxis and the deco-fabulous Chrysler Building. (p162)

Brooklyn Bridge Featured in countless films, TV shows and music videos, this neo-Gothic wonder is one of the world's most handsome connectors. (p28)

Best
Sports &
Activities

Although hailing cabs in New York City can feel like a blood sport and waiting on subway platforms in summer heat is steamier than a sauna, New Yorkers still love to stay active in their spare time. And considering how limited the green spaces are in New York, it's surprising for some visitors just how active the locals can be.

Running & Cycling

The 1.6-mile path surrounding the Jacqueline Kennedy Onassis Reservoir is for runners and walkers only. Also try the paths along the Hudson River in Lower Manhattan or FDR Dr and the East River in the UES. NYC has added more than 250 miles of bike lanes in the last decade, but the uninitiated should stick to the less hectic trails in parks and along rivers.

Indoor Sports & Activities

Yoga and Pilates studios dot the city. For a gym workout, try your luck at scoring a complimentary pass from one of the franchised studios.

Best Spectator Sports

New York Yankees

(☏718-293-4300, tours 646-977-8687; www.yankees.com; E 161st St, at River Ave; tours $20; ⑤B/D, 4 to 161st St-Yankee Stadium) Even if you're not a baseball enthusiast, it's worth trekking to Queens to experience the rabid fandom.

New York Mets (☏718-507-8499; www.mets.com; 123-01 Roosevelt Ave, Flushing; tickets $19-130; ⑤7 to Mets-Willets Pt) NYC's other loved baseball team.

New York Knicks (www.nyknicks.com; Madison Sq Garden, Seventh Ave btwn 31st & 33rd Sts, Midtown West; tickets from $75.50; ⑤A/C/E, 1/2/3 to 34th St-Penn Station) The basket-

ALESSANDRO RIZZI/GETTY IMAGES ©

☑ **Top Tips**

▶ Most teams sell tickets via **Ticketmaster** (☏800-745-3000; www.ticketmaster.com). The other major outlet is **StubHub** (www.stubhub.com).

ball team calls Madison Square Garden home.

Brooklyn Nets (www.nba.com/nets; tickets from $15; 🚌351 from Port Authority) Brooklyn's new pro basketball team plays at high-tech Barclays Center.

New York Giants (☏201-935-8222; www.giants.com; Meadowlands Stadium, East Rutherford, NJ; 🚌351 from Port Authority; 🚆NJ Transit from PennStation to Meadowlands) One of the National Football League's oldest teams; now in New Jersey.

Best
Parks

New York's parks, gardens and squares are its collective backyards. The larger parks are ideal for strolling or simply soaking up the sunshine, with plenty of seating as well as kiosks and nearby cafes. Smaller squares offer serendipitous moments of encounter, wonder and surprise.

Outdoor Activities

New Yorkers have perfected the art of turning their green spaces into places of recreation and encounter. During the summer months you'll find outdoor film screenings, Shakespeare performed in Central Park and concerts at Battery Park's Hudson River Park, not to mention Lincoln Center Dance Nights.

Beyond Manhattan

If you're looking for sprawling acres of green space beyond Central Park, it's best to head to Brooklyn. The borough's newest park is the 85-acre **Brooklyn Bridge Park** (☎718-802-0603; www.brooklynbridge park.org; East River Waterfront, btwn Atlantic Ave & Adams St; admission free; ⏰6am-1am; ♿; **S** A/C to High St; 2/3 to Clark St; F to York St), which has revitalized a once-barren stretch of shoreline, turning a series of abandoned piers into public parkland. Nearing completion, it will ultimately become the largest new park in Brooklyn since Calvert Vaux and Frederick Olmsted designed the 585-acre Prospect Park in the 19th century.

MATT MUNRO/LONELY PLANET ©

Best Parks

Central Park The city's famous park has more than 800 acres of rolling meadows and boulder-topped hillocks. (p178)

The High Line A thin stripe of green that unfurls up the western slice of downtown. (p86)

Gramercy Park NYC exclusivity at its finest: this park is cut off from the public by wrought-iron fences, but it's oh-so wonderful to peek in. (p116)

Madison Square Park A refurbished green oasis that showcases large-scale sculptures, wields popular burgers from its Shake Shack and relieves visitors with its public restroom facility. (p116)

Riverside Park A 100-block park running alongside the Hudson on Manhattan's west side – an ideal spot for a bike ride. (p185)

Bryant Park A welcome respite from the restless motion of Midtown, Bryant Park offers film screenings in summer and ice-skating in winter. (p146)

Best
Tours

While the streets of New York lend themselves well to unguided discovery, it's often worth joining a tour to gain greater insight into the city's rich history and lesser-known anecdotes.

SIVAN ASKAYO/LONELY PLANET ©

Big Apple Greeter Program

(☏ 212-669-8159; www.bigapplegreeter.org; admission free) Set up an intimate stroll in the neighborhood of your choice, led by a local volunteer who just can't wait to show off his or her city to you. Reserve four weeks in advance.

Big Onion Walking Tours

(☏ 888-606-9255; www.bigonion.com; tours $20) Choose from nearly 30 tours, exploring history, culture and neighborhood lore throughout NYC.

Bike the Big Apple

(☏ 877-865-0078; www.bikethebigapple.com; tours incl bike & helmet around $95) Offers a variety of tours including a six-hour Ethnic Apple Tour that covers a bit of Queens, northern Brooklyn and the Lower East Side of Manhattan.

Foods of New York

(☏ 212-913-9964; www.foodsofny.com; tours from $52) The official foodie tour of NYC & Company offers various three-hour tours that help you eat your way through the city. Prepare thyself for a moving feast of fresh Italian pasta, sushi, global cheeses and real New York pizza.

On Location Tours

(☏ 212-683-2027; www.onlocationtours.com; tours $25-49) Offers various tours covering TV shows and both small and silver screen locations, letting you live out your entertainment-obsessed fantasies.

Wildman Steve Brill

(☏ 914-835-2153; www.wildmanstevebrill.com; tours up to $20) New York's best-known naturalist has been leading folks on foraging expeditions through city parks for more than 30 years.

Strayboots

(☏ 877-787-2929; www.strayboots.com; tours from $12) Self-guided hybrid tours that fuse interesting urban info and a scavenger hunt element to help New York neophytes find their way around the neighborhood of their choice. Go at your own pace as you text in your answers to central command to receive your next clue.

Municipal Art Society

(☏ 212-935-3960; www.mas.org; tours from adult/child $20/15; S F to 57th St) Various scheduled tours focusing on architecture and history, including a popular walking tour of Grand Central Terminal.

Survival Guide

Survival Guide

Before You Go

When to Go

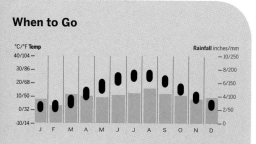

°C/°F **Temp**
40/104 —
30/86 —
20/68 —
10/50 —
0/32 —
-10/14 —

Rainfall inches/mm
— 10/250
— 8/200
— 6/150
— 4/100
— 2/50
— 0

J F M A M J J A S O N D

➡ **Winter (Dec–Feb)**
Snowfalls and sub-zero temperature. The holiday season keeps things light despite the shivers.

➡ **Spring (Mar–May)**
Eager cafes drag their patio furniture out at the first hint of warm weather.

➡ **Summer (Jun–Aug)**
Oppressively hot at the height of summer. Locals flock to their Hamptons share on weekends.

➡ **Fall (Sep–Nov)** Brilliant bursts of red and gold illuminate the city's parks.

Book Your Stay

➡ The average room rate is well over $300. But don't let that scare you: there are great deals to be had – almost all of which can be found through savvy online snooping.

➡ Unlike many destinations, New York City doesn't have a 'high season.' Sure, there are busier times of the year when it comes to tourist traffic, but with more than 50 million visitors per year, the Big Apple never loses sleep over filling up beds. As such, room rates fluctuate based on availability; in fact, most hotels have a booking algorithm in place that spits out a price quote relative to the number of rooms already booked on the same night. The busier the evening, the higher the price.

➡ If you're looking to find the best room rates, flexibility is key – weekdays are often cheaper and you'll generally find that accommodations in winter months have smaller price tags. If you are visiting over a weekend, try the business hotels in the Financial District, which tend to empty out when the working week ends.

→ If you do have an inkling of where you'd like to stay, it's best to start at your desired hotel's website as it'll often include deals and package rates.

Useful Websites

→ **Newyorkhotels.com** (www.newyorkhotels. com) The self-proclaimed official website for hotels in NYC.

→ **NYC** (www.nycgo.com/ hotels) Loads of listings from the NYC Official Guide.

→ **Lonely Planet** (www. lonelyplanet.com) Author-recommendation reviews and online booking.

Best Budget

→ **Local NYC** (www.the localny.com) Affordable dorms and doubles with rooftop views and a great Long Island City location.

→ **New York Loft Hostel** (www.nylofthostel.com) Converted warehouse with a buzzing vibe in boho-loving Bushwick.

→ **Harlem Flophouse** (www.harlemflophouse. com) A charming town house in the heart of Harlem.

→ **Jane Hotel** (www. thejanenyc.com) The cabin-sized rooms are tiny, but the gorgeous ballroom and bar looks like it belongs in a five-star hotel.

→ **St Mark's Hotel** (www. stmarkshotel.net) This East Village budget option draws a young, nightlife-loving crowd, which enjoys being within strolling distance of the city's best concentration of bars and cocktail lounges.

Best Midrange

→ **Citizen M** (www. citizenm.com) Contemporary, high-tech rooms near the heart of Times Square.

→ **Wall Street Inn** (www.thewallstreetinn. com) Comfy beds and colonial-style rooms in the Financial District.

→ **Boro Hotel** (www.boro hotel.com) High design with panoramic views in Long Island City.

→ **3B** (www.3bbrooklyn. com) Charming four-room Brooklyn haunt run

by a creative, arts-loving collective.

→ **Bubba & Bean Lodges** (www.bblodges.com) Upper East Side town house with kitchenettes and a welcoming vibe.

→ **1871 House** (www.1871house.com) Has the feel of a quaint 19th-century inn, but is walking distance of sprawling Central Park.

Best Top End

→ **Ace Hotel** (www. acehotel.com/newyork) A hipster funhouse with DJs spinning beats in the lobby, and first-rate coffee and cocktails on hand.

→ **Knickerbocker** (http:// theknickerbocker.com) Luxurious Midtown option with a fabulous rooftop bar.

→ **Bowery Hotel** (www. theboweryhotel.com) Gorgeous rooms, a model-draped lobby, and great eating and cocktailing options.

→ **Hôtel Americano** (www.hotel-americano. com) This designer's dream is the boutique sleep of the future, stocked with an international assortment of upscale treats.

➜ **Plaza** (www.theplaza. com) Spoil yourself at this luxurious icon on Central Park South.

➜ **Crosby Street Hotel** (www.firmdalehotels. com) Uber-stylish guest rooms on a cobblestone street downtown.

Arriving in New York City

☑ **Top Tip** For the best way to get to your accommodations, see p17.

John F Kennedy International Airport

John F Kennedy International Airport (JFK), 15 miles from Midtown in southeastern Queens, has eight terminals, serves nearly 50 million passengers annually and hosts flights coming and going from all corners of the globe.

➜ **Taxi** A yellow taxi from Manhattan to the airport will use the meter. Prices depend on traffic (often about $60) and it can take 45 to 60 minutes.

From JFK, taxis charge a flat rate of $52 to any destination in Manhattan (not including tolls or tip).

➜ **Vans and car service** Shared vans cost around $20 to $26 per person, depending on the destination. If traveling to the airport from NYC, car services have set fares from $45.

➜ **Express bus** The NYC Airporter runs to Grand Central Terminal, Penn Station or the Port Authority Bus Terminal from JFK. The one-way fare is $17.

➜ **Subway** The AirTrain ($5, payable before you exit) links JFK to the subway. Take the AirTrain to Howard Beach–JFK Airport station for the A line through Brooklyn and into Manhattan, or opt for Sutphin Blvd–Archer Ave (Jamaica Station) for the E, J or Z line to Queens and Manhattan.

➜ **Long Island Rail Road (LIRR)** Take the AirTrain to Jamaica Station, from where LIRR trains depart frequently to Penn Station in Manhattan or to Atlantic Terminal in Brooklyn. One-way fares to either Penn Station or Atlantic Terminal cost $7.50 ($10 at peak times).

LaGuardia Airport

Used mainly for domestic flights, LaGuardia is smaller than JFK but only eight miles from Midtown Manhattan; it sees about 26 million passengers per year.

➜ **Taxi** A taxi to/from Manhattan costs about $42 for the approximately half-hour ride.

➜ **Car service** A car service from LaGuardia costs around $35.

➜ **Express bus** The NYC Airporter costs $14.

➜ **Subway and bus** It's less convenient to use public transportation to get from LaGuardia into the city. The best subway link is the 74th St–Broadway station (7 line, or the E, F, M and R lines at the connecting Jackson Hts–Roosevelt Ave station) in Queens, where you can pick up the Q70 Express Bus to the airport (about 10 minutes to the airport).

Newark Liberty International Airport

Don't write off New Jersey when looking for airfares to New York. Newark's airport is 16 miles from Midtown, about the same distance from Midtown as JFK, and brings many New Yorkers out for flights – some 36 million passengers annually.

➡ **Car service and taxis** A car service runs about $45 to $60 for the 45-minute ride to Midtown; taxis run roughly the same. You only have to pay the $15 toll to go through the Lincoln Tunnel (at 42nd St) or Holland Tunnel (at Canal St) coming into Manhattan from Jersey; there's no charge going back through to NJ.

➡ **Subway/train** NJ Transit runs rail services (with an AirTrain connection) between Newark airport (EWR) and New York's Penn Station for $13 each way. The trip takes 25 minutes and runs every 20 or 30 minutes from 4:20am to about 1:40am. Hold onto your ticket, which you must show upon exiting at the airport.

➡ **Express bus** The Newark Airport Express has a bus service between the airport and Port Authority Bus Terminal, Bryant Park and Grand Central Terminal in Midtown ($16 one way). The 45-minute ride goes every 15 minutes from 6:45am to 11:15pm (and every half hour from 4:45am to 6:45am and 11:15pm to 1:15am).

Getting Around

Subway
☑ **Best for...** straight up or down trips in Manhattan, or reaching neighborhoods in the outer boroughs.

➡ The New York subway's 660-mile system, run by the **Metropolitan Transportation Authority** (MTA; ☎ 511; www.mta.info), is iconic, cheap ($2.75 per ride), round-the-clock and easily the fastest and most reliable way to get around the city. It's also safer and (a bit) cleaner than it used to be.

➡ All buses and subways use the yellow-and-blue MetroCard, which you can purchase or add value to at one of several easy-to-use automated machines at any station. You can use cash, or an ATM or credit card. Just select 'Get new card' and follow the prompts. Tip: if you're not from the US, enter 99999 when the machine asks for your zip code.

➡ The card itself costs $1. You then select one of two types of MetroCard. The 'pay-per-ride' is $2.75 per ride, though the MTA tacks on a 5% bonus on MetroCards over $5. (Buy a $20 card, and you'll receive $21 worth of credit. If you plan to use the subway quite a bit, you can also buy an 'unlimited ride' card ($31 for a seven-day pass).

➡ Subway maps are posted inside most stations. You can also get a free map from any attendant.

Taxi
☑ **Best for...** getting to and from the airports with luggage in tow, or zigzagging across Manhattan.

➡ The Taxi & Limousine Commission has set fares for rides (which can be paid with credit or debit card). It's $2.50 for the initial fare (first one-fifth of a mile), 50¢ for each additional one-fifth mile as well as per every 60 seconds of being

Subway Cheat Sheet

Numbers, letters and colors Subway train lines have a color and a letter or number. Trains with the same color run on the same tracks, often following roughly the same path through Manhattan before branching out into the other boroughs.

Express and local lines Each color-coded line is shared by local trains and express trains; the latter make only select stops in Manhattan (indicated by a white circle on subway maps). If you're covering a greater distance, you're better off transferring to the express train (usually just across the platform from the local) to save time.

Getting into the right station Some stations have separate entrances for downtown or uptown lines (read the sign carefully). If you swipe in at the wrong one, you'll either need to ride the subway to a station where you can transfer for free, or just lose the $2.75 and re-enter the station (usually across the street). Also look for the green and red lamps above the stairs at each station entrance; green means that it's always open, while red means that a particular entrance will be closed at certain hours, usually late at night.

Weekends All the rules switch on weekends, when some lines combine with others, some get suspended, some stations get passed and others are reached. Locals and tourists alike stand on platforms confused, sometimes irate. Check the www.mta.info website for weekend schedules. Sometimes posted signs aren't visible until after you reach the platform.

stopped in traffic. There's also a $1 peak surcharge (weekdays from 4pm to 8pm) and a 50¢ night surcharge (8pm to 6am), plus a NY State surcharge of 50¢ per ride.

➡ Tips are expected to be 10% to 15%, but give less if you feel in any way mistreated – and in that case be sure to ask for a receipt and use it to note the driver's license number.

➡ The TLC keeps a Passenger's Bill of Rights, which gives you the right to tell the driver which route you'd like to take, or ask your driver to stop smoking or turn off an annoying radio station. Also, the driver does not have the right to refuse you a ride based on where you are going. Tip: get in first, then say where you're going.

➡ Cabs are available if the light on the roof is illuminated. It's particularly difficult to score a taxi in the rain, at rush hour and around 4pm, when many drivers end their shifts.

➡ Green Boro Taxis operate in the outer boroughs and Upper Manhattan. They have the same fares and features as yellow cabs, and are a good way to get around (and between) Brooklyn and Queens.

Walking

Best for... exploring quaint neighborhoods such as the West Village, the East Village, Chinatown and SoHo.

→ Screw the subway, cabs and buses, and go green. New York, down deep, can't be seen until you've taken the time to hit the sidewalks: the whole thing, like Nancy Sinatra's boots, is made for pedestrian transport.

→ Broadway runs the length of Manhattan, about 13.5 miles. Crossing the East River on the pedestrian planks of the Brooklyn Bridge is a New York classic. Central Park trails can get you to wooded pockets from where you won't even see or hear the city.

Bus

Best for... taking in the city's atmosphere as you make your way across town.

→ Buses are operated by the MTA, the same folks that run the subway. They share an identical ticketing system.

→ The standard local bus fare is $2.75 ($6.50 for express buses), payable with MetroCard or exact change (no dollar bills or pennies).

→ Crosstown buses are numbered according to the street they traverse.

Boat

Best for... visiting the Statue of Liberty and snapping photos of the skyline.

→ **East River Ferry** (www. eastriverferry.com; 1-way $4-6) runs year-round services connecting a variety of locations in Manhattan, Queens and Brooklyn.

Citi Bike

New York has embraced two-wheeled transport over the last decade with new bike lanes and an extensive bike-sharing network. Hundreds of Citi Bike kiosks in Manhattan and parts of Brooklyn house the sturdy blue bicycles.

To use a Citi Bike, purchase a 24-hour or seven-day access pass (around $11 or $28 including tax) at any Citi Bike kiosk. You will then be given a five-digit code to unlock a bike. Return the bike to any station within 30 minutes to avoid incurring extra fees. Reinsert your credit card (you won't be charged) and follow the prompts to check out a bike again (you need wait only two minutes between check-outs). You can make an unlimited number of 30-minute check-outs during those 24 hours or seven days.

Helmets are highly recommended, but not obligatory.

→ **New York Water Taxi** (☎ 212-742-1969; www.nywatertaxi.com; hop-on, hop-off 1-day pass $31) has a fleet of zippy yellow boats that provide hop-on, hop-off services around Manhattan and Brooklyn.

→ Another bigger, brighter ferry (this one's orange) is the commuter-oriented **Staten Island Ferry** (www. siferry.com; Whitehall Terminal, 4 South St, at Whitehall; ◷ 24hr; **S** 1 to South Ferry), which makes constant free journeys across New York Harbor.

Essential Information

Business Hours

Standard business hours are as follows:

➡ **Banks** 9am to 6pm Monday to Friday; some banks are also open from 9am to noon on Saturdays.

➡ **Businesses** 9am to 5pm Monday to Friday.

➡ **Restaurants** Breakfast from 6am to 11am, lunch from 11am to 3pm, and dinner from 5pm to 11pm. Weekend brunch goes from 11am to 4pm.

➡ **Bars** 5pm to 4am.

➡ **Clubs** 10pm to 4am.

➡ **Shops** 10am to around 7pm Monday to Friday, and 11am to around 8pm Saturdays. Sunday hours are variable: some stores stay closed while others keep weekday hours. Stores tend to stay open later in the neighborhoods downtown.

Discount Cards

The following discount cards offer a variety of passes and perks to some of the city's must-sees. Check the websites for more details.

➡ **Downtown Culture Pass** (www.downtown culturepass.org)

➡ **Explorer Pass** (www. smartdestinations.com)

➡ **New York CityPASS** (www.citypass.com/ new-york)

➡ **The New York Pass** (www.newyorkpass.com)

Electricity

The US electric current is 110V to 115V, 60Hz AC. Outlets are made for flat two-prong plugs (which often have a third, rounded prong for grounding).

If your appliance is made for another electrical system (eg 220V), you'll need a step-down converter, which can be bought at hardware stores and drugstores for around $25 to $60. Most electronic devices (laptops, camera-battery chargers etc) are built for dual-voltage use, however, and will only need a plug adapter.

120V/60Hz

120V/60Hz

Emergency

→ **Police, Fire & Ambulance** ☎911

→ **Poison control** ☎800-222-1222

Money

☑ **Top Tip** US dollars are the only accepted currency in NYC. While debit and credit cards are widely accepted, it's wise to have a combination of cash and cards on hand.

ATMs

→ ATMs are on practically every corner. You can either use your card at banks – usually in a 24-hour-access lobby, filled with up to a dozen monitors at major branches – or you can opt for the lone wolves, which sit in delis, restaurants, bars and grocery stores, charging fierce service fees that average $3 but can go as high as $5.

Credit Cards

→ Major credit cards are accepted at most hotels, restaurants and shops throughout New York City. In fact, you'll find it difficult to perform certain transactions, such as purchasing tickets to

Money-Saving Tips

→ Browse our list of free attractions (p228).

→ Check museum websites to see when they offer free admission.

→ Save on theater tickets by buying tickets at the TKTS booth at Times Square or in Lower Manhattan.

→ Stock up on picnic goodies at the many outdoor farmers markets and gourmet grocers.

performances and renting a car, without one.

→ Stack your deck with a Visa, MasterCard or American Express, as these are the cards of choice.

Changing Money

→ Banks and moneychangers, found all over New York City (including all three major airports), will give you US currency based on the current exchange rate.

Public Holidays

This is a list of major NYC holidays and special events. These holidays may force the closure of many businesses or attract crowds, making dining and accommodations reservations difficult.

New Year's Day January 1

Martin Luther King Day Third Monday in January

Presidents' Day Third Monday in February

Easter March/April

Memorial Day Late May

Gay Pride Last Sunday in June

Independence Day July 4

Labor Day Early September

Rosh Hashanah & Yom Kippur Mid-September to mid-October

Halloween October 31

Thanksgiving Fourth Thursday in November

Christmas Day December 25

New Year's Eve December 31

Safe Travel

Crime rates in NYC remain at their lowest in years. There are few neighborhoods remaining where you might feel apprehensive, no matter what time of night (and they're mainly in the outer boroughs). Subway stations are generally safe, too, though in some low-income neighborhoods, they can be dicey. There's no reason to be paranoid, but it's better to be safe than sorry, so use common sense. Snatch-and-run thefts of smartphones aren't uncommon; be aware of your surroundings and don't walk around staring at your phone (especially when entering/exiting subway stations, and in crowded places). Don't walk around alone at night in unfamiliar, sparsely populated areas. Be aware of pickpockets particularly in mobbed areas, such as Times Square or Penn Station at rush hour.

Telephone

Cell Phones

Most US cell (mobile) phones, besides the iPhone, operate on CDMA, not the European standard GSM – make sure you check compatibility with your phone service provider. North Americans should have no problem, but it is best to check with your service provider about roaming charges.

If you require a cell phone, you'll find many storefronts – most of which are run by Verizon, T-Mobile or AT&T – where you can buy a cheap phone and load it up with prepaid minutes, thus avoiding a long-term contract.

Phone Codes

No matter where you're calling within New York City, even if it's just across the street in the same area code, you must always dial ☏1 + the area code first.

Manhattan ☏212, ☏646

Outer boroughs ☏347, ☏718, ☏929

All boroughs (usually cell phones) ☏917

International and Domestic Calls

Phone numbers within the USA consist of a three-digit area code followed by a seven-digit local number. If you're calling long distance, dial ☏1 + the three-digit area code + the seven-digit number. To make an international call from NYC call ☏011+ country code + area code + number. When calling Canada, there is no need to use the ☏011.

Toilets

☑ **Top Tip** The NY Restroom website (www.nyrestroom.com) is a handy resource for scouting out a loo.

Considering the number of pedestrians, there's a noticeable lack of public restrooms around the city. You'll find restrooms in Grand Central Terminal, Penn Station and Port Authority Bus Terminal, and in parks, including Madison Square Park, Battery Park, Tompkins Square Park, Washington Square Park and Columbus Park in Chinatown, plus several places scattered around Central Park. The good bet, though, is to pop into a Starbucks (there's one about every three blocks), a department store (Macy's, Century 21, Bloomingdale's) or a neighborhood park.

Tourist Information

In this web-based world you'll find infinite online

esources to get up-to-the-minute information about New York. In person, try one of the official bureaus of **NYC & Company** (www.nycgo.com).

Times Square (Map p134, D3; ☏ 212-484-1222; www.nycgo.com; Seventh Ave, at 44th St, Midtown West; ☺9am-6pm; Ⓢ N/Q/R, S, 1/2/3, 7 to Times Sq-42nd St)

Macy's Herald Square (Map p134, D5; ☏ 212-484-1222; www.nycgo.com; Macy's, 151 W 34th St, at Broadway; ☺9am-7pm Mon-Fri, from 10am Sat, from 11am Sun ; Ⓢ B/D/F/M, N/Q/R to 34th St-Herald Sq)

City Hall (Map p30, C4; ☏ 212-484-1222; www.

nycgo.com; City Hall Park, at Broadway; ☺9am-6pm Mon-Fri, 10am-5pm Sat & Sun; Ⓢ 4/5/6 to Brooklyn Bridge-City Hall; R to City Hall; J/Z to Chambers St)

The **Brooklyn Tourism & Visitors Center** (☏ 718-802-3846; www.nycgo.com; 209 Joralemon St, btwn Court St & Brooklyn Bridge Blvd, Downtown; ☺10am-6pm Mon-Fri; Ⓢ 2/3, 4/5 to Borough Hall) has all sorts of info on the much-loved borough.

Travelers with Disabilities

Federal laws guarantee that all government offices and facilities are accessible to the

disabled. For information on specific places, you can contact the mayor's **Office for People with Disabilities** (☏ 212-639-9675; www.nyc.gov/html/mopd; ☺9am-5pm Mon-Fri), which will also send you a free copy of its *Access New York* guide if you request it.

Big Apple Greeter (www.bigapplegreeter.org/what-is-the-access-program; admission free) has more than 50 volunteers with physical disabilities on staff who are happy to show off their corner of the city.

For detailed information on subway and bus wheelchair accessibility, call the **Accessible Line** (☏ 511; http://web.mta.

Dos & Don'ts

➜ Hail a cab only if the roof light is on.

➜ You needn't obey 'walk' signs – simply cross the street when there isn't oncoming traffic.

➜ When negotiating pedestrian traffic on the sidewalk, think of yourself as a vehicle; don't stop short; follow the speed of the crowd around you; and pull off to the side if you need to take out your map or umbrella. Most New Yorkers are respectful of personal space, but they will bump into you – and not apologize – if you get in the way.

➜ When boarding the subway, wait until the passengers disembark, then be assertive enough when you hop on so that the doors don't close in front of you.

➜ In New York you wait 'on line' instead of 'in line.'

➜ Oh, and Houston St is pronounced How-sten, not Hew-sten.

info/accessibility/stations. htm) for a list of subway stations with elevators or escalators. Also visit www. nycgo.com/accessibility.

Visas

The USA Visa Waiver Program (VWP) allows nationals from 38 countries to enter the US without a visa, provided they are carrying a machine-readable passport. For the updated list of countries included in the program and current requirements, see the **US Department of State** (http://travel.state.gov/ visa) website.

Citizens of VWP countries need to register with the **US Department of Homeland Security** (http://esta.cbp.dhs.gov) three days before their visit. There is a $14 fee for registration application; when approved, the registration is valid for two years or until your passport expires, whichever comes first.

You must obtain a visa from a US embassy or consulate in your home country if you:

➡ do not currently hold a passport from a VWP country;

➡ are planning to stay longer than 90 days; or

➡ are planning to work or study in the US.

Index

DRINKING

Behind the Scenes

Send Us Your Feedback

We love to hear from travelers – your comments help make our books better. We read every word, and we guarantee that your feedback goes straight to the authors. Visit **lonelyplanet.com/contact** to submit your updates and suggestions.

Note: We may edit, reproduce and incorporate your comments in Lonely Planet products such as guidebooks, websites and digital products, so let us know if you don't want your comments reproduced or your name acknowledged. For a copy of our privacy policy visit lonelyplanet.com/privacy.

Our Readers

Many thanks to the travelers who used the last edition and wrote to us with helpful hints, useful advice and interesting anecdotes:

Rick Geldman, Katy Mcgreal and Mary Nash.

Regis' Thanks

I'm grateful to many folks who shared tips on their favorite places in the city. Special thanks to my talented co-authors Cristian Bonetto and Zora O'Neill for their excellent contributions that showcase this ever-changing city, and to Wesley Clark for providing a home away from home. As always, biggest thanks go to my wife Cassandra and our daughters, Genevieve and Magdalena, who make this whole enterprise worthwhile.

Cristian's Thanks

Sincere thanks to Kathy Stromsland, Charles Isherwood, Eben Freeman, Chris Crowley, Kim Anderson, Christa Larwood, Mark Webster and Steven Ritzel for their tips, insight and friendship. Also, a big shout-out to my ever-diligent co-writers, Regis St Louis and Zora O'Neill.

This Book

This 6th edition of *Pocket New York City* was written and researched by Regis St Louis and Cristian Bonetto. Zora O'Neill contributed content for MoMA PS1. This guidebook was produced by the following: **Destination Editor** Rebecca Warren **Product Editors** Anne Mason, Susan Paterson **Senior Cartographer** Alison Lyall **Book Designers** Virginia Moreno, Jessica Rose **Assisting Editor** Michelle Bennett **Cover Researcher** Naomi Parker **Thanks to** Kate Chapman, Kate Kiely, Indra Kilfoyle, Benjamin Little, Kate Mathews, Catherine Naghten, Dianne Schallmeiner, Ellie Simpson, Lyahna Spencer, John Taufa, Angela Tinson, Tony Wheeler

Our Writers

Regis St Louis

A Hoosier by birth, Regis grew up in a sleepy riverside town where he dreamed of big-city intrigue and small, expensive apartments. In 2001 he settled in New York, which had all that and more. Since then he has explored vast swaths of the city, from the Bronx to Brighton Beach, ever in search of both classic and bizarre NYC experiences. Regis' work has appeared in more than 50 Lonely Planet guidebooks. When not on the road, he splits his time between Brooklyn and New Orleans.

Cristian Bonetto

Cristian has played both visitor and local in New York City, a place that won his heart way back in his *Sesame Street* diaper days. Indeed his passion for the city saw *New York Magazine* name him one of the 'Reasons to Love New York' in 2014. Gotham's constant reinvention continues to feed an insatiable curiosity that has seen the one-time scriptwriter shed light on everything from lesser-known art collections to cognoscenti dumpling dens.

Published by Lonely Planet Publications Pty Ltd
ABN 36 005 607 983
6th edition – Aug 2016
ISBN 978 1 74360 127 3
© Lonely Planet 2016   Photographs © as indicated 2016
10 9 8 7 6 5 4 3 2 1
Printed in China